Random House
Bad Speller's
Dictionary

Random House
Bad Speller's
Dictionary

Second Edition

Joseph Krevisky
and Jordan L. Linfield

RANDOM HOUSE
NEW YORK

ISBN: 0-679-76433-X

Manufactured in the United States of America
9 8 7 6 5 4 3 2 1

New York   Toronto   London   Sydney   Auckland

Introduction

It has been thirty years since we wrote the first book that answered the Catch-22 of spelling: *How do I find a word in the dictionary if I don't know how to spell it?* Our answer was simple: *Look it up by its wrong spelling.* So we compiled the first dictionary for bad spellers—which so many of us are (some of us even flaunt it as a badge of pride). The nearly two million copies of the *Bad Speller's Dictionary* that have been sold confirm the persistence of the spelling problem. In fact, our vast new collection of actual examples of misspellings from many sources—television, newspapers, magazines, advertisements, correspondence, essays, memos—suggests that the phenomenon has become much worse. That deterioration has been accelerated by our educational system, too much television, excessive reliance on electronic spell checkers, and the emergence of so many new words.

That's why we have prepared this new revised and enlarged edition for the 1990's. We have added thousands of current words from business, computers, entertainment, medicine, psychology, religion, science, and the law.

It's Our English Language

The main source of our problems with spelling is the irregular crazy pattern of English spelling. A late-night TV talk show displayed an ad for a bug killer that kills your *aunts* [ants]. A leading newspaper ran a headline about a boat race that read: "Neither knew who *one*" [won]. Another paper called a tough cop a *psyhco* [psycho]. The American Library Association, a model of correctness, passed out a flyer that read: "Information pollution: *whose* fouling our system?" [who's] And the diplomas for one year's graduates of the U.S. Naval Academy read, "U.S. *Navel* Academy."

The other source of our spelling problems is the fact that spelling and pronunciation often simply don't match. In other languages, such as Spanish, letters always have the same pronunciation. Spanish *i* is always pronounced like the *ee* in *feet,* the *a* like the *a* in *father,* the *u* like the *oo* in *fool.* English vowels, on the other hand, have many varied pronunciations. *A* is one sound in *hat,* another in *hate,* still another in *all,* in *care,* in *father. E* is *ee* in *cede, eh* in *sell, u* in *berth,* a little like the *ai* of *air* in the word *where,* and so on. Consonants are a bit easier to handle, but you still have the *c* of *cell* and the *s* of *sell,* the *c* of *coffee* and the *k* of *kernel.*

Turn it around and start with sounds, and it's just as confusing. The long *a* sound of *hate* is *ei* in *weight* or *feign* and *ai* in *wait*. The long *e* sound, as in *feet*, shows up as *feat, mien, believe, receive,* and *recede.*

While Spanish vowels are all pronounced distinctly, regardless of their location in the word, this is not so in English. In multisyllabic words we often pronounce only the vowel in the stressed syllable clearly and slur the other syllables. The other vowels often tend to have the same buried sound—something like "uh" or "ih," regardless of whether the vowel is *a, e, i, o,* or *u. Vacation* becomes "vuhcation," *innocent* is "insinent," *probably* is "probibly" or (running the two *b*'s together) "probly." We strongly urge you to rely on your dictionary to check the pronunciation of words, as this will often help you to spell correctly.

Words that look or sound alike create special difficulties. Confusion of words that seem as simple as *to, too,* and *two* and *there, their,* and *they're* are commonplace. We certainly can't rely on our computer spell checkers, which lack the capacity to spot look-alikes or sound-alikes. This popular poem describes the dilemma well:

Spellbound

I have a spelling checker,
It came with my PC;
It plainly marks four my revue
Mistakes I cannot sea.
I've run this poem threw it,
I'm sure your please too no,
Its letter perfect in it's weigh,
My checker tolled me sew.

How to Use This Dictionary

The *Bad Speller's Dictionary* has three sections—a list of incorrect and correct spellings, a list of words that look or sound alike, and a quick list of correct spellings.

Incorrect/Correct List

This section is a collection of thousands of commonly misspelled words arranged alphabetically by their misspellings so that you can find the word by looking for it either as you think it's spelled or by the way it sounds. The phonetic misspelling is a common source of error. Looking for this type of misspelling is the easiest way to find a word when you're not sure how to spell it.

You will find the incorrect spelling in the left-hand column of this section, and the correct spelling in the right-hand column. Thus, if you have an "addiction" to "CD-ROMs" for your "computer" and you're not sure of the spellings, you will find:

Incorrect	Correct
adiktion	addiction
ceedee rom	CD-ROM
seedy rom	CD ROM
cumputer	computer

It's important that you check the *complete* correct spelling in the right-hand column, for while we focus on initial errors, we have also included additional misspellings in other parts of the word. Thus, we show "innsomia" for "insomnia" to emphasize, at the beginning of the word, the common error of doubling a consonant; but we add the omission of the "n" near the end to underscore the tendency to drop consonants when they have a difficult sound like "mn."

Look/Sound Alikes Section

This section provides a carefully selected list of some of the most common and important words that are confused because they look or sound alike. A brief definition or key word enables you to distinguish the meanings of the pairs (or triplets, or quadruplets). Examples:

abject (spiritless), **object** (a material thing; to oppose)

infect (contaminate), **infest** (swarm), **invest** (to put in money)

Quick List of Correct Spellings

The Quick List of Correct Spellings includes all the words from the "Correct" part of the Incorrect/Correct list, plus all the main entries in the Look/Sound Alikes section. Thus, if you are reasonably confident about the spelling of a word, you can check this list first.

Double Asterisk (**)

A double asterisk after a correct spelling on the Incorrect/Correct List or on the Quick List means that the word also appears in the Look/Sound Alike section. Take the word "piece," meaning a portion. This is often misspelled "*peice*." But it is also sometimes confused with its homonym "peace," meaning absence of conflict.

We would welcome your sending us examples—clippings, memos, etc., for our future editions. Send them to us at Innovation Press, c/o Random House. Many thanks, and have some fun, too.

A

Incorrect	Correct	Incorrect	Correct
abait	**abate**	abuze	**abuse**
abaration	**aberration****	abzurd	**absurd**
abarent	**aberrant****	accademic	**academic**
abarigine	**aborigine**	acceed	**accede****
abawtion	**abortion**	accerasy	**accuracy**
abbandon	**abandon**	accidently	**accidentally**
abbatement	**abatement**	acclame	**acclaim**
abbet	**abet**	accnowledge	
abblaze	**ablaze**		**acknowledge**
abbolition	**abolition**	accoustics	**acoustics**
abborshun	**abortion**	accownt	**account**
abbort	**abort****	accrew	**accrue**
abbout	**about**	accrobat	**acrobat**
abbrasive	**abrasive**	accross	**across**
abbsorb	**absorb**	accrostic	**acrostic**
abbstinence	**abstinence**	accumen	**acumen**
abbstrak	**abstract****	accur	**occur****
abbuze	**abuse**	accurit	**accurate**
abby	**abbey**	accurred	**occurred**
abdeman	**abdomen**	accute	**acute**
abduck	**abduct**	acennd	**ascend**
abel	**able**	acertain	**ascertain**
abeld	**abled**	acheive	**achieve**
abelism	**ableism**	Ackilles heel	**Achilles heel**
aberation	**abrasion****	acktivist	**activist**
abharant	**abhorrent****	ackustics	**acoustics**
abhoar	**abhor**	ackwire	**acquire**
abillity	**ability**	acklame	**acclaim**
abiss	**abyss**	aclimate	**acclimate**
abjeck	**abject****	acnowledgement	
abley	**ably**		**acknowledgment**
abnoxious	**obnoxious**	acommodate	
abragate	**abrogate****		**accommodate**
abraid	**abrade**	acompany	**accompany**
abreviate	**abbreviate**	acompanyment	
abrup	**abrupt**		**accompaniment**
absalutuly	**absolutely**	acomplice	**accomplice****
abscence	**absence**	acomplish	**accomplish****
abserd	**absurd**	acord	**accord**
absess	**abscess****	acordion	**accordion**
absint	**absent**	acost	**accost**
abstanance	**abstinence**	acount	**account**
abstetrician	**obstetrician**	acountent	**accountant**
abt	**apt**		

Incorrect	Correct	Incorrect	Correct
acquantence		adenda	addenda
	acquaintance	adequatly	adequately
acquasition	acquisition	adged	aged
acquitle	acquittal	adict	addict
acrabat	acrobat	adige	adage
acredidation		adiktion	addiction
	accreditation	adinoma	adenoma
acredit	accredit	adishon	edition**
acrege	acreage	adition	addition**
acros	across	adjatent	adjutant
acrue	accrue	adjustible	adjustable
acselerate	accelerate	admanition	admonition
acsesery	accessory	admendment	amendment
acshual	actual	admerable	admirable
acsident	accident**	adminnistrater	
actavist	activist		administrator
acter	actor	admisable	admissible
actualy	actually**	admitance	admittance
acuire	acquire	admition	admission
acumenacal	ecumenical	adolesent	adolescent
acumulate	accumulate	adoor	adore
acurecy	accuracy	adop	adopt**
acuse	accuse	adress	address
acustom	accustom	aduce	adduce**
acwitt	acquit	advanse	advance
adam	atom	advantige	advantage
adaquete	adequate	advizable	advisable
addams apple		advizer	adviser
	Adam's apple	advisery	advisory
addement	adamant	advurtize	advertise
addhere	adhere	adyou	adieu**
addhesion	adhesion	afair	affair**
addick	addict	afect	affect**
addmanition	admonition	affire	afire
addministeration		affraid	afraid
	administration	Affrica	Africa
addmiral	admiral	afgan	Afghan
addmit	admit	afible	affable
addorible	adorable	afidavit	affidavit
addrenal	adrenal	afiliate	affiliate
addult	adult	afinity	affinity
addvantagous		afirm	affirm
	advantageous	afirmative	affirmative
addvertisement		afix	affix
	advertisement	aflict	afflict
adelesense	adolescence	afluence	affluence

Incorrect	Correct	Incorrect	Correct
aford	**afford**	airea	**area****
aforizm	**aphorism**	aireel	**aerial**
afrade	**afraid**	Aireh	**Eire****
afront	**affront**	airis	**heiress**
afrontry	**effrontery**	airlume	**heirloom**
aftakare	**aftercare**	airobic	**aerobic**
aftanoon	**afternoon**	airoplane	**airplane**
aftawerds	**afterwards**	Aisha	**Asia**
afthalmologist		aithe	**eighth**
	ophthalmologist	ajacent	**adjacent**
afurmative	**affirmative**	ajed	**aged**
agany	**agony**	ajeism	**ageism**
agast	**aghast**	ajenda	**agenda**
ageing	**aging**	ajile	**agile**
agenst	**against**	ajudication	**adjudication**
agensy	**agency**	ajurn	**adjourn****
agern	**adjourn****	ajustable	**adjustable**
agervate	**aggravate**	ajutent	**adjutant**
aggrarian	**agrarian**	akademy	**academy**
aggree	**agree**	ake	**ache**
aggreshun	**aggression****	aker	**acre**
aggriculture	**agriculture**	aklaim	**acclaim**
agground	**aground**	akne	**acne****
ague	**ague**	aknolege	**acknowledge**
agillity	**agility**	akolite	**acolyte**
agincys	**agencies**	akording	**according**
aginise	**agonize**	aks	**axe****
agism	**ageism**	akseed	**accede****
agoe	**ago**	aksel	**axle****
agrafobia	**agoraphobia**	akselerate	**accelerate**
agrandize	**aggrandize**	aksent	**accent****
agreable	**agreeable**	akses	**axis****
agread	**agreed**	aksess	**access****
agregate	**aggregate**	aksidents	**accidents****
agreing	**agreeing**	aktiv	**active**
agressive	**aggressive**	akute	**acute**
agrieved	**aggrieved**	akward	**awkward**
ahmond	**almond**	akyupunkcher	
ahmz	**alms****		**acupuncture**
ahnroot	**en route**	alagy	**allergy****
ahntray	**entrée**	albyumin	**albumin**
ahnwee	**ennui**	alcahole	**alcohol**
ahts	**arts**	aleby	**alibi**
aile	**aisle****	aleet	**elite**
ainshent	**ancient**	alege	**allege****
air aparent	**heir apparent**	alegiance	**allegiance**

Incorrect	Correct	Incorrect	Correct
alegro	**allegro**	altoe	**alto**
alergy	**allergy****	altrueizm	**altruism**
aleveate	**alleviate**	alturnit	**alternate****
alfabet	**alphabet**	alude	**allude****
alfanoomeric		alure	**allure**
	alphanumeric	alurgic	**allergic**
alfer	**alpha**	alyanation	**alienation**
alian	**alien**	amallgamated	
aliance	**alliance**		**amalgamated**
aline	**align**	amature	**amateur****
aljee	**algae**	amaty	**amity****
alkamy	**alchemy**	ambbasador	**ambassador**
alkohol	**alcohol**	ambbiguous	**ambiguous**
alkoholic	**alcoholic**	ambeance	**ambiance** or
alla kart	**à la carte**		**ambience**
allanon	**Al-anon**	ambolism	**embolism**
albino	**albino**	ambyalance	**ambulance**
alldenty	**al dente**	amealiorate	**ameliorate**
allee	**alley****	ameeba	**amoeba**
allert	**alert**	ameritus	**emeritus**
allgorythm	**algorithm**	amerous	**amorous**
allie	**ally****	amfetamine	**amphetamine**
allimoney	**alimony**	aminable	**amenable**
allkoholism	**alcoholism**	amiosentesis	
allmanac	**almanac**		**amniocentesis**
allmighty	**almighty**	ammalgam	**amalgam**
allmost	**almost**	ammbition	**ambition**
allone	**alone**	ammend	**amend****
alloof	**aloof**	Ammerican	**American**
allottment	**allotment**	ammex	**AMEX**
allowence	**allowance**	ammity	**amity****
allready	**already****	ammount	**amount**
allso	**also**	ammplafacation	
allthough	**although**		**amplification**
alltogether	**altogether****	ammtrack	**Amtrak**
alluminum	**aluminum**	amneezha	**amnesia**
allways	**always****	amonia	**ammonia**
almer matter	**alma mater**	amoor	**amour****
alocate	**allocate**	amoung	**among**
alot	**allot**	ampeer	**ampere**
alow	**allow****	amplafy	**amplify**
alowed	**allowed****	ampp	**amp**
alright	**all right**	ampythitter	**amphitheater**
alsoeran	**also ran**	ampyutate	**amputate**
altar ego	**alter ego**	amuk	**amok**
altenate	**alternate****	amunition	**ammunition**

Incorrect	Correct	Incorrect	Correct
amusment	**amusement**	annew	**anew**
amuze	**amuse**	annger	**anger**
amyable	**amiable****	anngora	**angora**
analise	**analyze****	annima	**anima****
analitic	**analytic**	annimal	**animal****
anamal	**animal****	annimus	**animus**
anamoly	**anomaly**	annoint	**anoint**
anaversary	**anniversary**	annomaly	**anomaly**
anbolic	**anabolic**	annomy	**anomie****
anceint	**ancient**	anntartika	**Antarctica**
ancologist	**oncologist**	anntasid	**antacid**
aneemic	**anemic**	anntena	**antenna**
anend	**anent**	anntrax	**anthrax**
anereksia nervous		annuel	**annual****
	anorexia nervosa	annull	**annul****
anewity	**annuity**	anologous	**analogous**
anewrism	**aneurism or**	anonimus	**anonymous**
	aneurysm	anotate	**annotate**
anex	**annex**	anouncement	
anfetamine	**amphetamine**		**announcement**
angery	**angry**	anoyence	**annoyance**
angwish	**anguish**	anplifier	**amplifier**
angziety	**anxiety**	anpule	**ampule****
anihilate	**annihilate**	anputation	**amputation**
anilgesic	**analgesic**	anputee	**amputee**
anilist	**analyst****	anpyatate	**amputate**
anjina	**angina**	anser	**answer**
anjioma	**angioma**	ansester	**ancestor**
anjycardeogram		ansestree	**ancestry**
	angiocardiogram	anshent	**ancient**
ank	**ankh**	antabody	**antibody**
ankaman	**anchorman**	antaganist	**antagonist**
ankel	**ankle**	antartic	**antarctic**
anker	**anchor**	antaseptic	**antiseptic**
ankshus	**anxious**	antatoksin	**antitoxin**
ankst	**angst**	antchovy	**anchovy**
annalasis	**analysis**	ante-American	
annaljesic	**analgesic**		**anti-American**
annalog	**analog****	antebiotic	**antibiotic**
annalogy	**analogy**	antedepresent	
annatomy	**anatomy**		**antidepressant**
anndroyd	**android**	anteek	**antique****
annecdotal	**anecdotal**	antehistomin	
annecdote	**anecdote**		**antihistamine**
annerexia	**anorexia**	antisapate	**anticipate**
annesthetic	**anesthetic**	antisedent	**antecedent**

Incorrect	Correct	Incorrect	Correct
antiseed	**antecede**	appauled	**appalled**
antybody	**antibody**	appeel	**appeal**
anual	**annual****	appeerence	**appearance**
anualee	**annually**	appellete	**appellate**
anuity	**annuity**	appenndisitis	**appendicitis**
anull	**annul****	appere	**appear**
anulled	**annulled**	apperence	**appearance**
anurism	**aneurism or**	applys	**applies**
	aneurysm	appnia	**apnea**
anuther	**another**	appointy	**appointee**
anwee	**ennui**	appologize	**apologize**
any where	**anywhere**	appology	**apology****
apagee	**apogee**	appostrophe	**apostrophe**
aparatus	**apparatus**	appraisel	**appraisal**
aparel	**apparel**	apprenntise	**apprentice**
aparent	**apparent**	appreshible	**appreciable**
apartide	**apartheid**	appropo	**apropos**
apathesis	**apotheosis**	apptitude	**aptitude**
apaul	**appall**	apraise	**appraise****
apeal	**appeal**	apreciate	**appreciate**
apear	**appear**	aprecot	**apricot**
apease	**appease**	aprehend	**apprehend**
apeks	**apex**	aprentice	**apprentice**
apell	**apple**	aprin	**apron**
apellate	**appellate**	aproach	**approach**
apend	**append**	apropriate	**appropriate**
apendectomy		aprove	**approve**
	appendectomy	aproximate	**approximate**
apendix	**appendix**	aquaintance	**acquaintance**
apetite	**appetite****	aquire	**acquire**
aphrocentric	**Afrocentric**	aquisition	**acquisition**
aplacater	**applicator**	aquittal	**acquittal**
aplaud	**applaud**	aquitted	**acquitted**
apliance	**appliance**	aragant	**arrogant**
aplicant	**applicant**	araign	**arraign****
aplication	**application**	arange	**arrange****
aplum	**aplomb**	aray	**array**
aply	**apply**	arbatrate	**arbitrate**
apoinment	**appointment**	arber	**arbor**
apoint	**appoint**	arbitery	**arbitrary**
apokriful	**apocryphal**	ardeco	**art deco**
apologize	**apologize**	aready	**already****
apologys	**apologies**	arears	**arrears**
aposle	**apostle****	arebag	**airbag**
apparentally	**apparently**	areena	**arena**
appartment	**apartment**	arest	**arrest**

Incorrect	Correct	Incorrect	Correct
arewaves	**airwaves**	artical	**article**
argo	**argot**	artilery	**artillery**
arguement	**argument**	artissticly	**artistically**
argyue	**argue**	artry	**artery**
arial	**aerial**	artwear	**artware**
ariola	**areola**	arye	**awry**
ariseing	**arising**	arythimia	**arrhythmia**
arithmatic	**arithmetic**	asadosis	**acidosis**
arithmia	**arrhythmia**	asalt	**assault**
arive	**arrive**	asanine	**asinine**
arkade	**arcade**	asasinate	**assassinate**
arkaic	**archaic**	asassin	**assassin**
arkangel	**archangel**	asault	**assault**
arkatipe	**archetype**	asay	**assay****
arkeology	**archeology**	asaylent	**assailant**
Arkinsaw	**Arkansas**	ascance	**askance**
arkitect	**architect**	asemble	**assemble**
arkives	**archives**	asent	**assent****
armastice	**armistice**	aserb	**acerb**
armfull	**armful**	asert	**assert****
arodynamics		asess	**assess**
	aerodynamics	aset	**asset**
arogance	**arrogance**	asetone	**acetone**
arogant	**arrogant**	asfalt	**asphalt**
aronautics	**aeronautics**	asfixia	**asphyxia**
aroogala	**arugula**	ashaimed	**ashamed**
arosol	**aerosol**	ashawr	**ashore**
arow	**arrow**	ashin	**ashen**
arrabesk	**arabesque**	ashure	**assure**
arraingment	**arrangement**	asid	**acid**
arrane	**arraign****	asign	**assign**
arrcive	**archive**	asimilationist	
arressted	**arrested**		**assimilationist**
arrise	**arise**	asist	**assist**
arristocrat	**aristocrat**	asistent	**assistant**
arrivel	**arrival**	askee	**ASCII**
arround	**around**	asma	**asthma**
arrouse	**arouse****	asociate	**associate**
arrsenic	**arsenic**	asorbtion	**absorption**
artafakt	**artifact**	asparation	**aspiration**
artaficial	**artificial**	aspirent	**aspirant****
arte	**art**	asprin	**aspirin****
artee	**arty**	assale	**assail**
arterosklerosis		assalt	**assault**
	arteriosclerosis	assesed	**assessed**
artic	**arctic**	assimilateable	**assimilable**

Incorrect	Correct	Incorrect	Correct
assinement	**assignment****	atrosity	**atrocity**
assinine	**asinine**	attavism	**atavism**
assistence	**assistance****	attom	**atom**
assoshiation	**association**	attone	**atone**
asspargis	**asparagus**	aturney	**attorney**
assperin	**aspirin****	audable	**audible**
asspire	**aspire**	audeofile	**audiophile**
asstigmatizm	**astigmatism**	audiance	**audience**
asstonish	**astonish**	Augest	**August**
asstrigent	**astringent**	augziliary	**auxiliary****
asstronimy	**astronomy**	aukward	**awkward**
assylum	**asylum**	auntitoksin	**antitoxin**
ast	**asked**	aunuled	**annulled**
astablish	**establish**	autabigraphy	
asternot	**astronaut**		**autobiography**
astoot	**astute**	autaimunity	
astrangement			**autoimmunity**
	estrangement	autamatic	**automatic**
asume	**assume**	autamobile	**automobile**
asurence	**assurance****	autapilot	**autopilot**
asurtive	**assertive**	auther	**author**
atach	**attach****	authority	**authority**
atack	**attack****	autoefocus	**autofocus**
atact	**attacked**	automashun	
atain	**attain**		**automation****
atashay	**attaché****	auxilary	**auxiliary****
atemt	**attempt**	avalable	**available**
atend	**attend**	avan-guard	**avant-garde**
atendence	**attendance****	avantage	**advantage**
atendent	**attendant**	aveary	**aviary**
atenshun	**attention**	aveater	**aviator**
atenyuate	**attenuate**	aved	**avid**
atest	**attest**	aventitious	**adventitious**
athalete	**athlete**	avilanch	**avalanche**
athaletic	**athletic**	avocate	**advocate**
athritis	**arthritis**	avoidible	**avoidable**
athyist	**atheist**	avrage	**average**
atic	**attic**	avursion	**aversion**
atire	**attire**	avvenue	**avenue**
atitude	**attitude****	avvokado	**avocado**
atmisfere	**atmosphere**	aw	**awe****
atract	**attract**	awdacious	**audacious**
atrafy	**atrophy**	awdiance	**audience**
atreum	**atrium**	awdio	**audio**
atribute	**attribute**	awdit	**audit**
atrition	**attrition**	awditoriem	**auditorium**

Incorrect	Correct	Incorrect	Correct
awear	**aware**	ayclair	**éclair**
awefel	**awful****	ayelash	**eyelash**
aweight	**await**	ayeth	**eighth**
awktion	**auction**	ayker	**acre**
awkwid	**awkward**	ayleet	**élite**
awra	**aura**	ayleus	**alias**
aw revoir	**au revoir**	aymanorea	**amenorrhea**
awrgee	**orgy**	aymen	**amen**
awsome	**awesome**	aynus	**anus****
awsteer	**austere**	ayorta	**aorta**
awt	**ought****	aypron	**apron**
awthentick	**authentic**	ayress	**heiress**
awthorety	**authority**	ayrobics	**aerobics**
awtimaticly		aysentric	**acentric****
	automatically	aysian	**Asian**
awtism	**autism**	aytheist	**atheist**
awtum	**autumn**	azbestos	**asbestos**
axident	**accident**	Azher	**Asia**
axxed	**asked**	azma	**asthma**

			B

Incorrect	Correct	Incorrect	Correct
babeesit	**babysit**	balence	**balance**
bachler	**bachelor**	balerina	**ballerina**
backinal	**bacchanal**	baleywick	**bailiwick**
backround	**background**	balistics	**ballistics**
backwerd	**backward**	balital	**belittle**
bagage	**baggage**	balkany	**balcony**
bagd	**bagged**	ballid	**ballad****
bage	**badge**	ballit	**ballot****
baggs	**bags**	baloon	**balloon**
bagin	**begin**	balpoint	**ballpoint**
baheemoth	**behemoth**	bambu	**bamboo**
bahn	**barn**	bamitsvah	**Bar Mitzvah**
baige	**beige**	bamy	**balmy**
baist	**baste**	banana	**banana**
bakbone	**backbone**	bancwet	**banquet****
bakkstabber	**backstabber**	bandige	**bandage**
baklog	**backlog**	baner	**banner**
bakon	**bacon**	bangoes	**banjos**
bakteria	**bacteria**	banista	**banister**
baktrack	**backtrack**	bankrup	**bankrupt**
balay	**ballet****	bankrupcy	**bankruptcy**
bale out	**bailout**	bannana	**banana**

Incorrect	Correct	Incorrect	Correct
banndana	**bandana**	batton	**baton**
banndit	**bandit**	battry	**battery**
bannish	**banish**	baught	**bought****
banwaggen	**bandwagon**	bawd rait	**baud rate**
bapptise	**baptize**	bawk	**balk**
baptiss	**Baptist**	bawsht	**borscht**
baracks	**barracks**	baybe	**baby**
barage	**barrage**	baye	**bey**
barate	**berate**	baygel	**bagel**
barbacue	**barbecue**	baysball	**baseball**
barbeturate	**barbiturate**	bayshing	**Beijing**
bareeved	**bereaved**	baysment	**basement**
barell	**barrel**	bazzoka	**bazooka**
bargin	**bargain**	beap	**beep**
baricuda	**barracuda**	bearfaced	**barefaced**
barier	**barrier**	beatle	**beetle**
barikade	**barricade**	beautyful	**beautiful**
barish	**bearish**	becomeing	**becoming**
barly	**barley**	becon	**beacon**
barmshell	**bombshell**	becum	**become**
barnfire	**bonfire**	becuz	**because**
barrberian	**barbarian**	beddbug	**bedbug**
barrometer	**barometer**	bedder	**better****
basall	**basal**	beddmate	**bedmate**
bashe	**bash**	bedspred	**bedspread**
basicly	**basically**	beealy	**bialy**
basik	**basic**	bee-bee-ess	**BBS**
basitracin	**bacitracin**	beefor	**before**
basiz	**basis****	beegan	**began**
bassin	**basin**	beehaf	**behalf**
bassk	**bask**	beenball	**beanball**
bassketbawl	**basketball**	beeoh	**B.O.**
bassmitzve	**Bas Mitzvah**	beeref	**bereft**
bassque	**Basque**	beest	**beast**
bastid	**bastard****	beestial	**bestial**
bata	**beta**	beestro	**bistro**
batallian	**battalion**	beever	**beaver**
batared baby		beeware	**beware**
	battered baby	beewilder	**bewilder**
batchler	**bachelor**	befor	**before**
baten	**batten**	befrend	**befriend**
baterd wimmen		begel	**bagel**
	battered women	beger	**beggar**
batered wife	**battered wife**	beginer	**beginner**
batery	**battery**	begining	**beginning**
batray	**betray**	behavier	**behavior**

Incorrect	Correct	Incorrect	Correct
beir	**bier****	bestyal	**bestial**
beladona	**belladonna**	beuty	**beauty**
beleaf	**belief**	bevrage	**beverage**
beleive	**believe**	biakemistry	**biochemistry**
belicose	**bellicose**	Bibel	**Bible**
beligerant	**belligerent**	biche	**bitch**
belitel	**belittle**	bied	**bide****
bellfree	**belfry**	bigest	**biggest**
beltweigh	**Beltway**	biggamy	**bigamy**
belweather	**bellwether**	biggot	**bigot**
bely	**belie****	biggshot	**big shot**
benafit	**benefit**	biggwig	**bigwig**
bended	**bent**	bilbord	**billboard**
benefishal	**beneficial**	bild	**build****
benefishery	**beneficiary**	bilet	**billet**
beneith	**beneath**	biliard	**billiard**
benifited	**benefited**	biline	**byline**
benine	**benign**	bilion	**billion**
bennevelent	**benevolent**	bilionnaire	**billionaire**
bennzacane	**benzocaine**	billyus	**bilious**
benshmark	**benchmark**	bilofair	**bill of fare**
benz	**bends**	bilt	**built**
beogrephy	**biography**	bilyus	**bilious**
beond	**beyond**	bimmbo	**bimbo**
beopsy	**biopsy**	binay brith	**B'nai B'rith**
bequethe	**bequeath**	binery	**binary**
beray	**beret**	binnoculars	**binoculars**
berbin	**bourbon**	biosentrism	**biocentrism**
berden	**burden**	bipass	**bypass**
berger	**burger**	birdy	**birdie**
bergler	**burglar**	bisek	**bisect**
berglery	**burglary**	biseps	**biceps**
berial	**burial**	bisk	**bisque**
berieved	**bereaved**	biskit	**biscuit**
berlap	**burlap**	bisy	**busy**
berlesk	**burlesque**	biten	**bitten**
bernout	**burnout**	biter	**bitter**
bernt	**burnt**	bivawhacked	**bivouacked**
berryberry	**beriberi**	bivwak	**bivouac**
berser	**bursar****	biyou	**bayou**
bersitis	**bursitis**	bizness	**business**
berst	**burst**	bizz	**biz**
berthmother	**birthmother**	blader	**bladder**
berthstone	**birthstone**	blair	**blare**
beseige	**besiege****	blakbord	**blackboard**
beserk	**berserk**	blakgard	**blackguard**

Incorrect	Correct	Incorrect	Correct
blakhed	**blackhead**	boch	**botch****
blakmale	**blackmail**	bodd	**bod**
blamless	**blameless**	boddy	**body**
blanche	**blanch**	boddygard	**bodyguard**
blankit	**blanket**	bodiss-ripper	
blasay	**blasé**		**bodice-ripper**
blasfemy	**blasphemy**	boggocity	**bogosity**
blasst	**blast**	bogin	**bogon**
blasster	**blaster**	bogis	**bogus**
blaytant	**blatant**	boicot	**boycott**
blead	**bleed**	boid	**bird**
bleap	**bleep****	boistrous	**boisterous**
bledd	**bled**	bokay	**bouquet**
bleech	**bleach**	bolester	**bolster**
bleek	**bleak**	bom	**bomb****
blerb	**blurb**	bombox	**boombox**
blest	**blessed**	bonde	**boned**
bleve	**believe**	bondfire	**bonfire**
blined	**blind**	bone vivante	**bon vivant**
blisster	**blister**	bonet	**bonnet**
blite	**blight**	boney	**bony****
blith	**blithe**	bonion	**bunion**
blits	**blitz**	bonis	**bonus**
blizard	**blizzard**	bon swar	**bon soir**
blobb	**blob**	bonz	**bones**
blockaid	**blockade**	boobu	**bubo**
blodbathe	**bloodbath**	boodwar	**boudoir**
blok	**block****	booey	**buoy****
blonnd	**blond**	bookay	**bouquet**
bloos	**blues**	bookeeping	**bookkeeping**
blosom	**blossom**	boorzhwa	**bourgeois**
blote	**bloat****	boose	**booze**
bloted	**bloated**	boosom	**bosom**
bloter	**blotter**	booteek	**boutique**
blowse	**blouse**	bord	**board****
blubaby	**blue baby**	bordaline	**borderline**
blubery	**blueberry**	borow	**borrow**
blublud	**blueblood**	bosa noeva	**bossa nova**
blud	**blood**	bost	**boast**
bluf	**bluff**	bosy	**bossy**
blugen	**bludgeon**	botelneck	**bottleneck**
blunnder	**blunder**	botes	**boats**
blunnt	**blunt**	botom	**bottom**
bluprint	**blueprint**	botsun	**boatswain**
blurr	**blur**	bottel	**bottle**
boan	**bone**	bottimless	**bottomless**

Incorrect	Correct	Incorrect	Correct
botyalism	**botulism**	brokin	**broken**
boundry	**boundary**	brokrage	**brokerage**
bouyant	**buoyant**	bronkiel	**bronchial**
boykot	**boycott**	broshure	**brochure**
boyler plait	**boiler plate**	brounstone	**brownstone**
bozzo	**bozo**	browz	**browse****
brade	**braid****	brue	**brew**
bragart	**braggart**	bruk	**brook**
brah	**bra**	brunkitis	**bronchitis**
brail	**Braille**	brusk	**brusque**
brakeven	**break-even**	bruthers	**brothers**
brakout	**breakout**	bruz	**bruise****
brakup	**breakup**	brybe	**bribe**
brandee	**brandy**	buckel	**buckle**
brane	**brain**	Buda	**Buddha**
branestorm	**brainstorm**	budee	**buddy****
bran-new	**brand-new**	buety	**beauty**
braselet	**bracelet**	bufalo	**buffalo**
braul	**brawl**	bufer	**buffer**
bravry	**bravery**	buffay	**buffet**
bravvado	**bravado**	bufoon	**buffoon**
brawdway	**Broadway**	bugd	**bugged**
brayces	**braces**	buge	**budge**
braysen	**brazen**	bugel	**bugle**
brazere	**brassiere**	bugg	**bug**
breakible	**breakable**	bujet	**budget**
breakthru	**breakthrough**	buk	**buck**
bredth	**breadth****	buke	**book**
breefkase	**briefcase**	buket	**bucket**
breif	**brief**	buksom	**buxom**
brekfast	**breakfast**	buldje	**bulge**
brest	**breast**	buldozer	**bulldozer**
brethren	**brethren**	bulean	**Boolean**
breze	**breeze**	bulit	**bullet**
bridgroom	**bridegroom**	bulitin	**bulletin**
brige	**bridge**	bullemia	**bulemia**
briggader	**brigadier**	bullivard	**boulevard**
briliant	**brilliant**	bullwork	**bulwark**
brissel	**bristle**	bullyon	**bouillon****
Britanica	**Britannica**	buly	**bully**
brite	**bright**	bumbelbee	**bumblebee**
Britin	**Britain****	bumer	**bummer**
britle	**brittle**	bumfog	**BOMFOG**
broak	**broke**	bummper	**bumper**
brocalli	**broccoli**	bundel	**bundle**
broe	**bro'**	bunglow	**bungalow**

Incorrect	Correct	Incorrect	Correct
bunz	**buns**	buyproduct	**byproduct**
burbin	**bourbon**	buz	**buzz**
burch	**birch**	buze	**booze**
burglery	**burglary**	buzwords	**buzzwords**
buriel	**burial**	byass	**bias**
buro	**bureau**	bycultural	**bicultural**
burth mark	**birthmark**	bycuspid	**bicuspid**
burthrite	**birthright**	bycycle	**bicycle**
busibody	**busybody**	byenial	**biennial****
busness	**business**	byeout	**buy-out**
busom	**bosom**	bye-sink	**bissync**
bussel	**bustle**	byfokal	**bifocal**
bussted	**busted**	byin	**buy-in**
busteeay	**bustier**	byle	**bile**
busyly	**busily**	bylingwal	**bilingual**
bute	**boot****	bynary	**binary**
butician	**beautician**	byofeedback	**biofeedback**
butiful	**beautiful**	byology	**biology**
butsher	**butcher**	byonics	**bionics**
butten	**button**	byopsy	**biopsy**
bux	**bucks**	bypolar	**bipolar**

	C		
cabage	**cabbage**	calipso	**calypso**
cabanet	**cabinet**	calizhun	**collision****
cabel	**cable****	calkulus	**calculus**
cach	**catch**	callamity	**calamity**
caddenza	**cadenza**	callender	**calendar****
cafateria	**cafeteria**	callisthenics	**calisthenics**
cafay olay	**café au lait**	calocwiel	**colloquial**
cafeine	**caffeine**	calry	**calorie**
caffay	**café**	calsium	**calcium**
caffs	**calves**	camafloge	**camouflage**
cafkaesk	**Kafkaesque**	camalot	**Camelot**
caigy	**cagey**	camara	**camera**
cairtaker	**caretaker**	camelia	**camellia**
cakafony	**cacophony**	cameradery	**camaraderie**
caktus	**cactus**	camfer	**camphor**
calaco	**calico**	cammcorda	**camcorder**
Calafornia	**California**	canalony	**canneloni**
calcalate	**calculate**	canibis	**cannabis**
caleber	**caliber**	cansel	**cancel**
calidiscope	**kaleidoscope**	canser	**cancer**

Incorrect	Correct	Incorrect	Correct
canvis	**canvas****	carnul	**carnal****
canyen	**canyon**	caroner	**coroner****
caos	**chaos**	carot	**carrot****
capachino	**cappucino**	carowse	**carouse**
capashus	**capacious**	carravan	**caravan**
capcher	**capture**	carrbon dyoxide	
capible	**capable**		**carbon dioxide**
capilary	**capillary**	carrbuncle	**carbuncle**
capitchulate	**capitulate**	carredboard	**cardboard**
capitil	**capital****	carrees	**carries****
caposies sarkoma		carress	**caress**
	Kaposi's Sarcoma	carriage	**carriage**
capp	**cap**	carrjack	**carjack**
cappacity	**capacity**	carrnadge	**carnage**
caprese	**caprice**	carrotid	**carotid**
caprishous	**capricious**	carrpal	**carpal**
capsel	**capsule**	carsinogen	**carcinogen**
capshun	**caption**	cart blansh	**carte blanche**
capt	**capped**	cartalige	**cartilage**
captan	**captain**	cartell	**cartel**
captation fee		cartin	**carton**
	capitation fee	cartune	**cartoon**
carabean	**Caribbean**	carworn	**careworn**
caracter	**character**	carying	**carrying**
caratea	**karate**	casarole	**casserole**
carateen	**carotene**	cascaid	**cascade**
carbahidrate		caset	**cassette**
	carbohydrate	casheer	**cashier**
carben	**carbon**	cashmear	**cashmere**
carberater	**carburetor**	cashoe	**cashew**
carbin monoxide		caskit	**casket**
	carbon monoxide	casmint	**casement**
cardiak	**cardiac**	casock	**cassock**
cardnil	**cardinal**	cassel	**castle**
carear	**career**	cassenova	**Casanova**
carees	**caries****	cassino	**casino**
carefull	**careful**	casstrait	**castrate**
careing	**caring**	castagate	**castigate**
caricatour	**caricature**	castinet	**castanet**
caried	**carried**	casulty	**casualty**
carit	**carat****	cataclysm	**cataclysm****
carkass	**carcass**	catagory	**category**
carm	**calm****	catapiller	**caterpillar**
carma	**karma**	catar	**catarrh**
carmel	**caramel**	catastrofy	**catastrophe**
carnivul	**carnival**	catelogue	**catalog**

Incorrect	Correct	Incorrect	Correct
cateract	**cataract**	cemicle	**chemical**
cathater	**catheter**	cenchury	**century**
catheedral	**cathedral**	cencus	**census****
Cathlic	**Catholic**	cennter	**center**
caticomb	**catacomb**	cenotta	**sonata**
catilyon	**cotillion**	censitivity	**sensitivity**
catipult	**catapult**	centegrade	**centigrade**
catotonic	**catatonic**	centrel	**central**
catridge	**cartridge**	centrifigle	**centrifugal**
CATT skan	**CAT scan**	cerabelum	**cerebellum**
cattfish	**catfish**	cereberal	**cerebral**
cattlike	**catlike**	cerfue	**curfew**
cauff	**cough****	ceriff	**serif**
cavelcaid	**cavalcade**	cerimony	**ceremony**
caveleir	**cavalier**	certin	**certain**
cavernus	**cavernous**	chace	**chase**
caviatt	**caveat**	chagrinned	**chagrined**
cavvity	**cavity**	chaif	**chafe**
cawcashon	**Caucasian**	chaist	**chaste****
cawcus	**caucus**	chalenge	**challenge**
cawk	**caulk**	champeen	**champion**
cawleflower	**cauliflower**	champoo	**shampoo**
cawny	**corny**	chane	**chain**
caws sayleb	**cause célèbre**	chanel	**channel****
cawshun	**caution**	changable	**changeable**
cawz	**cause****	chanoocah	**Chanukah** or
cayjin	**Cajan or Cajun**		**Hanukah**
caynsian	**Keynesian**	chaplin	**chaplain**
cazm	**chasm**	chapple	**chapel**
cazoo	**kazoo**	charaty	**charity**
ceder	**cedar**	chare	**chair**
cee e oh	**CEO**	chariet	**chariot**
ceedee rom	**CD-ROM**	charrter	**charter**
ceese	**cease****	chartible	**charitable**
celabacy	**celibacy**	chastaty	**chastity**
celalite	**cellulite**	chater	**chatter**
celebrait	**celebrate****	chatt	**chat**
cellebrity	**celebrity**	chauffuer	**chauffeur****
celophane	**cellophane**	chawk	**chalk**
celtser	**seltzer**	chawk tawk	**chalk talk**
celulitis	**cellulitis**	chawtle	**chortle**
celuloid	**celluloid**	cheder	**cheddar**
celulose	**cellulose**	cheep	**cheap****
celyaler	**cellular**	cheet	**cheat**
cemantics	**semantics**	cheez	**cheese**
cematary	**cemetery****	cheif	**chief**

Incorrect	Correct	Incorrect	Correct
cheiftin	**chieftain**	cigret	**cigarette**
chelo	**cello**	cilynder	**cylinder**
chemest	**chemist**	ciment	**cement**
cherbert	**sherbet**	cinagog	**synagogue**
cherch	**church**	cinamon	**cinnamon**
cherib	**cherub**	Cinncinatti	**Cincinnati**
cherning	**churning**	cinoshure	**cynosure**
cherrish	**cherish**	circal	**circle**
chesnut	**chestnut**	circomstance	
chestity	**chastity**		**circumstance**
chieftin	**chieftain**	circuler	**circular**
chikkenpoks	**chicken pox**	circumfrence	
children	**children**		**circumference**
chimny	**chimney**	cirkit	**circuit**
chints	**chintz**	cirkumsize	**circumcise**
chipendale	**Chippendale**	cirrcumvent	**circumvent**
chipp	**chip**	cirviks	**cervix**
chivelrus	**chivalrous**	cist	**cyst**
chivelry	**chivalry**	cisterhood	**sisterhood**
chizel	**chisel**	cistitis	**cystitis**
choclit	**chocolate**	cistoscopy	**cystoscopy**
choper	**chopper**	citazen	**citizen**
chorkole	**charcoal**	citris	**citrus**
chossen	**chosen**	cival	**civil**
chouder	**chowder**	civlisation	**civilization**
chow main	**chow mein**	clamer	**clamor**
choyce	**choice**	clamidia	**chlamydia**
chrisanthemun		clanish	**clannish**
	chrysanthemum	clarevoiant	**clairvoyant**
chrisen	**christen****	clarvoiance	**clairvoyance**
Christyan	**Christian****	clasify	**classify**
chuby	**chubby**	clauz	**clause****
chuk	**chuck**	cleanex	**kleenex**
chumy	**chummy**	clearinse	**clearance**
chunel	**Chunnel**	cleek	**clique****
chynatown	**Chinatown**	cleeshay	**cliché**
cibercrud	**cybercrud**	clense	**cleanse**
cibernetics	**cybernetics**	cleptamania	**kleptomania**
ciberspace	**cyberspace**	cleracle	**clerical**
ciborg	**cyborg**	clere	**clear**
ciclamate	**cyclamate**	clevige	**cleavage**
cicle	**cycle**	clientell	**clientele**
ciclone	**cyclone**	climit	**climate**
cicofant	**sycophant**	clincker	**clinker**
cieling	**ceiling****	clinnic	**clinic**
ci-fi	**sci-fi**	cliper	**clipper**

Incorrect	Correct	Incorrect	Correct
clitteris	**clitoris**	cokpit	**cockpit**
cloan	**clone****	cokroch	**cockroach**
clober	**clobber**	coktale	**cocktail**
clok	**clock**	colaborate	**collaborate**
cloke	**cloak**	colapse	**collapse**
cloraform	**chloroform**	colar	**collar****
cloral hidrate		colateral	**collateral**
	chloral hydrate	coldslaw	**coleslaw**
closh	**cloche**	colebluded	**cold-blooded**
closit	**closet**	colect	**collect**
cloun	**clown****	colecter	**collector**
cloyster	**cloister**	coled	**cold**
cloz	**clothes****	coleegue	**colleague**
clozing	**closing**	colege	**college****
clozout	**closeout**	colegiate	**collegiate**
clozure	**closure**	colen	**colon****
clubb	**club**	coler	**color****
cluby	**clubby**	colera	**cholera**
cluch	**clutch**	colerachura	**coloratura**
cludge	**kludge**	Coleseum	**Colosseum**
clumzy	**clumsy**	colestral	**cholesterol**
clyent	**client**	colick	**colic**
clymax	**climax**	collander	**colander**
cnish	**knish**	collapsable	**collapsible**
coad	**code**	colleck	**collect**
coak	**coke**	collegit	**collegiate**
coam	**comb**	collition	**coalition**
coar	**core****	collitis	**colitis**
coardump	**core dump**	collonic	**colonic**
cobawl	**cobol**	collosal	**colossal**
cobler	**cobbler**	colloseum	**coliseum**
cocane	**cocaine**	collostomy	**colostomy**
coch	**coach**	colonaid	**colonnade**
codeen	**codeine**	colone	**cologne****
coersion	**coercion**	colslaw	**coleslaw**
cofee	**coffee**	colum	**column**
coff	**cough****	colusion	**collusion****
coffeklotsh	**kaffeeklatsch**	colyumist	**columnist**
cofin	**coffin**	comemorate	
cognative	**cognitive**		**commemorate**
cogulate	**coagulate**	comendable	
cohearint	**coherent**		**commendable**
coherce	**coerce**	comenshurite	
coinsidence	**coincidence**		**commensurate**
cojitait	**cogitate**	comercial	**commercial**
cokanut	**coconut**	comftable	**comfortable**

Incorrect	Correct	Incorrect	Correct
comikazi	**kamikazi**	comunicate	**communicate**
comission	**commission**	comunity	**community**
comit	**commit****	comurce	**commerce**
comited	**committed**	comute	**commute**
comittee	**committee****	conasseur	**connoisseur**
commedian	**comedian**	conceed	**concede**
commedy	**comedy****	concensus	**consensus**
commen	**common**	concequence	**consequence**
commet	**comet****	concer	**concur****
commic	**comic**	conciention	
comming	**coming**		**conscientious****
comminism	**communism**	concieve	**conceive**
commoon	**commune**	conclaive	**conclave**
commpendum		concock	**concoct**
	compendium	concorse	**concourse**
commplementry		concreet	**concrete**
	complementary**	concurense	**concurrence**
commpression		concushin	**concussion**
	compression	condaminimum	
commyuter	**commuter**		**condominium**
comodity	**commodity**	condamint	**condiment**
comotion	**commotion**	condem	**condemn****
companyon	**companion**	condesend	**condescend**
comparitive	**comparative**	condinsashun	
compatable	**compatible**		**condensation**
compatense	**competence**	condishun	**condition**
compeet	**compete**	condoe	**condo**
compeled	**compelled**	condrum	**condom**
compell	**compel**	conduck	**conduct**
compermize	**compromise**	conect	**connect**
competant	**competent**	conection	**connection**
compinsashun		confadense	**confidence**
	compensation	confascate	**confiscate**
compis	**compass**	confederit	**confederate**
compitition	**competition**	confekshinery	
complacate	**complicate**		**confectionary**
complexshun	**complexion**	confered	**conferred**
complience	**compliance**	conferm	**confirm**
composishun	**composition**	confes	**confess**
compoze	**compose**	confinment	**confinement**
comprahend	**comprehend**	confligrashun	
comprible	**comparable**		**conflagration**
compulsery	**compulsory**	confortable	**comfortable**
compyuter	**computer**	confrence	**conference**
comred	**comrade**	Confushus	**Confucius**
comtroller	**comptroller**	congagate	**conjugate**

Incorrect	Correct	Incorrect	Correct
congell	**congeal**	conseed	**concede**
congenyal	**congenial****	conseive	**conceive**
congradulate		consentrait	**concentrate**
	congratulate	consentrick	**concentric**
congrigashun		consept	**concept**
	congregation	consert	**concert**
congrous	**congruous**	conservitory	**conservatory**
conjer	**conjure**	consession	**concession**
conjeture	**conjecture**	conshunse	**conscience****
conjugle	**conjugal**	conshuss	**conscious****
conker	**conquer****	consil	**consul****
conncentrate	**concentrate**	consiliate	**conciliate**
Connecticut	**Connecticut**	consinement	**consignment**
connglomerate		consintration	
	conglomerate		**concentration**
conngres	**congress**	consise	**concise**
connisseur	**connoisseur**	consistant	**consistent**
connjunction	**conjunction**	consitter	**consider**
connjunctivitis		consoladate	**consolidate**
	conjunctivitis	consomate	**consummate**
connosewer	**connoisseur**	consoul	**console**
connsidrable	**considerable**	constible	**constable**
connspicuous		constilashun	**constellation**
	conspicuous	constint	**constant**
connstitution	**constitution**	consumtion	**consumption**
connstruck	**construct**	consynment	**consignment**
connsultent	**consultant**	consyurge	**concierge**
conntest	**contest**	contajus	**contagious**
conntraseptive		contane	**contain**
	contraceptive	contanent	**continent**
conntrast	**contrast**	contempry	**contemporary**
connvalecent		contemtable	**contemptible**
	convalescent	conterary	**contrary**
connvent	**convent**	conterception	
connvention	**convention**		**contraception**
connvertable	**convertible**	contimplate	**contemplate**
connvick	**convict**	continense	**countenance****
connviktion	**conviction****	continnualy	**continually**
conotashun	**connotation**	continnuous	**continuous****
conote	**connote**	contore	**contour**
conpute	**compute**	contractual	**contractual**
consanent	**consonant**	contrarywise	**contrariwise**
consavation		contratan	**contretemps**
	conservation**	contravershil	
conseal	**conceal**		**controversial**
conseat	**conceit**	contraversy	**controversy**

Incorrect	Correct	Incorrect	Correct
contribeaut	**contribute**	coridor	**corridor**
controled	**controlled**	corigated	**corrugated**
controll	**control**	coril	**coral****
contry	**country**	corn-beef	**corned beef**
conture	**contour**	cornise	**cornice**
conubeal	**connubial**	cornor	**corner****
conviless	**convalesce**	coroborate	**corroborate**
convilute	**convolute**	corperal	**corporal****
convinient	**convenient**	corpisle	**corpuscle**
convirge	**converge**	corpration	**corporation**
convirse	**converse**	corraled	**corralled**
convirtable	**convertible**	corrona	**corona**
convolse	**convulse**	corronary	**coronary**
conyak	**cognac**	corsarge	**corsage**
coo daytah	**coup d'état**	corse	**course****
coo di gra	**coup de grâce**	corsit	**corset**
cood	**could**	cort	**court****
coodent	**couldn't**	cortazone	**cortisone****
cookee cutter		cortison	**courtesan****
	cookie cutter	cortmarshal	**courtmartial**
cookoo	**cuckoo**	cortroom	**courtroom**
cookry	**cookery**	corz	**corps****
cooky jar	**cookie jar**	cosher	**kosher**
cooly	**coolly****	costic	**caustic**
coopay	**coupé**	cosy	**cozy**
coopon	**coupon**	cotage	**cottage**
cooprate	**cooperate**	cotin	**cotton**
cootour	**couture**	counsler	**counselor****
coper	**copper**	counterseptive	
copeus	**copious**		**contraceptive**
cople	**couple**	courticy	**courtesy****
copyriter	**copywriter**	covrage	**coverage**
copywright	**copyright**	cowch potatoe	
cor	**corps****		**couch potato**
coral	**corral****	cowerd	**coward****
coralation	**correlation**	cowhyde	**cowhide**
corderoy	**corduroy**	cowndown	**countdown**
cordnation	**coordination**	cownterfit	**counterfeit**
coreandar	**coriander**	cowntes	**countess**
corect	**correct**	cowwboy	**cowboy**
corectness	**correctness**	coytus	**coitus**
coredless	**cordless**	Cozak	**Cossack**
corelate	**correlate**	cozmanaut	**cosmonaut**
corenia	**cornea**	cozmapolitan	
coreografy	**choreography**		**cosmopolitan**
corespond	**correspond**	cozmic	**cosmic**

Incorrect	Correct	Incorrect	Correct
cozzin	**cousin****	critisise	**criticize**
craby	**crabby**	crittic	**critic****
cradenchle	**credential**	crokadile	**crocodile**
craffty	**crafty**	crokay	**croquet****
crain	**crane**	crokete	**croquette****
craion	**crayon**	crome	**chrome**
crak	**crack**	cronic	**chronic**
crakel	**crackle**	cronology	**chronology**
cramberry	**cranberry**	croocial	**crucial**
cramm	**cram**	crood	**crude**
crashendo	**crescendo**	crool	**cruel**
craul	**crawl**	croop	**croup**
craws-egsamine		croopya	**croupier**
	cross-examine	crooze	**cruise****
crawssrode	**crossroad**	crosection	**cross section**
craydal	**cradle**	crosepurposes	
craynium	**cranium**		**cross-purposes**
craypes	**crepes****	crosreference	
cream de la cream			**cross-reference**
	creme de la creme	croud	**crowd**
creap	**creep**	cround	**crowned**
creashun	**creation**	crowch	**crouch**
credable	**credible**	crowen	**crone**
creddit	**credit**	crowshay	**crochet****
credeter	**creditor**	crsanthemun	
credlus	**credulous**		**chrysanthemum**
creedence	**credence**	cruch	**crutch**
creem	**cream****	crue	**crew**
creese	**crease****	cruely	**cruelly**
cresh	**crèche**	cruesade	**crusade**
cressent	**crescent**	crulty	**cruelty**
creture	**creature**	crum	**crumb**
crewelty free	**cruelty free**	crussty	**crusty**
criket	**cricket**	crute	**cruet**
crimnal	**criminal**	cruzer	**cruiser**
crimsin	**crimson**	cryed	**cried**
criple	**cripple**	cubbard	**cupboard**
cripptografer		cubbicle	**cubicle**
	cryptographer	Cuber	**Cuba**
cript	**crypt**	cuepay	**coupé**
criptic	**cryptic**	cuhoots	**cahoots**
Crismas	**Christmas**	cukie	**cookie**
Cristian	**Christian****	culcher	**culture**
cristilize	**crystallize**	culd	**culled****
critacal	**critical**	cule	**cool**
criteek	**critique****	culer	**color****

Incorrect	Correct	Incorrect	Correct
cullesterole	**cholesterol**	cupon	**coupon**
cullinary	**culinary**	curancy	**currency**
cultavate	**cultivate**	curchef	**kerchief**
cumand	**command****	curent	**current****
cumense	**commence**	curiculum	**curriculum**
cumfortable	**comfortable**	curige	**courage**
cuming	**coming**	curios	**curious**
cumpound	**compound**	curiousity	**curiosity**
cumprehension		curley	**curly**
	comprehension	curnel	**kernel****
cumputer	**computer**	curonel	**colonel****
cunclude	**conclude**	currare	**curare**
cundemm	**condemn****	curree	**curry**
cundone	**condone**	curretage	**curettage**
cundum	**condom**	cursere	**cursor**
cunferr	**confer**	curst	**cursed**
cungressional		curteous	**courteous**
	congressional	curtesy	**courtesy****
cuning	**cunning**	custid	**custard**
cunjugale	**conjugal**	custidy	**custody**
cunservative	**conservative**	custimor	**customer****
cunspiracy	**conspiracy**	cuting edge	**cutting edge**
cunstitoot	**constitute**	cuttup	**cutup**
cunstruktion	**construction**	cuver	**cover**
cunsult	**consult**	cuvinant	**covenant**
cunsume	**consume**	cwafeur	**coiffure**
cuntaminate	**contaminate**	cyder	**cider**
cuntralto	**contralto**	cynecure	**sinecure**
cuntraption	**contraption**	cypher	**cipher**
cuntrive	**contrive**	cyropracter	**chiropractor**
cuntry	**country**	cyubic	**cubic**
cunvention	**convention**	cyumin	**cumin**

D

Incorrect	Correct	Incorrect	Correct
dabate	**debate**	dakiri	**daiquiri**
dable	**dabble**	dakron	**dacron**
dabochery	**debauchery**	dakshound	**dachshund**
dacolté	**décolleté**	dalapadate	**dilapidate**
dadda	**Dada**	dalia	**dahlia**
dafodile	**daffodil**	dalinkwent	**delinquent**
dager	**dagger**	daluge	**deluge**
dait rape	**date rape**	damenshin	**dimension**
daity	**deity**	damige	**damage**

Incorrect	Correct	Incorrect	Correct
danderuf	**dandruff**	deefensive	**defensive**
dandylion	**dandelion**	deeflate	**deflate**
dane	**deign**	deel	**deal**
danjros	**dangerous**	deelete	**delete**
dary	**dairy****	deelusion	**delusion**
dassiay	**dossier**	deepression	**depression**
daterbass	**data base**	deesel	**diesel**
datta	**data**	deesensitize	**desensitize**
dauter	**daughter**	deestruck	**destruct**
davelop	**develop**	deetached	**detached**
dawg	**dog**	deetoxification	
dawk	**dork**		**detoxification**
dawne	**dawn**		
daybu	**debut**	deeture	**detour**
daycore	**decor**	deeva	**diva**
dayly	**daily****	deeviant	**deviant**
dayne	**deign**	deeviation	**deviation**
daysy-	**daisy-wheel**	deevower	**devour**
daytabase	**data base**	def	**deaf**
dazel	**dazzle**	defakate	**defecate**
debaner	**debonair**	defalt	**default**
debry	**debris**	defanitely	**definitely**
debths	**depths**	defanition	**definition**
decarate	**decorate**	defeet	**defeat**
deceive	**deceive**	defence	**defense**
decend	**descend**	defendent	**defendant**
decese	**decease**	defensable	**defensible**
deciet	**deceit**	defered	**deferred**
decleration	**declaration**	defficit	**deficit**
decmal	**decimal**	deffinit	**definite****
decon	**deacon****	defie	**defy**
decreese	**decrease**	definitly	**definitely**
decription	**decryption**	defishent	**deficient**
ded	**dead****	defiunce	**defiance**
deddline	**deadline**	deflaytion	**deflation**
dedecate	**dedicate**	defrence	**reference**
dedlock	**deadlock**	defyed	**defied**
deduse	**deduce****	dehidrate	**dehydrate**
deebug	**debug**	dekaid	**decade**
deeception	**deception**	dekonjestant	
deecompression			**decongestant**
	decompression	delagate	**delegate**
deeconstruck	**deconstruct**	deleetion	**deletion**
deecumposed		delemma	**dilemma**
	decomposed	delite	**delight**
deeductable	**deductible**	delivry	**delivery**
		dellhuge	**deluge**

Incorrect	Correct	Incorrect	Correct
delliberate	**deliberate**	derje	**dirge**
dellicacy	**delicacy**	derrivative	**derivative**
dellicatessan	**delicatessen**	desabl	**decibel**
dellicious	**delicious**	desastrous	**disastrous**
dellv	**delve**	descover	**discover**
delly	**deli**	descrepancy	**discrepancy**
delt	**dealt**	descriminate	**discriminate**
delux	**deluxe**	desease	**disease**
demacrat	**democrat**	desecant	**desiccant**
demeening	**demeaning**	Desember	**December**
deminish	**diminish**	desency	**decency**
deminstrate	**demonstrate**	desent	**decent****
demmented	**demented**	desicion	**decision**
demmocrasy	**democracy**	desicrate	**desecrate****
demmography		desided	**decided**
	demography	desifer	**decipher**
demogogue	**demagogue**	desine	**design**
demonstratable		desireable	**desirable**
	demonstrable	desolit	**desolate****
demytass	**demi-tasse**	desparate	**desperate**
dence	**dense**	despare	**despair**
denie	**deny**	desprit	**desperate**
dentafrice	**dentifrice**	dessertion	**desertion**
denteen	**dentine**	dessicate	**desiccate****
dentel	**dental**	dessmal	**decimal**
dentice	**dentist**	desstop	**desktop**
dentle damn	**dental dam**	desstructive	**destructive**
denyal	**denial**	destenation	**destination**
deoderant	**deodorant**	destribute	**distribute**
depature	**departure**	det	**debt**
dependant	**dependent****	detale	**detail**
dependible	**dependable**	deteck	**detect**
depervation	**deprivation**	deteriate	**deteriorate**
depo	**depot**	detestible	**detestable**
depot-prevera		deth	**death**
	depo-provera	detocks	**detox**
deppilitary	**depilatory**	detter	**debtor**
depresent	**depressant**	detterent	**deterrent**
depreshiation		dettergent	**detergent**
	depreciation	dettermine	**determine**
depricate	**deprecate****	dettour	**detour**
deprieve	**deprive**	deveant	**deviant**
deps	**depths**	deveate	**deviate**
depudy	**deputy**	devel	**devil**
derick	**derrick**	devellop	**develop**
derileck	**derelict**	deversity	**diversity**

Incorrect	Correct	Incorrect	Correct
devert	**divert**	dilligent	**diligent**
devest	**divest**	dillute	**dilute**
devide	**divide**	dilog	**dialogue**
devine	**divine**	dilusion	**delusion**
devistate	**devastate**	dimeen	**demean**
devius	**devious**	dimensha precox	
devorce	**divorce**		**dementia praecox**
devulge	**divulge**	dimminative	**diminutive**
dewoe	**duo**	dimmwit	**dimwit**
dexterous	**dextrous**	dimolish	**demolish**
dezign	**design**	dimond	**diamond**
dezil	**diesel**	dinamic	**dynamic**
diacese	**diocese**	dinate	**dinette**
diafram	**diaphragm****	dingee	**dingy****
diatishn	**dietitian**	dinomite	**dynamite**
dicesion	**decision**	dint	**didn't**
dich	**dish**	diper	**diaper**
dichwasher	**dishwasher**	dipleat	**deplete**
dicksie	**Dixie**	diplomer	**diploma**
dicline	**decline**	diposit	**deposit**
didjital	**digital**	dipprived	**deprived****
diebetes	**diabetes**	dirdy	**dirty**
dieing	**dying****	direcshon	**direction**
dielaprare	**dial-a-prayer**	dirive	**derive**
dielation	**dilation****	dirogatory	**derogatory**
dier	**dire**	dirth	**dearth**
dierea	**diarrhea**	diry	**diary****
difakto	**de facto**	dis	**diss**
diference	**difference**	disadent	**dissident**
diftheria	**diphtheria**	disagrement	**disagreement**
difibralate	**defibrillate**	disallusion	**disillusion**
dificult	**difficult**	disalow	**disallow**
difrenshal	**differential**	disanent	**dissonant**
difuse	**diffuse**	disapate	**dissipate**
digestable	**digestible**	disaprobashon	
diggnity	**dignity**		**disapprobation**
diggress	**digress**	disaray	**disarray**
diggs	**digs**	disasterous	**disastrous**
diging	**digging**	disatisfy	**dissatisfy**
dihard	**diehard**	disavantaged	
dijest	**digest**		**disadvantaged**
dijitallus	**digitalis**	disaybled	**disabled**
diktionery	**dictionary**	disbersment	**disbursement**
dilect	**dialect**	discod	**discard**
dillema	**dilemma**	disconsilite	**disconsolate**
dilletant	**dilettante**	disconsurt	**disconcert**

Incorrect	Correct	Incorrect	Correct
discribe	**describe**	disqualafy	**disqualify**
discrimanate	**discriminate**	disrepitible	**disreputable**
discription	**description**	disrup	**disrupt**
discurtius	**discourteous**	dissability	**disability**
discwalafy	**disqualify**	dissagree	**disagree**
disdane	**disdain**	dissapoint	**disappoint**
disect	**dissect**	dissappear	**disappear**
disegragate	**desegregate**	dissastrous	**disastrous**
disembowl	**disembowel**	dissc	**disc** or **disk**
disemenate	**disseminate**	disscharge	**discharge**
disenfermation		disscorse	**discourse**
	disinformation	disscount	**discount**
disent	**dissent****	disscover	**discover**
disentery	**dysentery**	disscretion	**discretion**
disertion	**desertion**	disscusion	**discussion**
disfunctional		dissern	**discern**
	dysfunctional	dissheveled	**disheveled**
disgize	**disguise**	dissinfect	**disinfect**
disiduos	**deciduous**	dissinflation	**disinflation**
disign	**design**	dissinter	**disinter**
disimalar	**dissimilar**	dissipline	**discipline**
disipal	**disciple**	dissk	**disc** or **disk**
disipline	**discipline**	disskette	**diskette**
disklosher	**disclosure**	dissmis	**dismiss**
disko	**disco**	dissmount	**dismount**
diskretionery		dissplay	**display**
	discretionary	dissposil	**disposal**
disleksia	**dyslexia**	dispute	**dispute**
dismantel	**dismantle**	dissrespect	**disrespect**
dismissel	**dismissal**	disstemper	**distemper**
disociate	**dissociate**	disstracation	**distraction**
disolution	**dissolution**	distaf	**distaff**
disolve	**dissolve**	distastful	**distasteful**
disonest	**dishonest**	distence	**distance**
dispair	**despair**	disterb	**disturb**
disparije	**disparage**	distilation	**distillation**
dispasition	**disposition****	distingwish	**distinguish**
dispensery	**dispensary**	distint	**distinct**
dispeptic	**dyspeptic**	distraut	**distraught**
disperporshin		distres	**distress**
	disproportion	districk	**district**
dispicible	**despicable**	distrofy	**dystrophy**
displacment	**displacement**	distroy	**destroy**
disposess	**dispossess**	distruction	**destruction**
disposible	**disposable**	disuade	**dissuade**
dispurse	**disperse****	disy	**dicey**

Incorrect	Correct	Incorrect	Correct
disy	**dizzy**	dont	**don't**
dito	**ditto**	donut	**doughnut**
ditretis	**detritus**	doosh	**douche**
divaden	**dividend**	dooty	**duty**
divice	**device****	dopomine	**dopamine**
divied	**divide**	dorible	**durable**
divise	**devise****	dormatory	**dormitory**
divoid	**devoid**	dormint	**dormant**
divoshin	**devotion**	dosege	**dosage**
divurje	**diverge**	dosile	**docile**
divver	**diver**	dosseay	**dossier**
divvertikulosis		dott	**dot**
	diverticulosis	doubble dipper	**double-dipper**
divvestiture	**divestiture**		
divvine	**divine**	doubel diget	**double-digit**
divvision	**division**	doudy	**dowdy**
dizaster	**disaster**	douner	**downer**
dizease	**disease**	dounfall	**downfall**
diznee	**Disney**	doungrade	**downgrade**
do process	**due process**	dounside	**downside**
doal	**dole**	dounsize	**downsize**
doam	**dome**	dountime	**downtime**
dockudramer	**docudrama**	dourger	**dowager**
docter	**doctor**	dout	**doubt**
doctrinare	**doctrinaire**	dovtale	**dovetail**
docuementery		dowe	**Dow**
	documentary	dowenpour	**downpour**
dodel	**dawdle**	dowery	**dowry**
doenate	**donate**	downsoning	**downzoning**
doge	**dodge**	downtoun	**downtown**
doged	**dogged**	dragen	**dragon**
dogeral	**doggerel**	dramer	**drama**
dohmed	**domed**	dranege	**drainage**
dokument	**document**	draun	**drawn**
doledrums	**doldrums**	drawwback	**drawback**
dolfin	**dolphin**	dred	**dread**
doller	**dollar**	dreem	**dream**
domanere	**domineer**	drege	**dredge**
domasile	**domicile**	drery	**dreary**
dominent	**dominant**	drifwood	**driftwood**
dominyon	**dominion**	drivin	**drive-in**
domono	**domino**	drivven	**driven**
doner	**donor**	drivway	**driveway**
dongaree	**dungaree**	drizel	**drizzle**
donky	**donkey**	drol	**droll**
donstairs	**downstairs**	droping	**dropping**

Incorrect	Correct	Incorrect	Correct
droup	**droop**	dupplicate	**duplicate**
drouze	**drowse**	durby	**derby**
drownded	**drowned**	durma	**derma**
droyd	**droid**	durmatitis	**dermatitis**
drugery	**drudgery**	durration	**duration**
druggstore	**drugstore**	durres	**duress**
drugist	**druggist**	durring	**during**
drummstick	**drumstick**	duse	**deuce**
drunkeness	**drunkenness**	dussedup	**dust-up**
dryd	**dried**	dustee	**dusty**
dryvbuy	**drive-by**	dutyful	**dutiful**
dryve	**drive**	duve	**dove**
dubb	**dub**	duz	**does****
dubbel	**double**	duzen	**dozen**
dubbius	**dubious**	duzzens	**dozens**
duce	**deuce**	dwarve	**dwarf**
Duch	**Dutch**	dweam	**DWEM**
dudenum	**duodenum**	dwebe	**dweeb**
dueable	**doable**	dyagnose	**diagnose**
duely	**duly****	dyagonal	**diagonal**
dule	**dual****	dyal	**dial**
dulsit	**dulcet**	dyaretic	**diuretic**
dum	**dumb**	dyaspera	**diaspora**
dumby	**dummy**	dyce	**dice****
dume	**doom**	dycotomy	**dichotomy**
dumean	**demean**	dyet	**diet****
dumestic	**domestic**	dyitery	**dietary**
dumfound	**dumbfound**	dynasor	**dinosaur**
dumpee	**dumpy**	dyner	**diner****
dumpp	**dump**	dyning	**dining**
dungin	**dungeon****	dyoxen	**dioxin**
dunse	**dunce**	dyulog	**dialogue**
dupleks	**duplex**	dyve	**dive**
duplisity	**duplicity**	dyvon	**divan**

E

Incorrect	Correct	Incorrect	Correct
earing	**earring**	ebulient	**ebullient**
earlyer	**earlier**	eccise	**excise**
earwacks	**earwax**	ecconomic	**economic**
easly	**easily**	ech	**etch****
easment	**easement**	eckwity	**equity**
eavoke	**evoke**	eclesiestical	**ecclesiastical**
ebiny	**ebony**	eclips	**eclipse**

Incorrect	Correct	Incorrect	Correct
eco	**echo**	efishent	**efficient**
economacal	**economical**	efnocentric	**ethnocentric**
edable	**edible**★★	ege	**edge**★★
edatorial	**editorial**	eggs party	**ex parte**
eddit	**edit**	eggsecutive	**executive**
edima	**edema**	egoe	**ego**
edipiss complex		egplant	**eggplant**
	Oedipus complex	egsack	**exact**
edipus	**Oedipus**	egschange	**exchange**
editer	**editor**	egsit	**exit**
educatable	**educable**	egsplore	**explore**
edyucate	**educate**	egstempiraneus	
ee male	**E-mail**		**extemporaneous**
eeclampsia	**eclampsia**	egstink	**extinct**
eeger	**eager**	egstract	**extract**
eegle	**eagle**	egsume	**exhume**
eegocentric	**egocentric**	egzalt	**exalt**★★
eejaculate	**ejaculate**	egzert	**exert**
eelastic	**elastic**	egzist	**exist**
eelation	**elation**	egzotic	**exotic**
eele	**eel**	eibrow	**eyebrow**
eelection	**election**	eightteen	**eighteen**
eelectron	**electron**	eithernet	**Ethernet**
eeliptikal	**elliptical**	ejeck	**eject**
eemerging	**emerging**	ejiss	**aegis**
eemetic	**emetic**	ekcite	**excite**
eerake	**earache**	eklectic	**eclectic**
eerode	**erode**	ekology	**ecology**
eesop	**ESOP**	ekonomy	**economy**
eest	**east**	eks	**ex**
eether	**either**★★	eksalt	**exalt**★★
eethus	**ethos**	eksamorf	**exomorph**
eevakuate	**evacuate**	ekschange	**exchange**
eevaluate	**evaluate**	eksclude	**exclude**
eevent	**event**	eksclusive	**exclusive**
eeventially	**eventually**	ekscrewshiate	**excruciate**
eeviction	**eviction**	eksec	**exec**
eevocative	**evocative**	ekseed	**exceed**★★
eface	**efface**	eksillerate	**exhilarate**
efect	**effect**★★	eksist	**exist**
efedrin	**ephedrine**	eksistence	**existence**
efemminate	**effeminate**	eksize	**excise**
efervesent	**effervescent**	eksort	**exhort**
effert	**effort**	ekspadite	**expedite**
eficashus	**efficacious**	ekspansion	**expansion**
efishency	**efficiency**	ekspier	**expire**

Incorrect	Correct	Incorrect	Correct
eksploit	**exploit**	ellusadate	**elucidate**
ekspossure	**exposure**	elum	**elm**
ekspresway	**expressway**	elve	**elf**
ekspurt	**expert**	emagrint	**emigrant****
ekstacy	**ecstasy**	emale	**E-mail**
ekstend	**extend**	emanense	**eminence**
ekstermination		emarald	**emerald**
	extermination	embalism	**embolism**
ekstirpate	**extirpate**	embarassed	**embarrassed**
ekstole	**extol or extoll**	embasador	**ambassador**
ekstortion	**extortion**	embelish	**embellish**
ekstra	**extra**	embezle	**embezzle**
ekwater	**equator**	emblim	**emblem**
ekzonerate	**exonerate**	embomb	**embalm**
elafantisis	**elephantiasis**	embos	**emboss**
elagent	**elegant**	embrase	**embrace**
elagie	**elegy****	embrio	**embryo**
element	**element****	embroyder	**embroider**
elavate	**elevate**	emfasis	**emphasis**
elbo	**elbow**	emfizema	**emphysema**
eleck	**elect**	eminate	**emanate**
eleet	**elite**	emisary	**emissary**
elefent	**elephant**	emity	**enmity****
elegable	**eligible**	emmaskulatin	
elegants	**elegance**		**emasculation**
elektristy	**electricity**	emmbedded	**embedded**
elfs	**elves**	emmergancy	**emergency**
eliikser	**elixir**	emmployee	**employee**
elipse	**ellipse**	emolient	**emollient****
elipsis	**ellipsis**	emoshun	**emotion**
elisit	**elicit****	emperialism	**imperialism**
ellaberate	**elaborate**	empethy	**empathy**
ellaquent	**eloquent**	empier	**empire****
ellavation	**elevation**	emporer	**emperor**
elldoper	**L-dopa**	empotence	**impotence**
ellectercardagram		empressionism	
	electrocardiogram		**impressionism**
ellectorate	**electorate**	emptyness	**emptiness**
ellectronics	**electronics**	emty	**empty**
ellementary	**elementary****	emurge	**emerge****
ellevator	**elevator**	enamerd	**enamored**
elliminate	**eliminate****	enamy	**enemy****
ellisit	**elicit****	enchellada	**enchilada**
ellnino	**el Niño**	encite	**incite****
ellude	**elude****	encoed	**encode**
elluminate	**illuminate****	encompes	**encompass**

Incorrect	Correct	Incorrect	Correct
encorporate	**incorporate**	enterprenoor	
encript	**encrypt**		**entrepreneur**
endamorf	**endomorph**	enterview	**interview**
endere	**endear**	entier	**entire**
endever	**endeavor**	entimasy	**intimacy**
endoctrinate	**indoctrinate**	entise	**entice**
endorsment	**endorsement**	entolerance	**intolerance**
endouw	**endow**	entreet	**entreat**
enertia	**inertia**	entreprise	**enterprise**
enfarction	**infarction**	enuf	**enough**
enferior	**inferior**	enunsiate	**enunciate**
enfidell	**infidel**	envade	**invade**
enfiltrate	**infiltrate**	envaygle	**inveigle**
enfinite	**infinite**	envelup	**envelop****
enfisema	**emphysema**	envestigate	**investigate**
enflation	**inflation**	envie	**envy**
enfluence	**influence**	envirement	**environment**
enforcible	**enforceable**	envius	**envious**
enformercial	**informercial**	envoke	**invoke**
engeneer	**engineer**	envyable	**enviable**
Englind	**England**	enyuresis	**enuresis**
enhabit	**inhabit**	epacure	**epicure**
enhale	**inhale**	epademic	**epidemic**
enherit	**inherit**	epasod	**episode**
enigetic	**energetic**	epataf	**epitaph****
enitial	**initial**	epedermis	**epidermis**
enitiate	**initiate**	episcene	**epicine**
enivate	**enervate****	eplepsy	**epilepsy**
enncounter	**encounter**	eppick	**epic****
ennthoosiastic		eppok	**epoch****
	enthusiastic	equalibrium	**equilibrium**
enntry	**entry**	equaly	**equally**
enny	**any**	equanocks	**equinox**
enoble	**ennoble**	equidy	**equity**
enraige	**enrage**	equipt	**equipped**
enrap	**enwrap****	equivilent	**equivalent**
enrole	**enroll****	erace	**erase**
ensefalitis	**encephalitis**	eratic	**erratic****
ensime	**enzyme**	erb	**herb**
ensin	**ensign**	erban	**urban****
enstill	**instill**	erbs	**urbs**
entale	**entail**	erchin	**urchin**
entamology		eredrum	**eardrum**
	entomology**	erektion	**erection**
entatain	**entertain**	eresa	**ERISA**
enterance	**entrance**	ergency	**urgency**

Incorrect	Correct	Incorrect	Correct
erind	**errand****	ethacal	**ethical**
erithromicin		etikete	**etiquette**
	erythromycin	etsetra	**et cetera**
erje	**urge**	eufology	**ufology**
erk	**irk**	eunicorn	**unicorn**
erl	**earl**	euniform	**uniform**
erly	**early**	eunilatoral	**unilateral**
ermin	**ermine**	eutopia	**utopia**
ernest	**earnest**	evalushun	**evolution**
eroneus	**erroneous**	evapperate	**evaporate**
eror	**error****	evedence	**evidence**
erray	**array**	evenshul	**eventual**
errgo	**ergo**	evesdrop	**eavesdrop**
errgonomics	**ergonomics**	evick	**evict**
errosion	**erosion**	eviserate	**eviscerate**
errsatz	**ersatz**	evning	**evening**
erth	**earth**	evry	**every**
Ery	**Erie****	evrywear	**everywhere**
eryudite	**erudite**	evul	**evil**
esay	**essay****	evulve	**evolve**
escoriate	**excoriate**	evvaluate	**evaluate**
escourt	**escort**	evvaluation	**evaluation**
esculator	**escalator**	exackly	**exactly**
esence	**essence**	exacute	**execute**
esential	**essential**	exagarate	**exaggerate**
Eskamo	**Eskimo**	examanation	
eskeroll	**escarole**		**examination**
eskwisite	**exquisite**	exaust	**exhaust**
esofagus	**esophagus**	excape	**escape**
espianoge	**espionage**	excede	**exceed****
esscape	**escape**	excell	**excel****
esskwire	**esquire**	excentric	**eccentric****
essoteric	**esoteric**	excercise	**exercise****
esspousal	**espousal**	excitment	**excitement**
esstate	**estate**	exembank	**Eximbank**
essteemed	**esteemed**	exemt	**exempt**
esstimation	**estimation**	exessive	**excessive**
esstragin	**estrogen**	exgurshin	**excursion**
estamate	**estimate**	exhail	**exhale**
esteme	**esteem**	exhorbitant	**exorbitant**
Ester	**Easter**	exibit	**exhibit**
estract	**extract**	existance	**existence**
et	**ate****	exitus	**exodus**
etealogy	**etiology**	exkreet	**excrete**
eternaty	**eternity**	exort	**exhort**

Incorrect	Correct	Incorrect	Correct
expeled	**expelled**	extraordinary	
expell	**expel**		**extraordinary**
expence	**expense**	extravert	**extrovert**
expendible	**expendable**	extravigent	**extravagant**
experashun	**expiration****	extreem	**extreme**
experiance	**experience**	exurpt	**excerpt**
explaination	**explanation**	exxpedition	**expedition**
explative	**expletive**	exxperement	**experiment**
explisit	**explicit**	exxploit	**exploit**
expres	**express**	exxport	**export**
expresso	**espresso**	exxtent	**extent****
expurteez	**expertise**	exxterminate	**exterminate**
exray	**x-ray**	exxternal	**external**
exsecutive	**executive**	exxtort	**extort**
exseed	**exceed****	exxtract	**extract**
exsellent	**excellent**	exxtrapolate	**extrapolate**
exsept	**except****	exzema	**eczema**
exseptional	**exceptional****	exzile	**exile**
exsessive	**excessive**	exzilirate	**exhilarate**
exsist	**exist**	ey	**eye****
exsiteable	**excitable**	eyekon	**icon**
exsize	**excise**	eyesite	**eyesight**
exsperience	**experience**	eyesometric	**isometric**
exstacy	**ecstasy**	eyestrane	**eyestrain**
exstol	**extol or extoll**	Eyetalian	**Italian**
extateretorial		eyether	**either****
	extraterritorial	eyetinry	**itinerary**
extention	**extension**	eyris	**iris**
extersensery	**extrasensory**	eyudee	**IUD**
extracate	**extricate**	ezein	**ezine**
extracuricular		ezy	**easy**
	extracurricular	ezzampel	**example**

F

Incorrect	Correct	Incorrect	Correct
fabel	**fable**	facshun	**faction**
fabrakate	**fabricate**	facter	**factor**
fabrik	**fabric**	factery	**factory**
fabulus	**fabulous**	factsimile	**facsimile**
facalty	**faculty**	fadd	**fad**
faceing	**facing**	fadelity	**fidelity**
fachewal	**factual**	faery	**fairy****
fachuos	**fatuous**	faim	**fame**
facinate	**fascinate**	fain	**feign****

Incorrect	Correct	Incorrect	Correct
faiseoff	**face-off**	farse	**farce**
fakshus	**factious**	farsited	**farsighted**
faksimile	**facsimile**	fasaving	**facesaving**
fakt	**fact**	fase	**face**
faktual	**factual**	faseless	**faceless**
fakulty	**faculty**	fasen	**fasten**
falback	**fallback**	faseshus	**facetious**
fale	**fail**	fashial	**facial**
falibel	**fallible**	fashinable	**fashionable**
falicitate	**felicitate**	fashist	**fascist**
falicy	**fallacy**	fashon	**fashion**
falkin	**falcon**	fasilitate	**facilitate**
fallocrasy	**phallocracy**	fasility	**facility****
fallsafe	**failsafe**	fasill	**facile**
fallse	**false**	fasinate	**fascinate**
fallsees	**falsies**	fasithia	**forsythia**
fallshud	**falsehood**	fasodd	**façade**
fallter	**falter**	fassen	**fasten**
fallus	**phallus**	fassion	**fashion**
falopian tube		fasstidious	**fastidious**
	fallopian tube	fateeg	**fatigue**
falsafy	**falsify**	fatel	**fatal****
falseto	**falsetto**	faten	**fatten**
falt	**fault**	fatful	**fateful****
faluble	**fallible**	fathim	**fathom**
familar	**familiar**	fationable	**fashionable**
familyarize	**familiarize**	fattality	**fatality**
famin	**famine**	faty	**fatty**
famly	**family**	faught	**fought**
fammer	**farmer**	fauster	**foster**
fammished	**famished**	faverible	**favorable**
famus	**famous**	favrit	**favorite**
fanagle	**finagle**	fawce	**force**
fancyful	**fanciful**	fawceps	**forceps**
fane	**feign**	fawcet	**faucet****
fanntasise	**fantasize**	fawd	**ford**
fansy	**fancy**	fawklift	**forklift**
fanticy	**fantasy****	fawl	**fall**
fantom	**phantom**	fawmat	**format**
farely	**fairly**	fayed	**fade**
farenheit	**Fahrenheit**	faylure	**failure**
farfecht	**farfetched**	fayselift	**face-lift**
faringitis	**pharyngitis**	fayth	**faith**
farmacy	**pharmacy**	fayze	**faze****
faroe	**faro**	fead	**feed**
farrenheight	**Fahrenheit**	feadback	**feedback**

Incorrect	Correct	Incorrect	Correct
feald	**field**	fery	**ferry****
fealing	**feeling**	fesable	**feasible**
feasco	**fiasco**	fesster	**fester**
Febuary	**February**	festavil	**festival**
fech	**fetch****	feter	**fetter**
fedd	**Fed, the**	fether	**feather**
fedderals	**Federales**	fetle	**fettle**
feddora	**fedora**	fettish	**fetish****
fedeback	**feedback**	feu	**few**
fedral	**federal**	feuneril	**funeral****
feeansay	**fiancé****	feurius	**furious**
feeasco	**fiasco**	feva	**fever**
feeblely	**feebly**	fiatrap	**firetrap**
feeline	**feline**	fibbrilation	**fibrillation**
feemale	**female**	fiberoid	**fibroid**
feend	**fiend****	fichnet	**fishnet**
feesability	**feasibility**	ficks	**fix**
feest	**feast****	ficktion	**fiction**
feesta	**fiesta**	fidle	**fiddle**
feeture	**feature**	fiebrus	**fibrous**
feetus	**fetus**	fieder	**feeder**
feild	**field**	fierbug	**firebug**
feirce	**fierce**	fierfiter	**firefighter**
fella	**fellow**	fiesty	**feisty**
fellony	**felony**	figahead	**figurehead**
fellt	**felt**	figet	**fidget**
femenine	**feminine**	figger	**figure**
femer	**femur**	figyative	**figurative**
femminism	**feminism**	fikil	**fickle**
feness	**finesse****	fiksation	**fixation**
fennder	**fender**	fikticious	**fictitious**
fenobarbital		filagree	**filigree**
	phenobarbital	filanderer	**philanderer**
fenomenal	**phenomenal**	filanthropy	**philanthropy**
fenomenon	**phenomenon**	filately	**philately**
fense	**fence**	filay	**filet**
fere	**fear**	fileal	**filial**
ferett	**ferret**	filharmonic	**philharmonic**
ferget	**forget**	fillay	**filet**
fergive	**forgive**	fille	**faille**
fernish	**furnish**	fillibuster	**filibuster**
fersake	**forsake**	fillter	**filter**
ferst-rate	**first-rate**	fillthee	**filthy**
ferthermore	**furthermore**	fillum	**film**
fertil	**fertile**	filmsy	**flimsy**
ferver	**fervor**	filosophy	**philosophy**

Incorrect	Correct	Incorrect	Correct
finanse	**finance****	flayk	**flake**
finanshil	**financial**	flaykee	**flaky**
finatic	**fanatic**	flebitis	**phlebitis**
finese	**finesse****	flech	**flesh****
fingatip	**fingertip**	flecksible	**flexible**
fingger	**finger**	fleckstime	**flextime**
finil	**final**	fleebag	**fleabag**
finilize	**finalize**	fleese	**fleece**
finly	**finely****	flegeling	**fledgling**
finngerprint	**fingerprint**	flem	**phlegm**
fireing	**firing**	flert	**flirt**
firey	**fiery**	flete	**fleet**
firlo	**furlough**	flie	**fly**
firment	**ferment****	flikker	**flicker**
firoshus	**ferocious**	flipint	**flippant**
firther	**further****	flipp	**flip**
firtilise	**fertilize**	flirtacious	**flirtatious**
fishion	**fission**	flite	**flight**
fisically	**physically**	flix	**flicks**
fisiology	**physiology**	flochart	**flowchart**
fisscle	**fiscal****	flok	**flock****
fite	**fight**	flone	**flown**
fith	**fifth**	flook	**fluke**
fiting	**fitting**	floot	**flute**
fium	**fume**	flopy	**floppy**
flabagasted	**flabbergasted**	flor	**flaw****
flabergas	**flabbergast**	flore	**floor****
flachulent	**flatulent**	floresent	**fluorescent**
fladjelation	**flagellation**	floride	**fluoride****
flagg ship	**flagship**	floris	**florist**
flaging	**flagging**	floriscope	**fluoroscope**
flaim	**flame**	florish	**flourish**
flale	**flail**	Florrida	**Florida**
flambay	**flambé**	flote	**float**
flamible	**flammable**	flownder	**flounder**
flammboyant	**flamboyant**	flownse	**flounce**
flammenco	**flamenco**	flubb	**flub**
flaper	**flapper**	flucks	**flux**
flapp	**flap**	flucktuation	**fluctuation**
flasid	**flaccid**	flud	**flood**
flatary	**flattery**	fludder	**flutter**
flaten	**flatten**	flued	**fluid**
flater	**flatter**	fluint	**fluent**
flattfoot	**flatfoot**	flukshuate	**fluctuate**
flaver	**flavor**	flurine	**fluorine**
flaygrent	**flagrant****	flury	**flurry**

Incorrect	Correct	Incorrect	Correct
flys	**flies**	formadable	**formidable**
fobb	**fob**	formaly	**formally****
fobia	**phobia**	forman	**foreman**
focit	**faucet****	formelism	**formalism**
focks	**fox**	forment	**foment****
focksy	**foxy**	formil	**formal**
foe pas	**faux pas**	formost	**foremost**
foke	**folk**	forperson	**foreperson**
fokil	**focal**	forrensic	**forensic**
fokis	**focus**	forrest	**forest**
foks	**folks**	forrgon	**foregone**
foksel	**forecastle**	forrnication	
foled	**fold**		**fornication****
foleo	**folio**	forrum	**forum****
folicle	**follicle**	forsee	**foresee**
folige	**foliage**	forsful	**forceful**
foller	**follow**	forsight	**foresight**
foly	**folly**	forskin	**foreskin**
fom	**farm**	forstall	**forestall**
fome	**foam**	fortatude	**fortitude**
fomula	**formula**	forteen	**fourteen**
fondal	**fondle**	fosfate	**phosphate**
fonetic	**phonetic**	fosforescence	
fonics	**phonics**		**phosphorescence**
fonograph	**phonograph**	fosforus	**phosphorus**
fonte	**font****	fosil	**fossil**
fony	**phony**	fotagenic	**photogenic**
foolback	**fullback**	foto	**photo**
forcast	**forecast**	fotography	**photography**
forceable	**forcible**	fotosinthesis	
forchoon	**fortune**		**photosynthesis**
forck	**fork**	fountin	**fountain**
forclose	**foreclose**	fourthrite	**forthright**
forclozure	**foreclosure**	fourties	**forties**
forebid	**forbid**	fourtunately	**fortunately**
fored	**forehead**	fourtutuous	**fortuitous**
fore ever	**forever**	fourty	**forty**
forefit	**forfeit**	fow	**foe**
foremaldahide		foward	**forward****
	formaldehyde	fownd	**found****
foremer	**former**	fowndation	**foundation**
forfit	**forfeit**	foyble	**foible**
forgry	**forgery**	fraggment	**fragment**
forhead	**forehead**	fraim	**frame**
forin	**foreign**	fraim-up	**frame-up**
forje	**forge**	frajile	**fragile**

Incorrect	Correct	Incorrect	Correct
frakas	**fracas**	frought	**fraught**
frakcher	**fracture**	froun	**frown**
frale	**frail**	Froyd	**Freud**
frankfutter	**frankfurter**	froydian	**Freudian**
frannchize	**franchise**	frugl	**frugal**
frase	**phrase****	fruntend	**front-end**
frate	**freight**	fruntil	**frontal**
frawd	**fraud**	frusstate	**frustrate**
fraygrince	**fragrance**	frutful	**fruitful**
fraymwork	**framework**	Fryday	**Friday**
freaby	**freebie**	fue	**few**
freadom	**freedom**	fued	**feud**
freagint	**free agent**	fuedal	**feudal**
frealode	**freeload**	fugative	**fugitive**
freddy mack		fuge	**fugue**
	Freddie Mac	fuje	**fudge**
freek	**freak****	fulashus	**fallacious**
freese-dry	**freeze-dry**	fullfil	**fulfill**
frekel	**freckle**	fullfilment	**fulfillment**
frelance	**freelance**	fultime	**full-time**
frend	**friend****	fumbil	**fumble**
frendship	**friendship**	funcshin	**function**
frendsy	**frenzy**	fundew	**fondue**
frennetic	**frenetic**	fundimental	**fundamental**
frenonogy	**phrenology**	funel	**funnel**
frenship	**friendship**	funeril	**funeral****
frensic	**forensic**	fungis	**fungus**
frequincy	**frequency**	funkshunal	**functional**
freshin	**freshen**	funndementalist	
freway	**freeway**		**fundamentalist**
fricasee	**fricassee**	funy	**funny**
fricshin	**friction**	furee	**furry****
frier	**friar****	furlow	**furlough**
fril	**frill**	furm	**firm**
frinje	**fringe**	furnature	**furniture**
frite	**fright**	furst aide	**first aid**
friter	**fritter**	fuselage	**fuselage**
friternel	**fraternal**	fust	**first**
frivlous	**frivolous**	futball	**football**
frojalent	**fraudulent**	futil	**futile**
frok	**frock**	futlose	**footloose**
frollic	**frolic**	fuz	**fuzz****
fronteersman		fyancy	**fiancé****
	frontiersman	fyberglass	**fiberglass**
frontspiece	**frontispiece**	fyber optic	**fiber-optic**
frosen	**frozen**	fyfo	**FIFO**

Incorrect	Correct	Incorrect	Correct
fynite	**finite**	fyuror	**furor**
fyoog	**fugue**	fyushea	**fuchsia**
fyord	**fjord**	fyuture	**future**

G

Incorrect	Correct	Incorrect	Correct
gaberdeen	**gabardine**	garrish	**garish**
gaf	**gaffe****	gasalene	**gasoline**
gafilter fish	**gefilte fish**	gasha	**geisha**
gaget	**gadget**	gaskit	**gasket**
gail	**gale**	gasseous	**gaseous**
gaim	**game**	gasstritis	**gastritis**
gaitkeeper	**gatekeeper**	gastly	**ghastly**
galacksy	**galaxy**	gatfly	**gadfly**
galary	**gallery**	gauk	**gawk**
galeic	**Gaelic**	gavvel	**gavel**
galent	**gallant**	gawdy	**gaudy**
galick	**Gaelic**	gawge	**gorge**
galin	**gallon**	gawl	**gall**
galip	**gallop**	gawlbladder	**gallbladder**
gallaxy	**galaxy**	gawr	**gore**
gallvanize	**galvanize**	gawse	**gauze****
gally	**galley**	gaymee	**gamy**
galows	**gallows**	gaz	**gas**
galstone	**gallstone****	gazel	**gazelle**
gama globlin		gazet	**gazette**
	gamma globulin	gealogy	**geology**
gambul	**gamble****	geazer	**geezer**
gammer	**gamma**	geedesic	**geodesic**
gammit	**gamut****	geego	**GIGO**
ganda	**gander**	geehad	**jihad**
gangreen	**gangrene**	geeolegy	**geology**
ganishee	**garnishee**	geep	**jeep**
garantee	**guarantee****	geer	**gear**
gararge	**garage**	geestring	**G-string**
garbige	**garbage**	geetar	**guitar**
gard	**guard**	gelies	**jellies**
garder	**garter**	gellding	**gelding**
gardian	**guardian**	gemm	**gem**
gardin	**garden**	genacide	**genocide**
gardner	**gardener**	genarator	**generator**
garilus	**garrulous**	geneology	**genealogy**
garit	**garret**	genisis	**genesis**
garlick	**garlic**	gennerate	**generate**

Incorrect	Correct	Incorrect	Correct
genneric	**generic**	giography	**geography**
genrally	**generally**	giometry	**geometry**
genrus	**generous**	girdal	**girdle**
gentalia	**genitalia**	gise	**guise**
gentelman	**gentleman**	git	**get****
gentlely	**gently**	gittar	**guitar**
genuwine	**genuine**	givaway	**giveaway**
genyufleck	**genuflect**	givback	**giveback**
genyus	**genius****	gizzmo	**gizmo**
gerd	**gird**	glair	**glare**
geremiad	**jeremiad**	glajer	**glazier****
gergul	**gurgle**	glamerus	**glamorous**
gerl	**girl**	glammer	**glamour**
gerlfrend	**girlfriend**	glanse	**glance**
germain	**germane****	glase	**glaze**
Germin	**German****	glashul	**glacial**
gerrintology	**gerontology**	glass sealing	**glass ceiling**
gerrund	**gerund**	glawsy	**glossy**
gescher	**gesture****	gleem	**gleam**
geshtalt	**gestalt**	glew	**glue**
gess	**guess**	glich	**glitch****
gest	**guest****	glidder	**glider**
geswit	**Jesuit**	glimer	**glimmer**
gettaway	**getaway**	glimse	**glimpse**
getto	**ghetto**	gliserin	**glycerin**
gettset	**jet set**	gliter	**glitter**
gezundhite	**gesundheit**	glitratty	**glitterati****
giantism	**gigantism**	glits	**glitz****
gidance	**guidance**	globle	**global**
gide	**guide**	gloome	**gloom****
gidy	**giddy**	glorafy	**glorify**
gient	**giant**	glosary	**glossary**
gigal	**giggle**	glosies	**glossies**
gigg	**gig**	glotis	**glottis**
giggabit	**gigabit**	glowkoma	**glaucoma**
giggolo	**gigolo**	gluecose	**glucose**
gighurts	**gigahertz**	glutin	**glutton****
gilless	**guileless**	gnawshus	**nauseous**
gillotine	**guillotine**	goalden parashoot	
gilty	**guilty**		**golden parachute**
gimick	**gimmick**	goble	**gobble****
giminasium	**gymnasium**	goblit	**goblet**
gimnast	**gymnast**	goddless	**godless**
ginacology	**gynecology**	gode	**goad**
ginee	**guinea**	godess	**goddess**
gingam	**gingham**	goegoe	**go-go**

Incorrect	Correct	Incorrect	Correct
goenad	**gonad**	gramy	**Grammy**
goffer	**gopher****	granaid	**grenade**
gogles	**goggles**	grandaughter	
gokart	**gocart**		**granddaughter**
gole	**goal****	grandur	**grandeur**
golebrick	**goldbrick**	grane	**grain**
gon	**gone**	granfather	**grandfather**
gondala	**gondola**	granmal	**grand mal**
gonnarea	**gonorrhea**	grannmother	
goofee	**goofy**		**grandmother**
goolag	**gulag**	gransmanship	
goolash	**goulash**		**grantsmanship**
gooroo	**guru**	grany	**granny**
gootenburg	**Gutenberg**	granyule	**granule**
gord	**gourd**	grashus	**gracious**
gorgous	**gorgeous**	grassp	**grasp**
gormet	**gourmet**	gratooty	**gratuity**
gosamer	**gossamer**	grattis	**gratis**
goshe	**gauche****	gravaty	**gravity**
gosip	**gossip**	gravle	**gravel**
gosspel	**gospel**	grayhound	**greyhound**
gost	**ghost**	graysful	**graceful**
gote	**goat**	greanhouse	**greenhouse**
gotea	**goatee**	greatful	**grateful**
goten	**gotten**	greating	**greeting**
goun	**gown**	gredy	**greedy**
gowge	**gouge**	greengoe	**gringo**
gowss	**gauss**	greevence	**grievance**
goyter	**goiter**	greevus	**grievous**
grabb	**grab**	greif	**grief**
graber	**grabber**	greive	**grieve**
gradduate	**graduate**	greivence	**grievance**
graditude	**gratitude**	gremmlin	**gremlin**
gradjewal	**gradual**	grene	**green**
graf	**graph**	grenemail	**greenmail**
graffic	**graphic**	grete	**greet**
grafics	**graphics**	grewsome	**gruesome**
grafitti	**graffiti**	greze	**grease****
grafology	**graphology**	griddlock	**gridlock**
gragarious	**gregarious**	gridiern	**gridiron**
graid	**grade**	grill	**grille****
graipfruit	**grapefruit**	grimas	**grimace**
graive	**grave**	grinn	**grin**
grajuation	**graduation**	grissed	**grist**
gramer	**grammar**	gritt	**grit**
gramm	**gram**	gritz	**grits**

Incorrect	Correct	Incorrect	Correct
groanup	**grown-up**	gudlookin	**goodlooking**
groap	**grope**	gud will	**goodwill**
grone	**groan****	gufe	**goof**
groop	**group**	guidence	**guidance**
groopy	**groupie**	gullable	**gullible**
grose	**gross**	guner	**gunner**
grosry	**grocery**	gurder	**girder**
grotesk	**grotesque**	gurlee	**girlie**
grothe	**growth**	guse	**goose**
grovey	**groovy**	gussto	**gusto**
growch	**grouch**	guter	**gutter**
grownd	**ground**	guterul	**guttural**
grownwork	**groundwork**	gutts	**guts**
groyn	**groin**	guvernment	**government**
gruje	**grudge**	guvnor	**governor**
grume	**groom**	guynofobia	**gynophobia**
grummpy	**grumpy**	guyser	**geyser**
grunje	**grunge**	gwackamola	**guacamole**
grutootous	**gratuitous**	gwash	**gouache****
gruve	**groove****	gygerbite	**gigabyte**
gruvil	**grovel**	gyger counter	
gryme	**grime**		**Geiger counter**
grynd	**grind**	gyle	**guile**
guage	**gauge****	gypsim	**gypsum**

H

Incorrect	Correct	Incorrect	Correct
habbit	**habit**	halaluyah	**hallelujah**
habichawate	**habituate**	halatosis	**halitosis**
habillitate	**habilitate**	Halaween	**Halloween**
habitchual	**habitual**	halcean	**halcyon**
hach	**hatch**	hale mary	**Hail Mary**
hackneed	**hackneyed**	halfs	**halves**
hadick	**haddock**	halmark	**hallmark**
haf	**half**	haloosination	
haffway	**halfway**		**hallucination**
hagerd	**haggard**	halow	**hallow****
hagil	**haggle**	halsion	**halcyon**
hainus	**heinous****	halusinate	**hallucinate**
hairbrained	**harebrained**	halusinogen	**hallucinogen**
hairlip	**harelip**	hamberger	**hamburger**
hait	**hate**	hamer	**hammer**
hakk	**hack**	hamlit	**hamlet**
hakker	**hacker**	hammatoe	**hammer toe**

Incorrect	Correct	Incorrect	Correct
hammstring	**hamstring**	haterd	**hatred**
hanbag	**handbag**	havock	**havoc**
hanbook	**handbook**	Hawayi	**Hawaii**
hancraft	**handicraft**	hawse	**horse****
hancuffs	**handcuffs**	haybeas korpis	
handdriting	**handwriting**		**habeas corpus**
handel	**handle**	haylo	**halo****
handycap	**handicap**	hayness	**heinous****
handywork	**handiwork**	hayrdue	**hairdo**
hanful	**handful**	hayrim	**harem**
hangkerchif	**handkerchief**	haytee	**Haiti**
hanmedown		haytful	**hateful****
	hand-me-down	hayvin	**haven****
hanngover	**hangover**	hayzy	**hazy**
hanoocah	**Hanukah**	hazbin	**has-been**
hant	**haunt**	hazil	**hazel**
hapin	**happen**	hazzerd	**hazard**
happly	**happily**	headake	**headache**
haradin	**harridan**	headinist	**hedonist**
harange	**harangue**	headress	**headdress**
harber	**harbor**	hearafter	**hereafter**
harboild	**hardboiled**	heartally	**heartily****
hardisk	**hard disk**	hebroo	**Hebrew**
hardning	**hardening**	hecktic	**hectic**
harecut	**haircut****	heddy	**heady**
haredresser	**hairdresser**	hede	**heed****
haried	**harried**	hedhunter	**headhunter**
Harlacwin	**harlequin**	hedkwarters	**headquarters**
harmoenyus	**harmonious**	hedlight	**headlight**
harnis	**harness**	hedline	**headline**
harrass	**harass**	hed-on	**head-on**
harrdship	**hardship**	heeler	**healer**
harremless	**harmless**	heematoma	**hematoma**
harrvest	**harvest**	heep	**heap**
harrykrishna		heerby	**hereby**
	Hare Krishna	heero	**hero**
harth	**hearth**	heet	**heat**
hartware	**hardware**	heetstroke	**heatstroke**
harty	**hearty****	heffer	**heifer**
hary	**hairy**	heighth	**height**
hasard	**hazard**	heirarchy	**hierarchy**
hasen	**hasten**	heje	**hedge**
hasienda	**hacienda**	hejemonoy	**hegemony**
hasle	**hassle****	hekil	**heckle**
hassidim	**Hasidim**	heksigon	**hexagon**
hatchit	**hatchet****	hel	**hell****

Incorrect	Correct	Incorrect	Correct
helish	**hellish**	hevy	**heavy**
hellem	**helm**	hevywait	**heavyweight**
hellicopter	**helicopter**	hewmongis	**humongous**
hellmit	**helmet**	hiarkill file	
hellples	**helpless**		**hierarchical file**
hellyn	**hellion**	hi-ball	**highball**
helo	**hello**	hibonate	**hibernate**
helth	**health**	hibread	**hybrid**
hemaglobin	**hemoglobin**	hibrow	**highbrow**
hemeroids	**hemorrhoids**	hich	**hitch**
hemesphere	**hemisphere**	hickup	**hiccup or hiccough**
hemm	**hem**	hiden	**hidden**
hemmafilia	**hemophilia**	hidensity	**high density**
hemmorage	**hemorrhage**	hideus	**hideous**
h-em-oh	**HMO**	hidrafobia	**hydrophobia**
hena	**henna**	hidranja	**hydrangea**
hensfourth	**henceforth**	hidraulic	**hydraulic**
hepful	**helpful**	hidrint	**hydrant**
hepparin	**heparin**	hidrofoil	**hydrofoil**
heppetitis	**hepatitis**	hidrogen	**hydrogen**
herassment	**harassment**	hidrokloric acid	
heratige	**heritage**		**hydrochloric acid**
herbashus	**herbaceous**	hiejack	**hijack**
herdel	**hurdle****	hiemlick manoover	
hereoic	**heroic**		**Heimlich maneuver**
heresay	**hearsay**	hifen	**hyphen**
herild	**herald**	hi-fidelity	**high fidelity**
hering	**herring****	hi-frequensy	
herisy	**heresy**		**high frequency**
herl	**hurl**	higbernate	**hibernate**
hermafradite		highpothesis	**hypothesis**
	hermaphrodite	highskool	**high school**
hermatige	**hermitage**	highst	**heist**
heros	**heroes**	hight	**height**
herredity	**heredity**	hi-handed	**high-handed**
herron	**heron**	hikery	**hickory**
her's	**hers**	hi-level	**high-level**
herse	**hearse**	hillarius	**hilarious**
hert	**hurt**	himen	**hymen**
hertofore	**heretofore**	hinderance	**hindrance**
hesatate	**hesitate**	hindoo	**Hindu**
hetagenius	**heterogeneous**	hinesite	**hindsight**
hethin	**heathen**	hiness	**highness**
hetrosexual	**heterosexual**	hinj	**hinge**
heve	**heave**	hipadermic	**hypodermic**
heven	**heaven****		

Incorrect	Correct	Incorrect	Correct
hipathermia	**hyperthermia**	hoamboy	**homeboy**
hiper	**hyper**	hoap	**hope**
hiperaktive	**hyperacative**	hobbell	**hobble**
hiperbolee	**hyperbole**	hobsinz cherce	
hipersensetive			**Hobson's choice**
	hypersensitive	hoby	**hobby****
hipertension	**hypertension**	hocky	**hockey****
hipertext	**hypertext**	hoddog	**hotdog**
hipnosis	**hypnosis**	hoemefobia	**homophobia**
hipnotist	**hypnotist**	hojpoj	**hodgepodge**
hipocricy	**hypocrisy**	hokes	**hoax**
hipocrite	**hypocrite**	holagram	**hologram**
hipocritic oath		holea	**wholly****
	Hippocratic oath	holedings	**holdings**
hipoglycemia		holedout	**holdout**
	hypoglycemia	holeharted	**wholehearted**
hipopotimis		holesale	**wholesale**
	hippopotamus	holesome	**wholesome**
hipotnoose	**hypotenuse**	holeycause	**holocaust**
hippee	**hippy**	holindaze	**hollandaise**
hipphopp	**hiphop**	hollicust	**holocaust**
hippokrit	**hypocrite**	holliday	**holiday****
hirearky	**hierarchy**	hollistic	**holistic**
hiredditery	**hereditary**	holow	**hollow****
hireup	**higher-up**	holyness	**holiness**
hirezolution		homaker	**homemaker**
	high resolution	homaside	**homicide**
hirise	**high-rise**	homegeneous	
hirling	**hireling**		**homogeneous****
hiroglific	**hieroglyphic**	homerfobia	**homophobia**
hiroism	**heroism**	homless	**homeless**
hirpeas	**herpes**	homly	**homely**
hisself	**himself**	hommage	**homage**
hisstamine	**histamine**	hommonim	**homonym**
hissterical	**hysterical**	homoesexual	**homosexual**
histeria	**hysteria**	homsick	**homesick**
histerictomoy		homsted	**homestead**
	hysterectomy	homwork	**homework**
histry	**history**	honakah	**Hanukah**
hite	**height**	honerable	**honorable**
hi-teck	**high-tech**	honeydo	**honeydew**
hivv	**HIV**	honist	**honest**
hiway	**highway**	honner	**honor**
hiyena	**hyena**	honny	**honey**
hizpanic	**Hispanic**	honrary	**honorary**
		honshow	**honcho**

Incorrect	Correct	Incorrect	Correct
honymoon	**honeymoon**	howzes	**houses**
hoo	**who**	hoy polloy	**hoi polloi**
hoobress	**hubris**	hoyst	**hoist****
hoonta	**junta****	hoze	**hose****
hoor	**whore****	hoziery	**hosiery**
hoove	**hoof**	hubb	**hub**
hopefull	**hopeful**	hubbkap	**hubcap**
hopeing	**hoping**	hud	**hood**
hopless	**hopeless**	hudd	**HUD**
horafyd	**horrified**	hudel	**huddle**
horemone	**hormone**	huf	**hoof**
horenjus	**horrendous**	huk	**hook**
horey	**hoary****	hukelbery	**huckleberry**
horible	**horrible**	hukworm	**hookworm**
horizen	**horizon**	humain	**humane****
horney	**horny**	humbell	**humble****
hornit	**hornet**	humer	**humor**
horra	**horror**	humilliate	**humiliate**
horrizontal	**horizontal**	huming	**humming**
horrorscope	**horoscope**	hummanities	**humanities**
horsey	**horsy**	humpe	**hump**
horshoe	**horseshoe**	humrus	**humorous****
horspower	**horsepower**	hunderd	**hundred**
hortaculcher	**horticulture**	hungar	**hunger**
horty	**haughty**	hungery	**hungry****
hosh	**harsh**	hupbub	**hubbub**
hosheesh	**hashish**	huray	**hurray**
hosspice	**hospice**	huricane	**hurricane**
hosspital	**hospital****	hurnia	**hernia**
hosspitality	**hospitality**	hursoot	**hirsute**
hosstel	**hostel****	hury	**hurry**
hostige	**hostage**	husle	**hustle**
hostle	**hostile****	hussler	**hustler**
hothedded	**hotheaded**	hute	**hoot**
hothows	**hothouse**	hutzpah	**chutzpah**
hotileer	**hotelier**	huvel	**hovel**
hottbed	**hotbed**	huver	**hover**
hottel	**hotel**	huxter	**huckster**
houshold	**household**	huzbind	**husband**
houswife	**housewife**	huzy	**hussy**
houzbraker	**housebreaker**	hyatis	**hiatus**
houzing	**housing**	hygene	**hygiene**
howel	**howl**	hymnil	**hymnal**
howevver	**however**	hyoobriss	**hubris**
hownd	**hound**	hypacrite	**hypocrite**
howskeeper	**housekeeper**		

Incorrect	Correct	Incorrect	Correct
hypatheticle	**hypothetical**	hyumanity	**humanity**
hypocracy	**hypocrisy**	hyumid	**humid**
hystrung	**high-strung**	hyumidifer	**humidifier**
hyumanatarien		hyumility	**humility**
	humanitarian	hyuristics	**heuristics**

I

Incorrect	Correct	Incorrect	Correct
iadine	**iodine**	Ilinois	**Illinois**
ibaprofen	**ibuprofen**	iliterate	**illiterate**
icahn	**icon or ikon**	illagitimate	**illegitimate**
iceing	**icing**	illeetist	**elitist**
icey	**icy**	illiad	**Iliad**
ich	**itch**	illisit	**illicit****
idd	**id**	illude	**elude****
ideel	**ideal**	illyitis	**ileitis**
ideer	**idea**	ilness	**illness**
idendicle	**identical**	ilogigal	**illogical**
identafy	**identify**	iltempered	**illtempered**
ideosyncracy	**idiosyncrasy**	iluminate	**illuminate****
idget	**idiot**	ilusion	**illusion****
idiology	**ideology**	ilusstrious	**illustrious**
idium	**idiom**	ilustrate	**illustrate**
idollater	**idolater**	imaculate	**immaculate**
idylic	**idyllic**	imadgine	**imagine**
iern	**iron****	imagrint	**immigrant****
iffie	**iffy**	imatation	**imitation**
iggnite	**ignite**	imaterial	**immaterial**
ignamineus	**ignominious**	imature	**immature**
ignerant	**ignorant**	imbark	**embark**
ignor	**ignore**	imbezzler	**embezzler**
igominy	**ignominy**	imbicile	**imbecile**
igwana	**iguana**	imbiew	**imbue****
igzasprate	**exasperate**	imeasurable	
iknishun	**ignition**		**immeasurable**
ikon	**icon**	imediate	**immediate**
ikonaclass	**iconoclast**	imense	**immense**
ikthiology	**ichthyology**	imenslee	**immensely**
iland	**island**	imerging	**emerging**
ilastic	**elastic**	imerse	**immerse**
ile	**isle****	imidiately	**immediately**
ilectronic	**electronic**	imige	**image**
ilegal	**illegal**	imigry	**imagery**
ilegible	**illegible****	iminint	**imminent****

Incorrect	Correct	Incorrect	Correct
immagination		imployee	**employee**
	imagination	importence	**importance**
immegration	**immigration**	imposibility	**impossibility**
immemrable		impower	**empower**
	immemorable	imprasario	**impresario**
immesh	**enmesh**	impres	**impress**
immodest	**immodest**	impreshin	**impression**
immpact	**impact**	improovment	
immperative	**imperative**		**improvement**
immplore	**implore**	impuin	**impugn**
immport	**import**	impurfect	**imperfect**
immpregnate	**impregnate**	imput	**input****
immpropriety		impyaty	**impiety**
	impropriety	imune	**immune**
immpulse	**impulse**	inable	**enable****
immpuritiy	**impurity**	inacceptable	**unacceptable**
imobil	**immobile**	inaddmissible	
imoleate	**immolate**		**inadmissible**
imoral	**immoral****	inadekwit	**inadequate**
imortil	**immortal**	inadsesible	**inaccessible**
impare	**impair**	inain	**inane****
imparshal	**impartial**	inamel	**enamel**
impashent	**impatient**	inamored	**enamored**
impashoned	**impassioned**	inamy	**enemy****
impasition	**imposition**	inate	**innate**
impass	**impasse**	inaugarate	**inaugurate**
impaterbable		inavertent	**inadvertent**
	imperturbable	inavoidable	**unavoidable**
impatus	**impetus**	inawdible	**inaudible**
impecible	**impeccable**	inbalance	**imbalance**
impeech	**impeach**	inbieb	**imbibe**
impeed	**impede**	inbrolio	**imbroglio**
impeerial	**imperial**	incalcable	**incalculable**
impell	**impel**	incarnit	**incarnate**
impenitrible	**impenetrable**	incert	**insert****
impervize	**improvise**	incesint	**incessant**
impetense	**impotence**	incet	**inset****
impetent	**impotent**	inchant	**enchant**
impicunius	**impecunious**	inchoir	**enquire**
impinje	**impinge**	incidently	**incidentally**
impirtenant	**impertinent**	incidious	**insidious**
impius	**impious**	incinsere	**insincere**
implament	**implement**	incipid	**insipid**
implaquable	**implacable**	incircle	**encircle**
implie	**imply**	inclanation	**inclination**
implisit	**implicit**	inclemit	**inclement**

Incorrect	Correct	Incorrect	Correct
inclood	**include**	inditement	**indictment**
inclosher	**enclosure**	individuly	**individually**
inclyne	**incline**	indocternate	**indoctrinate**
incogneto	**incognito**	indomnitable	**indomitable**
incombent	**incumbent**	indores	**indoors**
incondecent	**incandescent**	indowment	**endowment**
incorijible	**incorrigible**	induce	**induce**
incourage	**encourage**	inducment	**inducement**
incrament	**increment**	induktive	**inductive**
incredable	**incredible**	indurance	**endurance**
increse	**increase**	industral	**industrial**
incroch	**encroach**	Indyan	**Indian**
incryption	**encryption**	inefable	**ineffable**
incum	**income**	inekscusible	**inexcusable**
incumpatable		iner	**inner**
	incompatible	inersha	**inertia**
incured	**incurred**	inervate	**innervate****
incuring	**incurring**	inevatable	**inevitable**
incyclopedia	**encyclopedia**	inexrable	**inexorable**
incyurible	**incurable**	infadel	**infidel**
indagent	**indigent**	infadelaty	**infidelity**
indagestion	**indigestion**	infalible	**infallible**
indago	**indigo**	infamashun	**information**
indalent	**indolent**	infanitly	**infinitely**
indascreet	**indiscreet****	infecshun	**infection**
indaspensible		infent	**infant**
	indispensable	inferaction	**infraction**
indastry	**industry**	infered	**infrared**
indavisible	**indivisible****	inferier	**inferior**
inddent	**indent**	inferm	**infirm**
indeesent	**indecent**	infermary	**infirmary****
indefensable	**indefensible**	infermation	**information**
indeks	**index**	inferstructure	
indelable	**indelible**		**infrastructure**
independant	**independent**	infimous	**infamous**
indesent	**indecent**	infinative	**infinitive**
indesirable	**undesirable**	infincy	**infancy**
indesposed	**indisposed**	infintile	**infantile**
indetted	**indebted**	infintry	**infantry**
indiferent	**indifferent**	infireority	**inferiority**
indiggnent	**indignant**	inflamable	**inflammable**
indight	**indite****	inflashin	**inflation**
indijinus	**indigenous****	infleckshun	**inflection**
indiketive	**indicative**	inflewenza	**influenza**
indiscribible	**indescribable**	inflooence	**influence**
indisisive	**indecisive**	influcks	**influx**

Incorrect	Correct	Incorrect	Correct
influinse	**influence**	inklined	**inclined**
influmatin	**inflammation**	inkognito	**incognito**
inforce	**enforce**	inkoherent	**incoherent**
inforemal	**informal**	inkompitent	**incompetent**
infrence	**inference**	inkomunicado	
infur	**infer**		**incommunicado**
infurtility	**infertility**	inkoncievable	
infuze	**infuse**		**inconceivable**
infyuriate	**infuriate**	inkongrous	**incongruous**
ingagement	**engagement**	inkonspicuous	
ingconclusive			**inconspicuous**
	inconclusive	inkontanent	**incontinent**
ingection	**injection**	inkorpperate	**incorporate**
ingine	**engine**	inkredulous	**incredulous**
Inglish	**English**	inkriminate	**incriminate**
ingrachiate	**ingratiate**	inkubater	**incubator**
ingrave	**engrave**	inkwest	**inquest**
ingreat	**ingrate**	inkwiry	**inquiry**
ingreedient	**ingredient**	inkwisitive	**inquisitive**
ingunction	**injunction**	inkyubater	**incubator**
inhabatint	**inhabitant**	inlighten	**enlighten**
inhabition	**inhibition**	innabsencha	**in absentia**
inhail	**inhale**	innacurate	**inaccurate**
inhancement		innapropriate	
	enhancement		**inappropriate**
inhanse	**enhance**	innarticulate	**inarticulate**
inherrit	**inherit**	inn as much as	
inhyuman	**inhuman**		**inasmuch as**
inibility	**inability**	innaugurate	**inaugurate**
inifective	**ineffective**	innauspicious	
iniksplicible	**inexplicable**		**inauspicious**
iniquality	**inequality**	innclusive	**inclusive**
inishal	**initial**	inncomprable	
inishialise	**initialize**		**incomparable**
inixpirienced		inncomprehensible	
	inexperienced		**incomprehensible**
injary	**injury**	innconvenient	
injeanius	**ingenious****		**inconvenient**
injek	**inject**	inndemity	**indemnity**
injery	**injury**	inndenture	**indenture**
injestion	**ingestion**	innduction	**induction**
injoyment	**enjoyment**	inndulge	**indulge**
inkapable	**incapable**	innebreate	**inebriate**
inkapacitate	**incapacitate**	innechative	**initiative**
inkarserate	**incarcerate**	innedible	**inedible**
inkeruptible	**incorruptible**	inneficient	**inefficient**

Incorrect	Correct	Incorrect	Correct
innept	**inept****	innventer	**inventor**
innfekshious	**infectious**	innvest	**invest****
innfermercial	**infomercial**	innvestigatin	
	or **informercial**		**investigation**
innfinitive	**infinitive**	innvolve	**involve**
innfinity	**infinity**	innvulnable	**invulnerable**
innflate	**inflate**	inocense	**innocence**
innflexible	**inflexible**	inocuous	**innocuous**
innfluenza	**influenza**	inordinant	**inordinate**
innformant	**informant**	inormous	**enormous**
innfringe	**infringe**	inovate	**innovate**
innfusion	**infusion**	inpail	**impale**
innhospitible	**inhospitable**	inpediment	**impediment**
innitiation	**initiation**	inpenitent	**impenitent**
innjustise	**injustice**	inpersonal	**impersonal**
innlaw	**in-law**	inpersonate	**impersonate**
innlay	**inlay**	inpitigo	**impetigo**
innoculate	**inoculate**	inplant	**implant**
innraktable	**intractable**	inplawsible	**implausible**
innrem	**in rem**	inpolite	**impolite**
innsekticide	**insecticide**	inpractical	**impractical**
innsert	**insert****	inprapritey	**impropriety**
innsignia	**insignia**	inpregnable	**impregnable**
innsist	**insist**	inprinting	**imprinting**
innsitutionalization		inprison	**imprison**
	institutionalization	inprobable	**improbable**
innsolvent	**insolvent**	inpromtu	**impromptu**
innsomia	**insomnia**	inproper	**improper**
innspection	**inspection**	inprovident	**improvident**
innstalation		inpulsive	**impulsive**
	installation**	inpunitiy	**impunity****
innstitution	**institution**	inquier	**inquire**
innstruction	**instruction**	inrich	**enrich**
innsult	**insult**	insalate	**insulate****
inntegrity	**integrity**	insalent	**insolent**
inntegument	**integument**	insanaty	**insanity**
inntermediary		inscrewtable	**inscrutable**
	intermediary	inseck	**insect**
inntestine	**intestine**	insekure	**insecure**
inntolerant	**intolerant**	insemble	**ensemble**
inntransagent		insendery	**incendiary**
	intransigent	insense	**incense**
inntrinsic	**intrinsic**	insentive	**incentive**
inntruder	**intruder**	inseprable	**inseparable**
innuit	**Inuit**	inserjint	**insurgent**
innveetro	**in vitro**	insest	**incest****

Incorrect	Correct	Incorrect	Correct
insibordinate		intavention	intervention
	insubordinate	intavil	interval
insident	incident	integeral	integral
insied	inside	intelectual	intellectual
insiggnificant		intelegance	intelligence
	insignificant	intemprate	intemperate
insiminate	inseminate	intensafy	intensify
insinerator	incinerator	intenshun	intention
insipient	incipient**	interceed	intercede
insise	incise	intercep	intercept
insision	incision	intercorse	intercourse
insisive	incisive	interduce	introduce
insistant	insistent	interferance	interference
insite	insight**	intergration	integration
inskription	inscription	interlewd	interlude
insolluble	insoluble	intermitent	intermittent
insparation	inspiration	intermural	intramural
instagate	instigate	internul	internal
instalment	installment	interpalate	interpolate**
instatute	institute	interpet	interpret
insted	instead	interrest	interest
instense	instance	intersede	intercede
instibility	instability	intersession	
instink	instinct		intercession**
instintaneus		interspection	
	instantaneous		introspection
instrament	instrument	interupt	interrupt
instruk	instruct	interusion	intrusion
insufrable	insufferable	interuterine	intrauterine
insurtion	insertion	intervenous	intravenous
insyulin	insulin	intervert	introvert
insyzer	incisor	intervue	interview
intacomm	intercom	inthrall	enthrall
intadick	interdict	inthusiasm	enthusiasm
intaface	interface	intifere	interfere
intagrate	integrate	intirior	interior**
intajection	interjection**	intooishun	intuition
intamarry	intermarry	intoragate	interrogate
intamate	intimate**	intoxacate	intoxicate
intamediete	intermediate	intraactive	interactive
intanational	international	intracacy	intricacy
intanet	Internet	intradependent	
intangle	entangle		interdependent
intanjible	intangible	intradisciplinary	
intaseck	intersect		interdisciplinary
intavenous	intravenous	intraface	interface

Incorrect	Correct	Incorrect	Correct
intrafereon	**interferon**	iradiation	**irradiation**
intranet	**Internet**	irafutable	**irrefutable**
intrap	**entrap**	irational	**irrational**
intrapersonal		iredeemable	**irredeemable**
	interpersonal	iredendist	**irredentist**
intraracial	**interracial**	ireguler	**irregular**
intreeg	**intrigue**	irelevence	**irrelevance**
intresting	**interesting**	iresistable	**irresistible**
intrist	**interest**	iresponsible	**irresponsible**
introod	**intrude**	irevocable	**irrevocable**
inturvene	**intervene**	irigate	**irrigate**
inuendo	**innuendo**	iriny	**irony**
inuendos	**innuendoes**	iritable	**irritable**
inumberable	**innumerable**	irn	**urn****
inurt	**inert**	irrascible	**irascible**
invallid	**invalid**	irregardless	**regardless**
invalyable	**invaluable**	irrelentless	**relentless**
invatation	**invitation**	irrevelant	**irrelevant****
invazhun	**invasion**	irridesent	**iridescent**
invegel	**inveigle**	isalate	**isolate**
invektive	**invective**	isberg	**iceberg**
invelop	**envelop****	isertope	**isotope**
invenerate	**inveterate**	ishue	**issue**
inveriably	**invariably**	ishuence	**issuance**
invesment	**investment**	ismus	**isthmus**
investagate	**investigate**	isreal	**Israel**
invey	**inveigh**	issometric	**isometric**
invidyus	**invidious**	ither	**either****
invigerate	**invigorate**	itily	**Italy**
invintory	**inventory**	itim	**item**
invironment	**environment**	itomise	**itemize**
invizable	**invisible****	ivary	**ivory**
invoise	**invoice**	ivey	**ivy****
invollintery	**involuntary**	I witness	**eyewitness**
invurtabrate	**invertebrate**	iyatrogenic	**iatrogenic**
inwerd	**inward**	i-you-d	**IUD**
ipacak	**ipecac**	Izlam	**Islam**
iradesense	**iridescence**	Izrael	**Israel**

J

Incorrect	Correct	Incorrect	Correct
jac	**jack**	jackuzi	**jacuzzi**
jackel	**jackal**	jaewak	**jaywalk**
jacknife	**jackknife**	jagantic	**gigantic**

Incorrect	Correct	Incorrect	Correct
jaged	**jagged**	jenny may	**Ginnie Mae**
jagg	**jag**	jenoside	**genocide**
jagwar	**jaguar**	jentile	**gentile****
jaid	**jade**	jenyus	**genius****
jakass	**jackass**	jepordy	**jeopardy**
jaket	**jacket**	jeramide	**jeremiad**
jakpot	**jackpot**	jere	**jeer**
jale	**jail**	jermicide	**germicide**
jallopy	**jalopy**	jerney	**journey****
jamaca	**Jamaica**	jerontology	**gerontology**
jamberee	**jamboree**	jerrimander	**gerrymander**
janator	**janitor**	jersy	**jersey**
janetic	**genetic**	jeryatricks	**geriatrics**
jangel	**jangle**	jestation	**gestation**
Januwery	**January**	jetison	**jettison**
Jappenese	**Japanese**	jetsome	**jetsam**
jargin	**jargon**	jett	**jet**
jarver	**java**	jettlagg	**jet lag**
jassy	**jazzy**	jety	**jetty**
javvlin	**javelin**	jeu jitsoo	**jujitsu**
jawndis	**jaundice**	jewdo	**judo**
jawz	**jaws**	jewdyism	**Judaism**
jaylbrake	**jailbreak**	jewellary	**jewelry**
jayride	**joyride**	jewls	**jewels**
jaysee	**Jaycee**	jewsy	**juicy**
jaz	**jazz**	Jezuit	**Jesuit**
jazmin	**jasmine**	jieb	**jibe****
jeanyal	**genial**	jiffiebag	**jiffybag**
jear	**jeer**	jify	**jiffy**
jeehad	**jihad**	jigabute	**gigabyte**
Jefersonien	**Jeffersonian**	jigel	**jiggle**
jejewne	**jejune****	jiger	**jigger**
jekill and hide		jigg	**jig**
	Jekyll and Hyde	jiggsaw	**jigsaw**
jelatin	**gelatine**	jimnastics	**gymnastics**
jellus	**jealous****	jimy	**jimmy**
jely	**jelly**	jingel	**jingle**
jembellia	**jambalaya**	jingivitis	**gingivitis**
jenatype	**genotype**	jingoe	**jingo**
jender	**gender**	jinjer	**ginger**
jenecide	**genocide**	jinjiva	**gingiva**
jeneration	**generation**	jinnie mays	**Ginny Maes**
jeneric	**generic**	jip	**gyp**
jenes	**jeans****	jipsee	**gypsy**
jenesis	**genesis**	jiraf	**giraffe**
jenetalia	**genitalia**	jirascope	**gyroscope**

Incorrect	Correct	Incorrect	Correct
jiters	**jitters**	joyne	**join**
jittney	**jitney**	joynt	**joint**
joak	**joke**	joyst	**joist**
jobb	**job****	joyus	**joyous**
jober	**jobber**	jubalee	**jubilee**
jogg	**jog****	judgement	**judgment**
joiful	**joyful**	judishary	**judiciary**
jokend	**jocund**	judism	**Judaism**
jokey	**jockey**	juganaut	**juggernaut**
jokker	**joker**	juge	**judge**
jokstrap	**jockstrap**	juggalar	**jugular****
jokular	**jocular**	jugler	**juggler****
jolet	**jolt**	jukstapose	**juxtapose**
joly	**jolly**	jumaika	**Jamaica**
jondarm	**gendarme**	jumbel	**jumble**
jonre	**genre**	jummp	**jump**
joobilunt	**jubilant**	jungel	**jungle**
joodaika	**Judaica**	jungshin	**junction**
joodas	**Judas**	junkee	**junkie** or **junky**
joodishal	**judicial**	junkit	**junket**
joodoe	**judo**	junkture	**juncture**
jooish	**Jewish**	junnkbond	**junk bond**
joojoo	**juju**	junnter	**junta****
jook box	**jukebox**	junque	**junk**
joolie	**July**	jurey	**jury****
joolip	**julep**	jurk	**jerk**
jools	**jewels**	jurnal	**journal**
joon	**June**	jurnlist	**journalist**
joonyer	**junior**	jurrooslim	**Jerusalem**
joorisdicshun	**jurisdiction**	jushe	**Jewish**
joorist	**jurist**	juss	**juice****
joose	**juice****	justefy	**justify**
joot	**jute****	justise	**justice**
josle	**jostle**	juvinile	**juvenile**
joting	**jotting**	jwa de veever	**joi de vivre**
jouns	**jounce**	jymnast	**gymnast**
joveal	**jovial**	jyrate	**gyrate**
joynder	**joinder**	jyve	**jive**

K

Incorrect	Correct	Incorrect	Correct
kache	**cache****	kafee klotch	
kadet	**cadet**		**kaffeeklatsch**
kadish	**Kaddish****	kaff	**calf**

Incorrect	Correct	Incorrect	Correct
kahki	**khaki**	kenard	**canard**
kameleon	**chameleon**	Kenedy	**Kennedy**
kameo	**cameo**	kenel	**kennel**
kangeroo	**kangaroo**	keosk	**kiosk**
kanish	**knish**	keoty	**coyote**
kanoo	**canoe**	kep	**kept**
kao	**kayo or K.O.**	kepe	**keep**
kaos	**chaos**	kerasene	**kerosene**
kapput	**kaput**	kerser	**cursor**
kaptive	**captive**	kersh	**kirsch**
karacter	**character**	kerst	**cursed**
karateen	**carotene**	kertin	**curtain**
karisma	**charisma**	kerupt	**corrupt**
karmer	**karma**	kerve	**curve**
karof	**carafe**	ketch	**catch**
karposee sarcoma		ketel	**kettle**
	Kaposi's sarcoma	kettosis	**ketosis**
karsinoma	**carcinoma**	keyo plan	**Keogh plan**
kasm	**chasm**	kiak	**kayak**
katar	**catarrh**	kibbitzer	**kibitzer**
kaveat empter		kible	**kibble**
	caveat emptor	kichin	**kitchen**
kavel	**cavil**	kiddnap	**kidnap**
kayle	**kale**	kidnee	**kidney**
kaynine	**canine**	kiebosh	**kibosh**
kaypok	**kapok**	kik-off	**kickoff**
k'bob	**kebob**	kilacicle	**kilocycle**
keal	**keel**	kilagram	**kilogram**
kean	**keen**	kilbassa	**kielbasa**
keaper	**keeper**	kiler	**killer**
keapunch	**keypunch**	kiljoy	**killjoy**
keatone	**ketone**	killabite	**kilobyte**
kechup	**ketchup**	killen	**kiln****
kee	**key****	killerbawd	**kilobaud**
keebored	**keyboard**	killerhertz	**kilohertz**
keekback	**kickback**	killometre	**kilometer**
keelo	**kilo**	killowatt	**kilowatt**
keenote	**keynote**	kimona	**kimono**
keepunch	**keypunch**	kindel	**kindle**
keesh	**quiche**	kindergarden	
keestone	**keystone**		**kindergarten**
keewee	**kiwi**	kindrid	**kindred**
kegg	**keg**	kinely	**kindly**
kellp	**kelp**	kiness	**kindness**
Keltic	**Celtic**	kingdum	**kingdom**
ken	**can**		

Incorrect	Correct	Incorrect	Correct
kiniscope	**kinescope**	kolyumnist	**columnist**
kinnetic	**kinetic**	komfortable	**comfortable**
kinpin	**kingpin**	koming	**coming**
kiper	**kipper**	kommunist	**communist**
kiropedy	**chiropody**	konclusion	**conclusion**
kist	**kissed**	konosewer	**connoisseur**
kitastrofy	**catastrophe**	kool	**cool**
kitin	**kitten**	koris	**chorus**
kiyoty	**coyote**	korz	**corps****
klak	**claque**	koytis	**coitus**
klandestin	**clandestine**	kraft	**craft**
klassified	**classified**	kriptic	**cryptic**
kleek	**clique****	kriptology	**cryptology**
klenser	**cleanser**	kronic	**chronic**
kloan	**clone****	kubism	**cubism**
klorine	**chlorine**	kudgel	**cudgel**
kloy	**cloy**	kul-de-sac	**cul-de-sac**
kneonatal	**neonatal**	kulture	**culture**
knewral	**neural**	kumpendium	
knewrosis	**neurosis**		**compendium**
knewspeak	**newspeak**	kurnel	**colonel****
knewt	**newt**	kurvashus	**curvaceous**
knewter	**neuter**	kusp	**cusp**
knifes	**knives**	kuspea	**cuspy**
knotation	**notation**	kwertee	**QUERTY**
knoted	**knotted**	kwier	**quire****
knowed	**knew****	kwik	**quick**
know-fault	**no-fault**	kwiksotic	**quixotic**
knowlege	**knowledge**	kwinella	**quinella**
knowmad	**nomad**	kwire	**choir****
kochere	**kosher**	kworem	**quorum**
kolic	**colic**	kwotidian	**quotidian**

L

labb	**lab**	lachkee kid	**latchkey kid**
labedo	**libido****	laciny	**larceny**
laber	**labor**	lacker	**lacquer**
labidinus	**libidinous**	lacksitive	**laxative**
labirinth	**labyrinth**	lacktose	**lactose**
lable	**label**	ladel	**ladle**
labotomy	**lobotomy**	lader	**ladder**
labratory	**laboratory**	ladys	**ladies**
lach	**latch**	laffable	**laughable**

Incorrect	Correct	Incorrect	Correct
laffter	**laughter**	larseny	**larceny**
lagard	**laggard**	lasatude	**lassitude**
lage	**large**	lase	**lace**
lagg	**lag**	laserate	**lacerate**
laging	**lagging**	lasivious	**lascivious**
lagune	**lagoon**	laso	**lasso**
lahiyime	**l'chaim**	lasseration	**laceration**
laim	**lame****	latatude	**latitude**
laim duck	**lame duck**	latenna	**Latina****
laison	**liaison**	laticework	**latticework**
lait	**late**	latly	**lately**
lakey	**lackey**	latril	**laetrile**
lakrimos	**lachrymose**	lattent	**latent**
laks	**lax**	latteral	**lateral**
laksadaysakle		lattin	**Latin**
	lackadaisical	lattino	**Latino****
laktation	**lactation**	laveleer	**lavaliere**
lakuna	**lacuna**	lavinder	**lavender**
lakwashus	**loquacious**	lavitory	**lavatory**
lamanate	**laminate**	lavva	**lava****
lambast	**lambaste**	lavvish	**lavish**
lamentible	**lamentable**	lawd	**lord****
lammentation		lawdanum	**laudanum**
	lamentation	lawdible	**laudable**
lamskin	**lambskin**	lawft	**loft**
lanalin	**lanolin**	lawnder	**launder**
langer	**languor**	lawndry	**laundry**
langwidge	**language****	lawnhand	**longhand**
langwish	**languish****	lawsoot	**lawsuit**
lanlady	**landlady**	layed	**laid**
lanlord	**landlord**	laytest	**latest**
lanmark	**landmark**	laytex	**latex**
lann	**LAN**	laywer	**lawyer**
lannedlocked	**landlocked**	lazyness	**laziness**
lanscape	**landscape**	leafs	**leaves**
lanse	**lance**	leakige	**leakage**
lantin	**lantern**	leanyent	**lenient**
lanyap	**lagniappe**	leasor	**lessor****
lanzheree	**lingerie**	leasure	**leisure**
lapce	**lapse**	leathil	**lethal**
lapell	**lapel**	leazon	**liaison**
laprascope	**laparoscope**	lecksacon	**lexicon**
laringitis	**laryngitis**	leconic	**laconic**
larinx	**larynx**	ledgislature	**legislature**
larrgess	**largesse**	leeder	**leader**
larrva	**larva****	leeg	**league**

Incorrect	Correct	Incorrect	Correct
leegenares disease		lettup	**letup**
	legionnaires' disease	levation	**levitation**
leejon	**legion**	leve	**leave****
lees	**least****	leven	**eleven**
leese	**lease**	levey	**levee****
leezon	**lesion**	levle	**level**
leff	**left**	levler	**leveler**
leffhanded	**left-handed**	levrage	**leverage**
leffovers	**leftovers**	levven	**leaven**
legallize	**legalize**	levver	**lever**
leger	**ledger**	lew	**lieu**
legil	**legal**	lewow	**luau**
legissy	**legacy**	leyoff	**layoff**
legitamate	**legitimate**	leyway	**layaway**
leif	**leaf****	lez majesty	**lese majesty**
leige	**liege**	lezbian	**lesbian**
leisurly	**leisurely**	libaterian	**libertarian**
lejable	**legible**	libbity	**liberty**
lejend	**legend**	liber	**LIBOR**
lejerdeman	**legerdemain**	liberalizm	**liberalism**
lejjer	**ledger**	liberry	**library**
lejon	**legion**	libility	**liability**
lekcher	**lecture**	lible	**libel****
lemenade	**lemonade**	libral	**liberal**
lemmen	**lemon**	libreto	**libretto**
lended	**lent**	lickrish	**licorice**
lenth	**length**	lickwidate	**liquidate**
lenz	**lens**	lieing	**lying**
leperd	**leopard**	lier	**liar****
lepersy	**leprosy**	lifboat	**lifeboat**
leprakon	**leprechaun**	lifes	**lives**
lept	**leaped**	liffoff	**liftoff**
lerch	**lurch**	lifgard	**lifeguard**
lern	**learn**	liftime	**lifetime**
lesen	**lessen****	ligiment	**ligament**
lessay fare	**laissez-faire**	ligiture	**ligature**
lesse majesty	**lese majesty**	likker	**liquor****
lessithin	**lecithin**	likly	**likely**
letahead	**letterhead**	likness	**likeness**
letchery	**lechery**	lillac	**lilac**
leter	**letter****	lilly	**lily**
lether	**leather**	lim	**limb****
lethergy	**lethargy**	limazine	**limousine**
letice	**lettuce**	limba	**limber**
lets	**let's**	limbow	**limbo**
letterd	**lettered**	lime disease	**Lyme disease**

Incorrect	Correct	Incorrect	Correct
limf	**lymph**	littligious	**litigious**
limfoma	**lymphoma**	littmus	**litmus**
limlite	**limelight**	livegard	**lifeguard**
limmbic	**limbic**	liven	**enliven**
limmit	**limit**	livlihood	**livelihood**
lims	**limps**	livly	**lively**
linament	**liniment****	livry	**livery**
Lincon	**Lincoln**	livstock	**livestock**
lingweeny	**linguine**	livvid	**livid****
lingwist	**linguist**	lizzard	**lizard**
linier	**linear****	loab	**lobe**
linkd	**linked**	loball	**lowball**
linkige	**linkage**	lobbie	**lobby**
linnen	**linen**	lobbster	**lobster**
linnger	**linger**	lobbster shift	**lobster shift**
linnoleum	**linoleum**	lobey	**lobby**
linnt	**lint**	lobrow	**lowbrow**
linx	**lynx****	locallize	**localize**
lionman	**lineman**	locamotive	**locomotive**
lippstick	**lipstick**	loccation	**location**
lipsink	**lip-sync**	lockket	**locket**
liqued	**liquid**	loecal	**low-cal**
liquify	**liquefy**	lofer	**loafer**
liric	**lyric**	loffty	**lofty**
lirk	**lurk**	logerithm	**logarithm**
lisence	**license**	loggic	**logic**
lisenshus	**licentious**	log off	**log-off**
lisergic acid	**lysergic acid**	logon	**log-on**
lisome	**lissome**	loial	**loyal**
lissed	**list**	loiyer	**lawyer**
lissen	**listen**	loje	**lodge****
litabug	**litterbug**	lokate	**locate**
litchen	**lichen****	lokist	**locust****
lite	**light**	lokjaw	**lockjaw**
liteharted	**lighthearted**	lokkout	**lockout**
litemotif	**leitmotiv**	lokus	**locus****
lite pen	**light pen**	lolode	**loload**
litergical	**liturgical**	lon	**lawn**
litewait	**lightweight**	lonch	**launch**
litheum	**lithium**	loneshark	**loanshark**
litle	**little**	longgwinded	**long-winded**
litorary	**literary**	lonjeray	**lingerie**
litracy	**literacy**	lonjevaty	**longevity**
litrature	**literature**	lonjitude	**longitude**
littany	**litany**	lonliness	**loneliness**
litteral	**literal**		

Incorrect	Correct	Incorrect	Correct
lonly	**lonely**	lozer	**loser**
lonsome	**lonesome**	lubercate	**lubricate**
loocrative	**lucrative**	lucksury	**luxury**
lood	**lewd**	ludacrus	**ludicrous**
looftmensh	**luftmensch**	luet	**lute****
looje	**luge**	lufa	**loofah**
looloo	**lulu**	lugage	**luggage**
loonatic	**lunatic**	luke	**luck**
looner	**lunar**	lukeism	**lookism**
loopus	**lupus**	lukemia	**leukemia**
loor	**lure**	lukout	**lookout**
loosid	**lucid**	lukra	**lucre**
lootenant	**lieutenant**	lukshurient	**luxuriant****
loover	**louver**	lukwarm	**lukewarm**
Loovre	**Louvre**	lulaby	**lullaby**
looze	**lose****	luminecent	**luminescent**
lor	**lore****	lummpectomy	
lorel	**laurel**		**lumpectomy**
loresoot	**lawsuit**	lunasy	**lunacy**
lornyet	**lorgnette**	lunchin	**luncheon**
lorre	**law****	lunchinet	**luncheonette**
los	**loss****	lunng	**lung**
losenge	**lozenge**	luny	**loony**
loshun	**lotion**	lupehole	**loophole**
lotery	**lottery**	lushous	**luscious**
lothe	**loathe****	lusster	**luster**
lothsum	**loathsome**	lusterous	**lustrous**
loto	**lotto**	luv	**love**
loveable	**lovable**	luxry	**luxury**
loveing	**loving**	luzer	**loser**
lovly	**lovely**	lydacaine	**lydocaine**
lowd	**loud**	lyeing	**lying**
lowdspeaker	**loudspeaker**	lykwise	**likewise**
lowgoe	**logo**	lyme	**lime****
lownje	**lounge**	lynchpin	**linchpin**
lowt	**lout**	lynup	**lineup**
loyter	**loiter**	lyon	**lion**

M

macanic	**mechanic**	maccaroni	**macaroni**
macarune	**macaroon**	machurashun	**maturation**
maccab	**macabre**	machure	**mature**
maccadim	**macadam**	macintosh	**mackintosh**

Incorrect	Correct	Incorrect	Correct
mackismo	**machismo**	malaze	**malaise**
mackrel	**mackerel**	malebox	**mailbox**
mackro	**macro**	maleman	**mailman**
madalion	**medallion**	malestorm	**maelstrom**
madd	**mad**	malfezence	**malfeasance**
maddame	**madame**	maliable	**malleable**
maddros	**madras**	maline	**malign**
madmwazel	**mademoiselle**	malingger	**malinger**
madona	**Madonna**	malishus	**malicious**
mafea	**Mafia**	mallady	**malady**
magesty	**majesty**	mallagusted	**maladjusted**
maggiler	**megillah**	mallaria	**malaria**
maggnanimous		mallformation	
	magnanimous		**malformation**
maggnesium	**magnesium**	mallignant	**malignant**
magizine	**magazine**	mallis	**malice**
magnatude	**magnitude**	mallnutrition	
magnifasense			**malnutrition**
	magnificence	mallpractice	**malpractice**
magnit	**magnet****	malpropism	**malapropism**
magot	**maggot**	mamagram	**mammogram**
mahchow	**macho**	mamal	**mammal**
mahiraja	**maharajah**	mamalade	**marmalade**
mahvlus	**marvelous**	mame	**maim**
maibe	**maybe****	mamell	**mammal**
maice	**mace**	mammery	**mammary**
maidnly	**maidenly**	mamosa	**mimosa**
mainger	**manger**	mamuth	**mammoth**
mainia	**mania**	manacure	**manicure**
maintainance		manafacture	**manufacture**
	maintenance	manafesto	**manifesto**
maionaize	**mayonnaise**	manafold	**manifold**
maitriarc	**matriarch**	managable	**manageable**
majer	**major**	managut	**manicotti**
majik	**magic**	manajer	**manager**
majistrat	**magistrate**	manakin	**mannequin**
majoraty	**majority**	mand	**manned**
Makavelian		mandable	**mandible**
	Machiavellian	manditory	**mandatory**
makeing	**making**	maneac	**maniac**
makismo	**machismo**	maneframe	**mainframe**
makrobiotic	**macrobiotic**	maneland	**mainland**
maksi	**maxi**	maner	**manner****
makup	**makeup**	manestream	**mainstream**
maladikshun	**malediction**	mangel	**mangle**
malaklusion	**malocclusion**	manginese	**manganese**

Incorrect	Correct	Incorrect	Correct
manicle	**manacle**	marvilus	**marvelous**
manje	**mange**	masaje	**massage**
manjer	**manger**	masaker	**massacre**
mannic depressive		masakist	**masochist**
	manic depressive	mascuelin	**masculine**
mannipulative		mashety	**machete**
	manipulative	mashinery	**machinery**
mannkind	**mankind**	Masichusetts	
manogamist	**monogamist**		**Massachusetts**
manoor	**manure**	masinry	**masonry**
manotinus	**monotonous**	masive	**massive**
manshun	**mansion**	maskerade	**masquerade**
mantlpeace	**mantelpiece**	maskuline	**masculine**
manule	**manual**	masooze	**masseuse**
manuscrip	**manuscript**	massala	**marsala**
manuver	**maneuver**	masscara	**mascara**
manyana	**mañana**	massokism	**masochism**
mapul	**maple**	masstektimy	**mastectomy**
maraskino	**maraschino**	masstermind	**mastermind**
marass	**morass**	masta	**master**
maratell	**marital****	mastacate	**masticate**
maratime	**maritime**	mastarpiece	**masterpiece**
marawana	**marijuana**	masterbait	**masturbate**
marawder	**marauder**	mastoyd	**mastoid**
marbel	**marble**	masur	**masseur**
marc	**mark****	matar	**matter**
marcdown	**markdown**	mater de	**maître d'**
mareen	**marine**	maternaty	**maternity**
marey	**marry****	mathamatics	
marige	**marriage****		**mathematics**
marjerin	**margarine**	matinay	**matinée**
marjin	**margin**	matramony	**matrimony**
markee	**marquis**	matrinly	**matronly**
markez	**marquise**	matris	**mattress**
markit	**market**	matterial	**material**
marksism	**Marxism**	mattriculate	**matriculate**
marow	**marrow**	maturnal	**maternal**
marragable	**marriageable**	mavrick	**maverick**
marrathon	**marathon**	mawdlin	**maudlin**
marrawder	**marauder**	maxamum	**maximum**
marrkup	**markup**	mayer	**mayor**
marryed	**married**	maylanje	**mélange**
marteeni	**martini**	maylay	**melée****
marter	**martyr**	maynage atwaw	
martygra	**Mardi Gras**		**ménage à trois**
marune	**maroon**	mayntane	**maintain**

Incorrect	Correct	Incorrect	Correct
maysa	**mesa**	melow	**mellow**
mayteeay	**métier****	memberane	**membrane**
maytreeark	**matriarch**	mementum	**momentum**
maytricks	**matrix**	memmber	**member**
maytrix	**matrix**	memmento	**memento**
mayvin	**maven**	memmorial	**memorial**
mazoleum	**mausoleum**	memrable	**memorable**
meaness	**meanness**	memrandum	
meanyal	**menial**		**memorandum**
meca	**mecca** or **Mecca**	memry	**memory**
mecanic	**mechanic**	memwar	**memoir**
mecksikin	**Mexican**	menajery	**menagerie**
Medacare	**Medicare**	menapause	**menopause**
medamorfisis		menise	**menace**
	metamorphosis	menningitis	**meningitis**
medecine	**medicine**	mennora	**menorah**
medekade	**Medicaid**	mennstration	
medel	**medal****		**menstruation**
medeocker	**mediocre**	menshun	**mention**
medetate	**meditate**	menstrate	**menstruate**
Mediteranean		ment	**meant**
	Mediterranean	mentch	**mensch**
medle	**meddle****	mentle	**mental**
medly	**medley**	meny	**many**
medow	**meadow**	menyu	**menu**
medyation	**mediation**	merandise	**Mirandize**
meedea	**media**	merang	**meringue**
meediate	**mediate**	meratocricy	**meritocracy**
meedjum	**medium**	merchindize	**merchandise**
meeger	**meager**	mercinery	**mercenary**
meeteor	**meteor****	merder	**murder**
meet market	**meat market**	merderer	**murderer**
meggerbite	**megabyte**	merdger	**merger**
meglomania		meret	**merit**
	megalomania	merje	**merge**
mein	**mien****	merly	**merely**
mekanize	**mechanize**	mermer	**murmur**
meklizine	**meclizine**	merryland	**Maryland**
meksako	**Mexico**	merryly	**merrily**
meldown	**meltdown**	mersy	**mercy**
melincoly	**melancholy**	merth	**mirth**
mellanoma	**melanoma**	mesenger	**messenger**
mellenen	**melanin**	mesing	**messing**
mellodious	**melodious**	messcline	**mescaline**
mellodrama	**melodrama**	mesure	**measure**
mellon	**melon**	mesy	**messy**

Incorrect	Correct	Incorrect	Correct
mesyur	**monsieur**	miligram	**milligram****
metafor	**metaphor**	milinary	**millinery****
metamfetimine		milionaire	**millionaire**
	methamphetamine	millicha	**militia**
metefisics	**metaphysics**	millyou	**milieu**
meteocrity	**mediocrity**	milogram	**myelogram****
meterial	**material**	miloma	**myeloma**
Methadist	**Methodist**	minamize	**minimize**
methe	**meth**	minamum	**minimum**
methed	**method**	Minasota	**Minnesota**
methedone	**methadone**	minature	**miniature**
metripolitan	**metropolitan**	mingel	**mingle**
metroe	**metro**	miniral	**mineral**
mettabolism	**metabolism**	minis	**minus**
mettalic	**metallic**	miniscule	**minuscule**
mettastasis	**metastasis**	minit	**minute**
metticulous	**meticulous**	minnimum	**minimum**
mettre de	**maitre d'**	minnister	**minister**
mettric	**metric**	minnyseries	**miniseries**
meucus	**mucous**	minoksidil	**minoxidil**
mezaneen	**mezzanine**	minoraty	**minority**
mezels	**measles**	minse	**mince****
mezmerize	**mesmerize**	minusha	**minutiae**
miakulper	**mea culpa**	miny	**mini**
micerorganism		minycomputer	
	microorganism		**minicomputer**
micersurgery		miopia	**myopia**
	microsurgery	miopic	**myopic**
micrascope	**microscope**	miricle	**miracle**
miday	**midday**	mirky	**murky**
middel	**middle**	miror	**mirror**
middwife	**midwife**	mirraje	**mirage****
midevil	**medieval**	mirtle	**myrtle**
midnite	**midnight**	mischevous	**mischievous**
mikerchip	**microchip**	mischif	**mischief**
mikerfilm	**microfilm**	miselaneous	
mikrafone	**microphone**		**miscellaneous**
mikro	**micro**	mishigan	**Michigan**
mikrobiology		mishin	**mission**
	microbiology	mishnary	**missionary**
mikrowave	**microwave**	Mississipi	**Mississippi**
mikture	**mixture**	miskast	**miscast**
milage	**mileage**	mislayed	**mislaid**
milameter	**millimeter**	mispell	**misspell**
milatery	**military**	mispropriate	
milenium	**millennium**		**misappropriate**

Incorrect	Correct	Incorrect	Correct
misquito	**mosquito**	mobd	**mobbed**
misrable	**miserable**	mobill	**mobile**
misry	**misery**	mobillize	**mobilize**
misscarage	**miscarriage**	mocassin	**moccasin**
missconception		moch	**mosh**
	misconception	moddality	**modality**
missconduct	**misconduct**	modderate	**moderate**
missdemeaner		modifyer	**modifier**
	misdemeanor	modil	**model****
missel	**missile****	modis operande	
misselaneous			**modus operandi**
	miscellaneous	modist	**modest**
missfit	**misfit**	modren	**modern**
missfortune	**misfortune**	modrenism	**modernism**
missgiving	**misgiving**	moedem	**modem**
misshap	**mishap**	moffia	**Mafia**
missin	**missing**	mogill	**mogul**
missojiny	**misogyny**	Mohamedin	
misstake	**mistake**		**Muhammadan**
misster	**mister**	mohoginy	**mahogany**
misstrial	**mistrial**	mojulate	**modulate**
missunderstand		moka	**mocha**
	misunderstand	mokery	**mockery**
mistacizm	**mysticism**	moksy	**moxie**
mistate	**misstate**	molatto	**mulatto**
mistep	**misstep**	moler	**molar**
misterious	**mysterious**	molify	**mollify**
mistery	**mystery**	mollases	**molasses**
misthenia graves		mollecule	**molecule**
	myasthenia gravis	mollestation	**molestation**
mistic	**mystic**	mombo	**mambo**
mistify	**mystify**	mommentus	**momentous**
mistris	**mistress**	monalith	**monolith**
mitabilism	**metabolism**	monalog	**monologue**
mitagate	**mitigate****	monarail	**monorail**
miterm	**midterm**	monark	**monarch**
mith	**myth**	monatery	**monetary**
mithical	**mythical**	mone	**moan**
mittin	**mitten**	moneter	**monitor**
mizanthrope	**misanthrope**	monistery	**monastery**
mizer	**miser**	monitone	**monotone**
mizerable	**miserable**	monnakrone	
mizuri	**Missouri**		**monochrome**
moal	**mole**	monniter	**monitor**
moap	**mope**	monnopolly	**monopoly**
mobb	**mob**	monnster	**monster**

Incorrect	Correct	Incorrect	Correct
monsterous	**monstrous**	mowse	**mouse****
mony	**money**	mowthpeace	**mouthpiece**
monyument	**monument**	moyschur	**moisture**
moomoo	**muumuu**	mozaic	**mosaic**
moovie	**movie**	muchroom	**mushroom**
morano	**Marrano**	mudy	**muddy**
morebid	**morbid**	mufin	**muffin**
morebund	**moribund**	muger	**mugger**
Moreman	**Mormon**	mugg	**mug**
moreon	**moron**	mukkup	**mockup**
moretality	**mortality**	mula	**mullah**
morfeen	**morphine**	mulagatanny	
morg	**morgue**		**mulligatawny**
morgage	**mortgage**	muleish	**mulish**
mornfull	**mournful**	mulltemillionaire	
moroco	**Morocco**		**multimillionaire**
morover	**moreover**	mulltinational	
morralty	**morality**		**multinational**
morrbidity	**morbidity**	mulltiple sklerosis	
morsal	**morsel**		**multiple sclerosis**
mortafy	**mortify**	mulltiplier	**multiplier**
mortaly	**mortally**	multaplex	**multiplex**
morter	**mortar**	multaply	**multiply**
mortuery	**mortuary**	multatude	**multitude**
mose	**most**	multykultural	
moseltough	**mazeltov**		**multicultural**
moshin	**motion**	multymedia	**multimedia**
moshroom	**mushroom**	multytasking	
mosk	**mosque**		**multitasking**
moskeeto	**mosquito**	mumbel	**mumble**
mosy	**mossy**	mummy trak	
motavate	**motivate**		**mommy track**
moteef	**motif****	mundain	**mundane**
moter	**motor**	munday	**Monday**
motled	**mottled**	munk	**monk**
motocycle	**motorcycle**	munkey	**monkey**
motse	**matza or matzoh**	munth	**month**
motserela	**mozzarella**	murcery	**mercury**
motta	**motto**	murchant	**merchant**
moufwash	**mouthwash**	murfy's lore	
mough	**muff**		**Murphy's Law**
mountage	**montage**	murge	**merge**
moustache	**mustache**	murmer	**murmur**
movment	**movement**	murrel	**mural**
mowdem	**modem**	musell	**muscle****
mowntain	**mountain**		

Incorrect	Correct	Incorrect	Correct
musilije	**mucilage**	myestrow	**maestro**
muskular distrophy		mygrane	**migraine**
	muscular dystrophy	mygrate	**migrate**
mussnt	**mustn't**	myke	**mike**
musster	**muster**	mynority	**minority**
mustid	**mustard****	myootation	**mutation**
mutha	**mother****	mytamicin C	
mutny	**mutiny**		**mitomycin C**
muzeem	**museum**	mytosis	**mitosis**
muzik	**music**	myuni	**muni**
muzlin	**muslin****	myunicipal	**municipal**
muzzel	**muzzle**	myutant	**mutant**
myazma	**miasma**	myute	**mute****
mycroprocesser		myutule	**mutual**
	microprocessor	mzuma	**mazuma**

N

Incorrect	Correct	Incorrect	Correct
nabb	**nab**	narrerband	**narrowband**
nabor	**neighbor**	narsisist	**narcissist**
nacent	**nascent**	narsistic	**narcissistic**
nachurally	**naturally**	nasent	**nascent**
nachuropathy		nash	**gnash**
	naturopathy	nashunel	**national**
nack	**knack**	nastershum	**nasturtium**
nacotics	**narcotics**	nastyness	**nastiness**
naddy	**natty**	nat	**gnat**
nafairius	**nefarious**	natchur	**nature**
naftha	**naphtha****	nattivity	**nativity**
naged	**nagged**	nausha	**nausea**
naiborhood	**neighborhood**	navagible	**navigable**
naivtay	**naïveté**	navey	**navy**
nale	**nail**	naw	**gnaw**
namless	**nameless**	nawm	**norm**
namonia	**pneumonia**	nawty	**naughty****
nany	**nanny**	naybor	**neighbor**
napsack	**knapsack**	naydir	**nadir**
naraminded		naytive	**native**
	narrow-minded	nazal	**nasal**
naration	**narration**	nazdack	**NASDAQ**
narative	**narrative**	neady	**needy**
narkalepsy	**narcolepsy**	nebulus	**nebulous**
narled	**gnarled**	necesery	**necessary**
narow	**narrow**	necesity	**necessity**

Incorrect	Correct	Incorrect	Correct
neckromansy		newmeric	numeric
	necromancy	newral	neural
nectereen	nectarine	newrologist	neurologist
nee	knee	newrosis	neurosis
neecap	kneecap	newsance	nuisance
neece	niece	newtor	neuter
needel	needle	newtral	neutral
neegrow	Negro	newtron	neutron
neelsens	Nielsen's	newvo rich	nouveau riche
neeo	neo	newzspaper	newspaper
neepotism	nepotism	nex	next
neersited	nearsighted	Niagra	Niagara
neet	neat	nializm	nihilism
neether	neither**	nianderthal	Neanderthal
nefew	nephew	nible	nibble**
nefritis	nephritis	nicateen	nicotine
negitive	negative	nich	niche**
neglajence	negligence	nickle	nickel
negleck	neglect	nicknack	knickknack
neglegay	negligee	nicly	nicely
negoshiate	negotiate	nietmare	nightmare
Negros	Negroes	nieve	naïve
neice	niece	nife	knife
nekkid	naked	nigate	negate
nekrology	necrology	night errend	
neks	next		knight errant
neksis	nexus	nikname	nickname
nelagism	neologism	nileism	nihilism
nell	knell**	nill	nil
nemisis	nemesis	nimbel	nimble
nemonic	mnemonic	nimf	nymph
nenersecond	nanosecond	nimmbee	NIMBY**
neppotizm	nepotism	ninedy	ninety
nerosis	neurosis	nineth	ninth
nerse	nurse	ninfamaniac	
nerture	nurture		nymphomaniac
nervanna	nirvana	ninteen	nineteen
nerviss	nervous	nionatal	neonatal
nesecery	necessary	nippal	nipple
nesessity	necessity	nirsery	nursery
nesle	nestle	nise	NYSE
nettwerk	network	nite	night**
neumonia	pneumonia	niteclub	nightclub
newbile	nubile	nitragen	nitrogen
newdist	nudist	nitting	knitting
newmatic	pneumatic	nives	knives

Incorrect	Correct	Incorrect	Correct
noatbook	**notebook**	noovo reesh	
nobb	**knob****		**nouveau riche**
nobles oblege		normel	**normal**
	noblesse oblige	normming	**norming**
noch	**notch**	northernly	**northerly**
nock	**knock****	noshun	**notion**
nocknee	**knock-knee**	nosis	**gnosis**
nock-offs	**knockoffs**	nosstril	**nostril**
nockternil	**nocturnal**	notafy	**notify**
noed	**node****	notchy	**gnocci**
noefrills	**no-frills**	notery	**notary**
noehitter	**no-hitter**	noth	**north**
noel	**knoll**	notible	**notable**
noesbleed	**nosebleed**	noticable	**noticeable**
noeshow	**no-show**	notise	**notice**
noevember	**November**	nottorious	**notorious**
nokshus	**noxious**	notworthy	**noteworthy**
nole	**knoll**	novacane	**Novocaine**
nolode	**no-load**	noval	**novel**
nomanal	**nominal**	noviss	**novice**
nome	**gnome**	no where	**nowhere**
nomminate	**nominate**	nowlege	**knowledge**
noneexempt	**nonexempt**	nown	**noun**
nonefat	**nonfat**	noyz	**noise**
nonesuport	**nonsupport**	nozgay	**nosegay**
nonndeductible		nozy	**nosy**
	nondeductible	nuckle	**knuckle**
nonnentity	**nonentity**	nucleous	**nucleus**
nonnprofit	**nonprofit**	nudal	**noodle****
nonock	**no-knock**	nudaty	**nudity**
nonshalant	**nonchalant**	nuetral	**neutral**
nonvilence	**nonviolence**	nukular	**nuclear**
noo	**new****	nulification	**nullification**
noobile	**nubile**	num	**numb**
nooclear	**nuclear**	numatic	**pneumatic**
nooge	**nudge**	numba	**number**
nooke	**nuke****	numb de plume	
noomatic	**pneumatic**		**nom de plume**
noomeral	**numeral**	nummerical	**numerical**
nooratic	**neurotic**	nummskull	**numskull**
nooron	**neuron**	numrous	**numerous**
noosance	**nuisance**	nuncom	**noncom**
noot	**newt**	nunery	**nunnery**
nooter	**neuter**	nunpairell	**nonpareil**
nootral	**neutral**	nunplus	**nonplus**

Incorrect	Correct	Incorrect	Correct
nunsektarian		nurve	nerve
	nonsectarian	nusecaster	newscaster
nunsekwiter	non sequitur	nusence	nuisance
nunsense	nonsense	nuspeak	newspeak
nunsizist	nonsizist	nustaljic	nostalgic
nunyou	non-U	nuthing	nothing
nupshal	nuptial	nutralise	neutralize
nuralja	neuralgia	nutrishon	nutrition
nurd	nerd	nuty	nutty
nurish	nourish	nyeev	naïve
nuritis	neuritis	nyether	neither**
nuroligist	neurologist	nyew	new**
nursary	nursery	nytffall	nightfall
nursmaid	nursemaid	nytragen	nitrogen

O

Incorrect	Correct	Incorrect	Correct
oaysis	oasis	obliderate	obliterate
obay	obey	oblidge	oblige
obayisence	obeisance	obligatto	obbligato
objjecshun	objection	oblikwey	obloquy**
obbligatory	obligatory	obnocshus	obnoxious
obblivus	oblivious**	obo	oboe
obblong	oblong	obsalecent	obsolescent
obbservatory	observatory	obsaleet	obsolete
obbstruction	obstruction	obsavation	observation
obbsurv	observe	obseekweus	obsequious
obcelete	obsolete	obseen	obscene
obderit	obdurate	obseshun	obsession
obedeance	obedience	obshay dart	objet d'art
obeecity	obesity	obskure	obscure
obees	obese	obstatrishin	obstetrician
obfaskate	obfuscate	obstickal	obstacle
obgective	objective	obstonite	obstinate
obhorent	abhorrent	obstruk	obstruct**
obichuary	obituary	obtane	obtain
obitrator	arbitrator	obtoos	obtuse
obitter diktum		obtusive	obtrusive
	obiter dictum	obveate	obviate
objeck	object**	obvius	obvious**
objecshunable		obvurse	obverse
	objectionable	obzervance	observance
oblagation	obligation	ocasion	occasion
obleek	oblique**	occassionel	occasional

Incorrect	Correct	Incorrect	Correct
occuler	**ocular**	ohpare	**au pair**
occulist	**oculist**	oister	**oyster**
occurance	**occurrence**	oklock	**o'clock**
oced	**OECD**	oklusion	**occlusion**
ociloscope	**oscilloscope**	oksymoron	**oxymoron**
octajenerion		oktal	**octal**
	octogenarian	oktane	**octane**
octapus	**octopus**	oktave	**octave**
ocult	**occult**	Oktober	**October**
ocupancy	**occupancy**	okupent	**occupant**
ocupyed	**occupied**	okyupation	**occupation**
ocurr	**occur****	olagarky	**oligarchy**
ocurred	**occurred**	olay	**olé**
od	**odd**	ole	**old**
oddisy	**odyssey**	oleboy network	
oddometer	**odometer**		**old-boy network**
odeous	**odious**	oledline	**old-line**
oder	**odor**	olefashioned	
oderus	**odorous**		**old-fashioned**
odlot	**odd lot**	olegirl network	
odorcolon	**eau de cologne**		**old-girl network**
ofbeet	**offbeat**	olfaktry	**olfactory**
ofer	**offer**	Olimpic	**Olympic**
offen	**often**	ollive	**olive**
offence	**offense**	ollygopoly	**oligopoly**
offring	**offering**	oltimer	**old-timer**
offshaw	**offshore**	omage	**homage**
ofhand	**offhand**	OME	**OEM**
ofice	**office****	ome	**ohm**
oficer	**officer**	omibus	**omnibus**
oficial	**official**	omishin	**omission**
ofishus	**officious**	omlet	**omelet**
ofline	**off-line**	omm	**om**
ofprice	**off-price**	ommbudsman	
ofputing	**off-putting**		**ombudsman**
ofsett	**offset**	omminous	**ominous**
ofspring	**offspring**	ommitt	**omit**
ofthamology		omnnipotent	**omnipotent**
	ophthalmology	omnepresent	**omnipresent**
of the record		omnishent	**omniscient**
	off-the-record	omniverus	**omnivorous**
ofyear	**off year**	onamatopea	
oggel	**ogle**		**onomatopoeia**
ogger	**ogre**	onarus	**onerous**
oh de colon		oncore	**encore**
	eau de cologne	onely	**only**

Incorrect	Correct	Incorrect	Correct
onesself	**oneself**	opptic	**optic**
onest	**honest**	opption	**option**
onis	**onus**	opra	**opera****
onkogene	**oncogene**	oprant	**operant**
on mass	**en masse**	oprate	**operate**
onncology	**oncology**	opress	**oppress**
onngoing	**ongoing**	opresser	**oppressor**
onnline	**on-line**	opreta	**operetta**
onnlooka	**onlooker**	oproprium	**opprobrium**
onnslawt	**onslaught**	opscurantism	
onofile	**oenophile**		**obscurantism**
onor	**honor**	opsequees	**obsequies**
onorable	**honorable**	opshen	**option**
onorary	**honorary**	opshinul	**optional**
onroot	**en route**	opsite	**op. cit.****
onsided	**one-sided**	opsteperus	**obstreperous**
onsomble	**ensemble**	optain	**obtain**
onsure	**onshore**	optamum	**optimum**
ontoroge	**entourage**	optishin	**optician**
ontraprenor	**entrepreneur**	optomism	**optimism**
ontray	**entrée**	optommotrist	**optometrist**
onvelope	**envelope**	opyulent	**opulent**
onwee	**ennui**	oragin	**origin****
ooz	**ooze**	orbut	**orbit**
opaik	**opaque**	orcherd	**orchard**
oparative	**operative**	orchester	**orchestra**
opatunist	**opportunist**	ordally	**orderly**
opeate	**opiate**	ordanation	**ordination**
opeck	**OPEC**	ordane	**ordain**
openess	**openness**	ordinence	**ordinance****
opin ended	**open-ended**	ordinry	**ordinary**
opin mined	**open-minded**	oredeal	**ordeal**
opinyun	**opinion**	oreganic	**organic**
opis	**opus**	oreint	**orient**
opner	**opener**	orentation	**orientation**
opning	**opening**	orevoir	**au revoir**
oponent	**opponent**	orfan	**orphan**
oportune	**opportune**	orful	**awful**
oportunity	**opportunity**	organisation	**organization**
opose	**oppose**	orgazm	**orgasm****
oposition	**opposition****	orgin	**organ****
opp-ed	**op-ed**	oricul	**oracle****
opperator	**operator**	orignal	**original**
oppeum	**opium**	oringe	**orange**
opponant	**opponent**	orjy	**orgy**
oppt	**opt****	orkid	**orchid**

Incorrect	Correct	Incorrect	Correct
ornathologist		outadate	out-of-date
	ornithologist	outkast	outcast
orniment	ornament	outkum	outcome
ornry	ornery	outlore	outlaw
orr	oar**	outtage	outage
orrator	orator	outter	outer
orrder	order	outtgoing	outgoing
orrganize	organize	outting	outing
orrnate	ornate	outtlay	outlay
orrthapedist	orthopedist	outtlet	outlet
ors d'oeurves		outtlook	outlook
	hors d'oeuvres	outtpatient	outpatient
orthadentist	orthodontist	outtput	output
orthentik	authentic	outwerd	outward
ortherdox	orthodox	ovabaring	overbearing
orthorety	authority	ovabite	overbite
orthorize	authorize	ovacum	overcome
oryental	oriental	ovahead	overhead
oscullatory	osculatory	ovakill	overkill
oshan	ocean	ovalation	ovulation
osheanography		ovar	over
	oceanography	ovarole	overall
osher	OSHA	ovatime	overtime
osify	ossify	ovature	overture
osillate	oscillate	ovaview	overview
osite	oocyte	ovazelus	overzealous
oskar	Oscar	ovel	oval
ossiloscope	oscilloscope	overate	overrate
osstensible	ostensible	overdoo	overdo**
ossteporosis	osteoporosis	overeach	overreach
osstrasize	ostracize	overeksposure	
ostintashus	ostentatious		overexposure
ostritch	ostrich	overide	override
ostypath	osteopath	overnite	overnight
otaman	ottoman	overought	overwrought
ote couture	haute couture	overrbord	overboard
ottee cee	OTC	overrthrow	overthrow
oth	oath**	overser	overseer
othawise	otherwise	overule	overrule
otour	auteur**	overun	overrun
oudo	outdo	overwelm	overwhelm
oudoor	outdoor	overy	ovary
our glass	hourglass	ovir the cownter	
ourhand	hour hand		over-the-counter
our's	ours	ovurt	overt**
ourselfs	ourselves		

Incorrect	Correct	Incorrect	Correct
ovvercompensate		owtline	**outline**
	overcompensate	owtporing	**outpouring**
ovverlok	**overlook**	owtragous	**outrageous**
ovyalate	**ovulate**	owtreach	**outreach**
owdated	**outdated**	owtsider	**outsider**
ownce	**ounce****	owtspoken	**outspoken**
owst	**oust**	owtstanding	**outstanding**
owt	**out****	owtwit	**outwit**
owtbord	**outboard**	oxagen	**oxygen**
owtbrake	**outbreak**	oxes	**oxen**
owtclass	**outclass**	oximoron	**oxymoron**
owtcry	**outcry**	oyl	**oil**
owtfeeld	**outfield**	oyntment	**ointment**
owtfit	**outfit**	ozmosis	**osmosis**

P

Incorrect	Correct	Incorrect	Correct
pachezi	**parcheesi**	pallit	**palate****
pachwerk	**patchwork**	pallsey	**palsy**
packige	**package**	palpatate	**palpitate**
Packistan	**Pakistan**	palpible	**palpable**
paddlock	**padlock**	palyative	**palliative**
padestrian	**pedestrian**	pam	**palm**
padjama	**pajama**	pament	**payment**
padray	**padre**	pamistry	**palmistry**
paeback	**payback**	pamphalet	**pamphlet**
paeyof	**payoff**	panaply	**panoply**
pagent	**pageant**	panash	**panache**
pailode	**payload**	pandamoneum	
pairent	**parent**		**pandemonium**
pajinate	**paginate**	pandar	**panda****
pakage	**package**	pandcake	**pancake**
pakking	**parking**	panerama	**panorama**
pakt	**pact****	panestaking	**painstaking**
palamino	**palomino**	panicea	**panacea**
palastine	**Palestine**	panicy	**panicky**
pallace	**palace**	panitela	**panatella**
pallacial	**palatial**	panjondum	**panjandrum**
pallasade	**palisade**	pankreas	**pancreas**
pallatable	**palatable**	panndemic	**pandemic**
palleontology		pannel	**panel**
	paleontology	pannhandle	**panhandle**
paller	**pallor**	panntheism	**pantheism**
pallindrome	**palindrome**	pantacostal	**Pentecostal**

Incorrect	Correct	Incorrect	Correct
pantamine	**pantomime**	parrenthasis	**parenthesis**
pantsnay	**pince-nez**	parrible	**parable**
panzy	**pansy**	parridy	**parody****
paola	**payola**	parrikeet	**parakeet**
papaloma	**papilloma**	parrish	**parish****
paper-mashay		parrishute	**parachute**
	papier-mâché	parrity	**parity****
papisy	**papacy**	parrking meter	
papp	**pap**		**parking meter**
pappaverine	**papaverine**	parrkinsons	**Parkinson's**
papperback	**paperback**	parrocheal	**parochial**
pappriker	**paprika**	parrole	**parole****
paprazy	**paparazzi**	parrson	**parson**
parafrase	**paraphrase**	parrthenogenesis	
paralise	**paralyze**		**parthenogenesis**
paraty	**parity****	parrturition	**parturition**
parce	**parse**	parrty	**party**
parchurition	**parturition**	parrymecium	
parden	**pardon**		**paramecium**
pardner	**partner**	parry-mutual	**pari-mutuel**
parfay	**parfait**	parsel	**parcel**
paridice	**paradise**	parshel	**partial**
paridime	**paradigm**	partasiple	**participle**
parifernalia		partickle	**particle**
	paraphernalia	partickuler	**particular**
parisite	**parasite**	partishun	**partition****
parkay	**parquet**	partisipate	**participate**
parlement	**parliament**	partizan	**partisan**
parler	**parlor**	partys	**parties**
Parmizan	**Parmesan**	parynoia	**paranoia**
parodocks	**paradox**	parypass	**pari passu**
parot	**parrot**	parypledgic	**paraplegic**
parraboler	**parabola**	parytal	**parietal**
parrade	**parade**	pasay	**passé**
parrafin	**paraffin**	pasenger	**passenger**
parragraf	**paragraph**	pashent	**patient**
parralel	**parallel**	pashion	**passion**
parralisis	**paralysis**	pasible	**passable****
parrameter	**parameter**	pasidge	**passage**
parramount	**paramount**	Pasific	**Pacific**
parraproffessional		pasify	**pacify**
	paraprofessional	pasive	**passive**
parrasychology		paso	**peso**
	parapsychology	pasover	**Passover**
parrathyon	**parathion**	pasport	**passport**
parratrooper	**paratrooper**	passay	**passé**

Incorrect	Correct	Incorrect	Correct
passification	**pacification**	paynter	**painter**
passifist	**pacifist**	payshent	**patient**
passta	**pasta**	paysley	**paisley**
passtell	**pastel**	paysmaker	**pacemaker**
passtime	**pastime**	paythos	**pathos****
passtrami	**pastrami**	paytriark	**patriarch**
pastachio	**pistachio**	paytron	**patron**
pasteing	**pasting**	paytronage	**patronage**
paster	**pastor****	payyee	**payee**
pastil	**pastille**	payyout	**payout**
pastrey	**pastry**	pean	**paean****
pasturize	**pasteurize**	peaphole	**peephole**
pastword	**password**	pearless	**peerless**
pastyer	**pasture****	peavish	**peevish**
patatoe	**potato**	pecunerary	**pecuniary**
patay	**pâté****	pedafilia	**pedophilia**
patermony	**patrimony**	pedagree	**pedigree**
patern	**pattern**	pedderast	**pederast**
patheing	**pathing**	peddiculosis	**pediculosis**
pathollogy	**pathology**	peddigog	**pedagogue**
paticular	**particular**	peddy	**petty**
patition	**petition****	pedent	**pedant**
patren	**patron**	pedistal	**pedestal**
patritism	**patriotism**	peeanist	**pianist**
patriyot	**patriot**	peeaza	**piazza**
patroleum	**petroleum**	peece	**PC**
pattedifoigra		peecework	**piecework**
	pâté de foie gras	peech	**peach**
pattela	**patella**	peedyatrics	**pediatrics**
pattent	**patent**	peekant	**piquant**
patternal	**paternal**	pee-m-ess	**PMS**
pattio	**patio**	peenil	**penal****
pattrol	**patrol**	peenis	**penis**
patune	**platoon**	peenut	**peanut**
paveing	**paving**	peepul	**people**
pavilon	**pavilion**	peeza	**pizza**
pavment	**pavement**	pegd	**pegged**
pawlbarer	**pallbearer**	pegoda	**pagoda**
pawltry	**paltry****	peice	**piece****
pawrter	**porter**	peicemeal	**piecemeal**
pawsity	**paucity**	peirce	**pierce**
pawtico	**portico**	pekan	**pecan**
pawtray	**portray**	peks	**pecs****
paycheck	**paycheck**	pektoral	**pectoral**
payed	**paid**	pelagra	**pellagra**
		pelet	**pellet****

Incorrect	Correct	Incorrect	Correct
pellvis	**pelvis**	perdominant	
pemanship	**penmanship**		**predominant**
penalogy	**penology**	perel	**peril**
penant	**pennant**	perfer	**prefer****
penatenshary		perferate	**perforate**
	penitentiary	perfered	**preferred**
penatint	**penitent**	perfessor	**professor**
penatrate	**penetrate**	perfict	**perfect****
penatration	**penetration**	perfume	**perfume**
penelty	**penalty**	pergatory	**purgatory**
pengwin	**penguin**	perge	**purge**
penife	**penknife**	peridontal	**periodontal**
penndyalum	**pendulum**	perliminary	**preliminary**
pennicilan	**penicillin**	perloin	**purloin**
penninsuler	**peninsula**	permenant	**permanent**
penntameter	**pentameter**	permenstrual	
penntathalon	**pentathlon**		**premenstrual**
penntegon	**Pentagon**	permiate	**permeate**
penntetok	**Pentateuch**	permisable	**permissible**
penntobarbital		permitt	**permit**
	pentobarbital	perogative	**prerogative**
penntup	**pent-up**	perpatrate	**perpetrate**
penoir	**peignoir**	perpatrater	**perpetrator**
penshent	**penchant**	perpensity	**propensity**
penshun	**pension**	perpettual	**perpetual**
pensil	**pencil**	perpicious	**propitious**
Pensylvania	**Pennsylvania**	perpindicular	
Pentacostal	**Pentecostal**		**perpendicular**
pentegram	**pentagram**	perple	**purple**
penus	**penis**	perponderant	
penyless	**penniless**		**preponderant**
peper	**pepper**	perport	**purport**
pepptic	**peptic**	perposterous	
perameter	**parameter**		**preposterous**
peraps	**perhaps**	perprietary	**proprietary****
percalator	**percolator**	perpubesent	**prepubescent**
percarious	**precarious**	perranum	**per annum**
percaution	**precaution**	perrascope	**periscope**
percept	**precept**	perrenial	**perennial**
percieve	**perceive**	perrifery	**periphery**
percise	**precise****	perrimter	**perimeter**
perclude	**preclude**	perriod	**period**
perculiar	**peculiar**	perrish	**perish****
percushion	**percussion**	perroxide	**peroxide**
perdikament	**predicament**	perrspective	**perspective**
		persacute	**persecute****

Incorrect	Correct	Incorrect	Correct
persavere	**persevere**	phaze	**phase****
perscribe	**prescribe****	Pheenix	**Phoenix**
perscription		pheenobarbatal	
	prescription**		**phenobarbital**
perse	**purse**	Philipino	**Filipino**
persent	**percent**	phillately	**philately**
persepectus	**prospectus**	Phillipines	**Philippines**
perser	**purser**	phinomenon	**phenomenon**
perserve	**preserve****	phisics	**physics**
persikute	**persecute****	phisionomy	**physiognomy**
persin	**person**	phisique	**physique****
persinality	**personality**	phisyology	**physiology**
perspacaous		phisyotherapy	
	perspicacious		**physiotherapy**
persue	**pursue**	phonettic	**phonetic**
persuit	**pursuit**	phonnics	**phonics**
persumption	**presumption**	phont	**font****
perswade	**persuade**	phosferous	**phosphorus**
pertanint	**pertinent**	phosforresence	
pertend	**pretend****		**phosphorescence**
perticulars	**particulars**	photagraph	**photograph**
pertonitis	**peritonitis**	phreek	**phreak****
peruet	**pirouette**	phylanthropy	
pervention	**prevention**		**philanthropy**
pervide	**provide**	physiclly	**physically**
pervue	**purview**	piana	**piano**
pesery	**pessary**	piarea	**pyorrhea**
pesimist	**pessimist**	piaza	**piazza**
pestaside	**pesticide**	picadilo	**peccadillo**
petteet	**petite**	piccyune	**picayune**
pettle	**petal**	pich	**pitch**
pettrify	**petrify**	pickcher	**picture****
pettulant	**petulant**	pickel	**pickle**
pettycoat	**petticoat**	picknic	**picnic**
petty mal	**petit mal**	picksel	**pixel**
peverse	**perverse****	picollo	**piccolo**
pezint	**peasant**	pidgeon	**pigeon****
phalus	**phallus**	pietty	**piety**
phamaceutical		piggeebak	**piggyback**
	pharmaceutical	piggment	**pigment**
phanntom lim		pijjin	**pigeon****
	phantom limb	pika	**pica****
phantastic	**fantastic**	piket	**picket**
Pharow	**Pharaoh**	pikkup	**pickup**
pharrinx	**pharynx**	pikpocket	**pickpocket**
phasician	**physician**	pilage	**pillage**

Incorrect	Correct	Incorrect	Correct
pilbox	**pillbox**	plaiyoff	**playoff**
pileing	**piling**	plajiarism	**plagiarism**
pilet	**pilot****	planetif	**plaintiff****
pilitis	**pyelitis**	plannet	**planet****
piller	**pillar****	plannetarium	
pillery	**pillory**		**planetarium**
pillfer	**pilfer**	planntation	**plantation**
pillgrim	**pilgrim**	plasa	**plaza**
pimmento	**pimento**	plasebo	**placebo**
pimpel	**pimple**	plasenta	**placenta**
pinacle	**pinnacle****	plassid	**placid**
pinapple	**pineapple**	plasster	**plaster**
pinkey	**pink eye**	plasstic	**plastic**
pinnochle	**pinochle****	plasted	**plastered**
pinnpoint	**pinpoint**	platow	**plateau**
pinnstripe	**pinstripe**	plattform	**platform**
pinnup	**pinup**	plattinum	**platinum**
pinsers	**pincers**	plattitude	**platitude**
pinurious	**penurious**	plattonic	**Platonic**
pionner	**pioneer**	plattoon	**platoon**
pipeing	**piping**	plausable	**plausible**
pipline	**pipeline**	plawdit	**plaudit**
piramid	**pyramid**	playwrite	**playwright**
pire	**pyre**	plazma	**plasma**
pirl	**purl****	pleab	**plebe**
piromaniac	**pyromaniac**	plebbacite	**plebiscite**
pirotechnics	**pyrotechnics**	plee	**plea**
pirpituity	**perpetuity**	pleed	**plead**
pisstil	**pistol****	pleet	**pleat**
pistin	**piston**	pleeze	**please****
pitchur	**picture****	plege	**pledge**
pitence	**pittance**	plenery	**plenary**
pittfall	**pitfall**	plenny	**plenty**
pittuitary	**pituitary**	plentyful	**plentiful**
pitty	**pity**	plesant	**pleasant**
pityful	**pitiful**	plesure	**pleasure**
pivit	**pivot**	pletherra	**plethora**
plaback	**playback**	pliewood	**plywood**
plabean	**plebeian**	plite	**plight**
placcate	**placate**	ploding	**plodding**
plackard	**placard**	ploi	**ploy**
placment	**placement**	ploorilism	**pluralism**
plad	**plaid**	plopp	**plop**
pladder	**platter**	plott	**plot****
plage	**plague****	plouw	**plow**
plaitlet	**platelet**	pluerisy	**pleurisy**

Incorrect	Correct	Incorrect	Correct
plugg	**plug**	polltagist	**poltergeist**
plukk	**pluck**	pollyethelene	
plumer	**plumber**		**polyethylene**
plunnder	**plunder**	pollygon	**polygon**
plurel	**plural**	pollygraf	**polygraph**
pluss	**plus**	polly si	**poli-sci**
pluttonium	**plutonium**	poltice	**poultice**
plya	**playa****	polute	**pollute**
plyable	**pliable**	polution	**pollution**
plye	**ply**	pome	**poem**
plyers	**pliers**	pommade	**pomade**
pockabook	**pocketbook**	pommel	**pummel**
pockit	**pocket**	pompidor	**pompadour**
podytry	**podiatry**	pompus	**pompous**
poetent	**potent**	poneytale	**ponytail**
poggrom	**pogrom****	ponsho	**poncho**
poinyant	**poignant**	pontif	**Pontiff**
poisin	**poison**	poobsesent	**pubescent**
poit	**poet**	pooding	**pudding**
poize	**poise**	poorim	**Purim**
poka	**polka****	pooshup	**push-up**
polen	**pollen**	pootsh	**putsch**
polerise	**polarize**	poppular	**popular****
poletry	**poultry****	poppulist	**populist**
Polianne	**Pollyanna**	popuree	**potpourri**
poliglot	**polyglot**	popuyulation	**population**
polisentric	**polycentric**	porcelin	**porcelain**
polisy	**policy**	poretal	**portal**
politikly korrect		poridge	**porridge**
	politically correct	pornagraphy	
poliunsaturated			**pornography**
	polyunsaturated	porposal	**proposal**
pollar	**polar**	porrthole	**porthole**
Pollaris	**Polaris**	portfollio	**portfolio**
Pollaroid	**Polaroid**	portible	**portable****
pollemic	**polemic**	porto ricco	**Puerto Rico**
pollice	**police**	portrit	**portrait**
polliester	**polyester**	posative	**positive**
polligamy	**polygamy****	poscard	**postcard**
pollimer	**polymer**	posedoffice	**post office**
pollio	**polio**	posemortem	**postmortem**
pollip	**polyp**	posepaid	**postpaid**
pollish	**polish**	posess	**possess**
pollite	**polite**	posession	**possession**
pollitics	**politics**	posible	**possible**
pollity	**polity**	posman	**postman**

Incorrect	Correct	Incorrect	Correct
pospone	**postpone**	precink	**precinct**
possefoot	**pussyfoot**	precoshious	**precocious**
possition	**position**	precure	**procure**
possta	**pasta**	predacate	**predicate**
possterity	**posterity**	predddnisone	**prednisone**
posstmaster	**postmaster**	preddesessor	**predecessor**
possy	**posse**	predeter	**predator**
postel	**postal**	predick	**predict**
postige	**postage**	predjidiss	**prejudice**
postirier	**posterior**	preeamble	**preamble**
postumus	**posthumous**	preech	**preach**
postyure	**posture**	preecher	**preacher**
potenshal	**potential**	preedictible	**predictable**
potery	**pottery**	preefabrikate	
poteum	**podium**		**prefabricate**
potry	**poetry**	preefered	**preferred**
pottasium	**potassium**	preemartial	**premarital**
potwhole	**pothole**	preemtory	**peremptory**
pouder	**powder**	preepare	**prepare**
pounse	**pounce**	preepuce	**prepuce**
pourus	**porous**	preesentation	
povety	**poverty**		**presentation**
powch	**pouch**	preesis	**paresis**
pownd	**pound**	preffer	**prefer****
powt	**pout**	prefice	**preface**
powwer	**power**	prefidious	**perfidious**
poynsetta	**poinsettia**	prefrence	**preference**
poyntless	**pointless**	pregenitor	**progenitor**
poyzin pill	**poison pill**	pregnent	**pregnant**
pozitron	**positron**	preist	**priest**
practologist	**proctologist**	prelood	**prelude**
prafound	**profound**	prema dona	**prima donna**
praggmatic	**pragmatic**	premere	**premier****
praier	**prayer**	preminent	**preeminent**
prairy	**prairie**	premiscuous	**promiscuous**
praize	**praise**	premiss	**premise**
praktical	**practical**	premiture	**premature**
praktise	**practice****	premival	**primeval**
praldahyde	**paraldehyde**	premmonition	
praliferate	**proliferate**		**premonition**
prataganist	**protagonist**	premyum	**premium**
pravincial	**provincial**	preocupation	
pravision	**provision**		**preoccupation**
preceed	**precede****	preperation	**preparation**
preceive	**perceive**	preposal	**proposal**
preception	**perception**		

Incorrect	Correct	Incorrect	Correct
preposition	**preposition****	priviledge	**privilege**
preprietor	**proprietor**	privisy	**privacy**
presadent	**president****	privitazation	
Presbaterian			**privatization**
	Presbyterian	privite	**private**
presedent	**precedent****	privvy	**privy**
preseed	**precede****	prizm	**prism**
presept	**precept**	prizon	**prison**
preshent	**prescient**	proab	**probe**
preshure	**pressure**	proaktiv	**proactive**
preshus	**precious**	probbate	**probate**
presice	**precise****	probbity	**probity**
presipatate	**precipitate**	probible	**probable**
prespiration	**perspiration**	problim	**problem**
prespire	**perspire**	proccreate	**procreate**
pressage	**presage**	procede	**proceed****
pressipiss	**precipice**	proceedure	**procedure**
presstige	**prestige**	procent	**percent**
pretsell	**pretzel**	prochoyce	**pro-choice**
prety	**pretty**	proclame	**proclaim**
prevade	**pervade**	procter	**proctor**
prevale	**prevail**	proddigious	**prodigious**
prevelant	**prevalent**	proddigy	**prodigy****
preversion	**perversion**	produck	**product**
previso	**proviso**	produktivity	**productivity**
previus	**previous**	produse	**produce**
prevue	**preview**	proe	**pro**
preycis	**precis****	proebation	**probation**
prezent	**present**	proebono	**pro bono**
prezide	**preside**	proechoyce	**pro-choice**
prezident	**president****	proejesterone	
prezume	**presume**		**progesterone**
priamplifier	**preamplifier**	proelife	**pro-life**
prickley	**prickly**	profalactic	
pricless	**priceless**		**prophylactic****
priemate	**primate**	profecy	**prophecy****
primative	**primitive**	profer	**proffer****
primerrily	**primarily**	profeshun	**profession**
primery	**primary**	proffesor	**professor**
primie	**preemie**	proffess	**profess**
prinsess	**princess**	proficient	**proficient**
priorty	**priority**	profile	**profile**
pritify	**prettify**	proffit	**profit****
prity	**pretty**	proflagate	**profligate**
privaricate	**prevaricate**	profuce	**profuse**
		profunctory	**perfunctory**

Incorrect	Correct	Incorrect	Correct
progection	**projection**	prosess	**process**
progeramer	**programmer**	prossecute	**prosecute****
proggnosis	**prognosis**	prosseser	**processor**
proggres	**progress**	prossession	**procession**
programm	**program****	prosspect	**prospect**
prohibbit	**prohibit**	prosstate	**prostate****
projeck	**project**	prosstatute	**prostitute**
projeny	**progeny**	prosstheesis	**prosthesis**
prokane	**procaine**	protatype	**prototype**
prokrastinate		proteck	**protect**
	procrastinate	protecoll	**protocol**
proktascope	**proctoscope**	protene	**protein**
prolive	**pro-life**	protezhay	**protégé**
proll	**prole**	prottaganist	**protagonist**
prollific	**prolific**	prottaplasm	**protoplasm**
prologgue	**prologue**	prottest	**protest**
prominade	**promenade**	Prottestent	**Protestant**
promisary	**promissory**	prottocoll	**protocol**
promm	**prom**	protton	**proton**
prommice	**promise**	protude	**protrude**
promminent	**prominent**	provadents	**providence**
prommiscuous		provoak	**provoke**
	promiscuous	provoe	**provost**
prommote	**promote**	provurb	**proverb**
promt	**prompt**	provvince	**province**
pronosticate		prowd	**proud****
	prognosticate	proxximity	**proximity**
pronounciation		proxxy	**proxy**
	pronunciation	prozaic	**prosaic**
prood	**prude**	pruddence	**prudence**
proove	**prove**	prufound	**profound**
properganda	**propaganda**	prunounce	**pronounce****
proppagate	**propagate**	prunto	**pronto**
proppel	**propel**	pruse	**peruse**
propper	**proper**	pruspectus	**prospectus**
propperty	**property****	prye	**pry**
propponent	**proponent**	pryemt	**preempt**
propportion	**proportion**	prymafacy	**prima facie**
proppose	**propose**	prymal scream	
propposition			**primal scream**
	proposition**	pryme	**prime**
propprietor	**proprietor**	pryority	**priority**
proppultion	**propulsion**	prypism	**priapism**
proprity	**propriety****	pryvitise	**privatize**
prosedure	**procedure**	psam	**psalm**
proseed	**proceed****	psico	**psycho**

Incorrect	Correct	Incorrect	Correct
psycology	**psychology**	purfector	**perfecta**
psyconalasis		purient	**prurient**
	psychoanalysis	puriferal	**peripheral**
pubb	**pub**	purile	**puerile**
pubblisity	**publicity**	puritis	**pruritis**
pubity	**puberty**	purjery	**perjury**
publacation	**publication**	purks	**perks**
publick	**public****	purmutation	**permutation**
puding	**pudding**	purnicious	**pernicious**
pudjy	**pudgy**	purp	**perp**
pue	**pew**	purpice	**purpose****
puggnatious	**pugnacious**	purplex	**perplex**
pulit	**pullet**	purquisite	**perquisite**
pulkritude	**pulchritude**	pursavere	**persevere**
pullminary	**pulmonary**	pursistance	**persistence**
pullp	**pulp**	pursona nongratis	
pullpit	**pulpit**		**persona non grata**
pullse	**pulse**	pursonnal	**personal****
pullser	**pulsar**	purspicacious	
pullverise	**pulverize**		**perspicacious**
pulside	**poolside**	pursuade	**persuade**
puly	**pulley**	purt	**PERT**
pumkin	**pumpkin**	purtain	**pertain**
pumpanickle		purterb	**perturb**
	pumpernickel	Purto Rico	**Puerto Rico**
punative	**punitive**	purvert	**pervert**
punctull	**punctual**	pussilanamous	
pungk	**punk**		**pusillanimous**
pungture	**puncture**	puthetic	**pathetic**
punjint	**pungent**	putina	**patina**
punktilious	**punctilious**	putred	**putrid**
punktuate	**punctuate**	putrify	**putrefy**
punnish	**punish**	puzzel	**puzzle**
punx	**punks**	pweblo	**pueblo**
pupe	**poop**	pyaneer	**pioneer**
pupet	**puppet**	pyedatear	**pied-à-terre**
pupull	**pupil****	pyela	**paella**
purception	**perception**	Pyric victory	
purch	**perch**		**Pyrrhic victory**
purchise	**purchase**	pyubes	**pubes**
pur deem	**per diem**	pyus	**pious****
purduction	**production**	pyutitive	**putative**

Incorrect	Correct	Incorrect	Correct

Q

Incorrect	Correct	Incorrect	Correct
quadd	**quad**	quepidity	**cupidity**
quaddrant	**quadrant**	quere	**queer**
quaddratic	**quadratic**	querk	**quirk****
quadrain	**quatrain**	queschun	**question**
quadrapledgic		questionaire	
	quadriplegic		**questionnaire**
quadrefonic		quibel	**quibble**
	quadrophonic	quicksotic	**quixotic**
quadrune	**quadroon**	quicsand	**quicksand**
quaf	**quaff**	quiddproko	
quafeur	**coiffure**		**quid pro quo**
quaik	**quake**	quier	**choir****
quak	**quack****	quik	**quick**
quakker	**Quaker**	quinntet	**quintet**
qualefy	**qualify**	quinntoplet	**quintuplet**
quallity	**quality****	quivver	**quiver****
quam	**qualm**	quized	**quizzed**
quanity	**quantity****	quizes	**quizzes**
quanntum	**quantum**	quizical	**quizzical**
quarc	**quark****	quizine	**cuisine**
quarel	**quarrel**	quodrangle	**quadrangle**
quarelled	**quarreled**	quoir	**choir****
quarentine	**quarantine**	quoshent	**quotient**
quarrtally	**quarterly**	quot	**quote****
quarrtet	**quartet**	quotashun	**quotation**
quary	**quarry****	quoter	**quota****
quashiokor	**kwashiorkor**	quynine	**quinine**
quater	**quarter**	qwadrepartite	
quawtaback	**quarterback**		**quadripartite**
quazar	**quasar**	qwantity	**quantity****
quazy	**quasi****	qwartz	**quartz****
qudrupul	**quadruple****	qwench	**quench**
queary	**query****	qwid	**quid**
queesh	**quiche**	qwill	**quill**
queezy	**queasy****	qwizz	**quiz**
quene	**queen****	qwurum	**quorum**
quepea	**kewpie**	qyayzar	**quasar**

Incorrect	Correct	Incorrect	Correct

R

Incorrect	Correct	Incorrect	Correct
rabbid	**rabid****	rajed	**raged**
rabees	**rabies****	rajeem	**regime**
rabi	**rabbi**	rakateer	**racketeer**
rabit	**rabbit****	raket	**racket**
rable	**rabble**	rakkish	**rakish**
racey	**racy**	rakoko	**rococo**
rachit	**ratchet**	rakontour	**raconteur**
raciosination		rakoon	**raccoon**
	ratiocination	raleroad	**railroad**
racizm	**racism**	ralley	**rally**
raconture	**raconteur**	rambil	**ramble**
racoon	**raccoon**	rameedial	**remedial**
raddicle	**radical**	ramm	**RAM****
raddiologist	**radiologist**	rammadam	**Ramadan**
raddish	**radish**	rammafication	
raddy	**ratty**		**ramification**
radeactivity	**radioactivity**	rammpage	**rampage**
radeation	**radiation**	rampint	**rampant**
radeator	**radiator**	randim	**random**
radeo	**radio**	ranecote	**raincoat**
radicks	**radix**	ranemaker	**rainmaker**
radiel	**radial**	rangle	**wrangle**
radient	**radiant**	rangler	**wrangler**
radisotope	**radioisotope**	ranje	**range**
radyis	**radius**	rankel	**rankle**
rafel	**raffle**	rannking	**ranking**
raff	**raft**	rannsak	**ransack**
rafia	**raffia**	ransid	**rancid**
rafined	**refined**	ransum	**ransom**
raform	**reform**	rapayshus	**rapacious**
ragga	**raga****	rapcher	**rapture**
ragid	**ragged**	rapel	**repel**
raglin	**raglan**	rapel	**rappel**
ragoo	**ragout****	rapore	**rapport**
rahtha	**rather**	rapp	**rap****
raign	**reign****	rappist	**rapist**
railling	**railing**	raproachment	
raindeer	**reindeer**		**rapprochement**
rainny	**rainy**	rapsody	**rhapsody**
raion	**rayon**	rarety	**rarity**
rait	**rate**	rarify	**rarefy**
raitable	**ratable**	rarly	**rarely**
raivin	**raven**	rascist	**racist**

Incorrect	Correct	Incorrect	Correct
rashanal	**rationale****	reanite	**reunite**
rashio	**ratio**	reapose	**repose**
rashnalize	**rationalize**	reapper	**reaper**
rashul	**racial**	reaserch	**research**
rashun	**ration**	reasessive	**recessive**
rasism	**racism**	reath	**wreath**
rasy	**racy**	reatort	**retort**
ratafy	**ratify**	reavaluate	**reevaluate**
rateing	**rating**	reawder	**reorder**
ratel	**rattle**	reazon	**reason**
rath	**wrath**	rebell	**rebel**
ratrap	**rattrap**	rebelyon	**rebellion**
rattlsnake	**rattlesnake**	reberthing	**rebirthing**
raught	**wrought**	rebiuk	**rebuke**
ravashing	**ravishing**	rebutil	**rebuttal**
raveel	**reveal**	recalsatrate	**recalcitrate**
ravije	**ravage**	recapichulate	**recapitulate**
ravnous	**ravenous**	recclamation	**reclamation**
ravvil	**ravel**	reccomend	**recommend**
ravvish	**ravish**	recconoyter	**reconnoiter**
rawkus	**raucous**	reccord	**record**
rawnchy	**raunchy**	reccreation	**recreation**
rawr	**raw****	reccumpense	**recompense**
rawshack	**Rorschach**	reccurrance	**recurrence**
rayce	**race**	recection	**resection**
raydar	**radar**	receed	**recede****
raydium	**radium**	receit	**receipt**
raydon	**radon**	recepy	**recipe**
raype	**rape**	reces	**recess**
rayshio	**ratio**	receshun	**recession**
raystrack	**racetrack**	recicle	**recycle**
rayth	**wraith**	recievable	**receivable**
rayting	**rating**	recieve	**receive**
rayz	**raze****	reck	**wreck****
rayzin	**raisin**	reckwisit	**requisite**
razer	**razor**	reclect	**recollect**
razidjual	**residual**	recloose	**recluse****
razon d'etre	**raison d'être**	reconisonce	
razzberry	**raspberry**		**reconnaissance**
reabuff	**rebuff**	reconize	**recognize**
reakshun	**reaction**	recooperate	**recuperate**
reakter	**reactor**	recovry	**recovery**
realaty	**reality**	recquire	**require**
realese	**release**	recrimnatory	
realise	**realize****		**recriminatory**
realy	**really**	recrute	**recruit**

Incorrect	Correct	Incorrect	Correct
rectafy	**rectify**	reep	**reap**
rectul	**rectal**	reepent	**repent**
reddhanded	**red-handed**	reeplacement	**replacement**
reddhearing	**red herring**	reeply	**reply****
reddline	**redline**	reeport	**report**
redekerate	**redecorate**	reeposess	**repossess**
redemshun	**redemption**	reepugnant	**repugnant**
reden	**redden**	reepulsive	**repulsive**
rederect	**redirect**	reesponse	**response**
redhed	**redhead**	reestriction	**restriction**
rediculous	**ridiculous**	reestrictive	**restrictive**
redily	**readily**	reetard	**retard**
reduceable	**reducible**	reetention	**retention**
redundent	**redundant**	reetred	**retread**
reduse	**reduce**	reetule	**retool**
redy	**ready**	reevene	**revenge**
reeact	**react**	reevoke	**revoke**
reebound	**rebound****	reevolver	**revolver**
reecapture	**recapture**	reevulsion	**revulsion**
reecepter	**receptor**	reeward	**reward**
reeceptionist	**receptionist**	reewind	**rewind**
reech	**reach**	referbish	**refurbish**
reeconstruct	**reconstruct**	refferendum	**referendum**
reedeme	**redeem**	reffermation	**reformation**
reeder	**reader**	reffugee	**refugee**
reed-only	**read-only**	reffuse	**refuse**
reedress	**redress**	refinment	**refinement**
reefraction	**refraction**	refirm	**reaffirm**
reefresher	**refresher**	refleks	**reflex**
reefund	**refund**	reflekshun	**reflection**
reeksamine	**reexamine**	refrance	**reference**
reelaps	**relapse**	refrane	**refrain**
reelent	**relent**	refree	**referee****
reel estate	**real estate**	refridgerator	**refrigerator**
reelizm	**realism**	refule	**refuel**
reeltor	**Realtor**	refun	**refund**
reem	**ream**	refuzal	**refusal**
reemarkable	**remarkable**	refyuge	**refuge**
reematch	**rematch**	refyute	**refute**
reemorse	**remorse**	regail	**regale****
reemote	**remote**	regarder	**regatta**
reenforcement		regay	**reggae****
	reinforcement	regestrer	**registrar**
reenkarnation		reggard	**regard**
	reincarnation	regilate	**regulate**
reenvent	**reinvent**	reglar	**regular**

Incorrect	Correct	Incorrect	Correct
regreshun	**regression**	relm	**realm**
regretible	**regrettable**	relucktinse	**reluctance**
regul	**regal****	relyd	**relied**
regurjatate	**regurgitate**	relyible	**reliable**
rehabbilitate	**rehabilitate**	remane	**remain**
rehersel	**rehearsal**	reme	**ream**
rehurse	**rehearse**	remidy	**remedy**
reignbow	**rainbow**	reminiss	**reminisce**
reishue	**reissue**	remishun	**remission**
rejament	**regiment**	remitence	**remittance**
rejensy	**regency**	remm	**REM**
rejestration	**registration**	remmark	**remark**
rejister	**register**	remmember	**remember**
rejon	**region**	remmit	**remit**
rejoyse	**rejoice**	remmonstate	**remonstrate**
rekall	**recall**	remoat	**remote**
rekapture	**recapture**	remoonerate	**remunerate**
rekin	**reckon**	remorsful	**remorseful**
rekline	**recline**	removeable	**removable**
reklis	**reckless**	removil	**removal**
reknown	**renown**	renact	**reenact**
rekombinant DNA	**recombinant DNA**	renagaid	**renegade**
		renaysense	**renascence**
rekonsile	**reconcile**	rendayvous	**rendezvous**
rekoop	**recoup**	reneg	**renege**
rekord	**record**	renevate	**renovate**
rektangul	**rectangle**	renforce	**reenforce**
rektim	**rectum**	renjin	**Roentgen**
rekwest	**request**	rennasonse	**renaissance**
rekweum	**requiem**	renownce	**renounce**
rekwital	**requital**	rentel	**rental**
rekwizit	**requisite**	rentry	**reentry**
relaition	**relation**	renue	**renew**
relakate	**relocate**	reoose	**reuse**
relaks	**relax**	reorgenise	**reorganize**
relavent	**relevant**	reostat	**rheostat**
relection	**reelection**	repare	**repair**
releif	**relief**	repatishun	**repetition**
releive	**relieve**	repatory	**repertory**
relie	**rely**	repawter	**reporter**
relient	**reliant**	repaytriate	**repatriate**
relinkwish	**relinquish**	repear	**reappear**
relitive	**relative**	repeel	**repeal**
rellegate	**relegate**	repelant	**repellent**
rellish	**relish**	reperation	**reparation**

Incorrect	Correct	Incorrect	Correct
reperbate	**reprobate**	resipient	**recipient**
reperduce	**reproduce**	resipracal	**reciprocal**
reperductive	**reproductive**	resiprosity	**reciprocity**
reperhensable		resitashun	**recitation**
	reprehensible	resle	**wrestle**
repersent	**represent**	resorse	**resource**
repetative	**repetitive**	resparator	**respirator**
repete	**repeat**	respectible	**respectable**
repetwar	**repertoire**	respit	**respite**
replaka	**replica**	responsable	**responsible**
replaysment	**replacement**	ressipea	**recipe**
repleet	**replete**	ressle	**wrestle**
repozatory	**repository**	resstriction	**restriction**
reppakushin	**repercussion**	resstructure	**restructure**
reppatee	**repartee**	restablish	**reestablish**
reppetition	**repetition**	restatution	**restitution**
repplenish	**replenish**	resterant	**restaurant**
repplicate	**replicate**	resteration	**restoration**
repport	**report**	restrane	**restrain**
reppublican	**Republican**	restrik	**restrict**
repputible	**reputable**	resumtion	**resumption**
reprable	**reparable**	resure	**reassure**
repramand	**reprimand**	resurtify	**recertify**
repreive	**reprieve**	resusitate	**resuscitate**
represed	**repressed**	resytul	**recital**
repreze	**reprise**	retale	**retail**
reprizal	**reprisal**	retalliate	**retaliate**
reproche	**reproach**	retane	**retain**
reproove	**reprove**	retaut	**retort**
reptil	**reptile**	retern	**return**
repyudiate	**repudiate**	retier	**retire**
rerite	**rewrite**	retirment	**retirement**
resadense	**residence**	retisent	**reticent**
resaleable	**resalable**	retna	**retina**
resalution	**resolution**	retorick	**rhetoric**
reseever	**receiver**	retreet	**retreat**
reseption	**reception**	retreive	**retrieve**
reserch	**research**	retroefit	**retrofit**
resessive	**recessive**	retrosay	**retroussé**
resevation	**reservation**	rettape	**red tape**
resevwar	**reservoir**	retterovirus	**retrovirus**
reshur	**reissue**	rettraction	**retraction**
residivism	**recidivism**	rettribushun	**retribution**
resind	**rescind****	rettroactive	**retroactive**
resint	**recent****	rettroe	**retro**

Incorrect	Correct	Incorrect	Correct
rettrogreshun		ricorder	recorder
	retrogression	ridel	riddle
rettrospeck	retrospect	ridence	riddance
retuch	retouch	ridgid	rigid
reveer	revere	rie	rye**
revelle	reveille**	RIET	REIT
revelution	revolution	rieterate	reiterate
revijun	revision	rifel	rifle**
revilation	revelation	rigermarole	rigmarole
revinew	revenue	rigerus	rigorous
revivle	revival	rigg	rig
revize	revise	right-in	write-in
revokashun	revocation	right-protect	
revrent	reverent**		write-protect
revult	revolt	rigle	wriggle
revursible	reversible	rigur	rigor
revurt	revert	riht	right**
revvarie	reverie**	rije	ridge
revvolve	revolve	rikity	rickety
revyoo	revue**	rikoshay	ricochet
reynion	reunion	rikota	ricotta
rezanense	resonance	rikshaw	rickshaw
rezemblence	resemblance	rilation	relation
rezent	resent**	rilegious	religious
rezerve	reserve	rince	rinse
rezerve	reserve	rinestone	rhinestone
rezidew	residue	ringger	ringer
rezign	resign	ringwurm	ringworm
rezilyens	resilience	rinitis	rhinitis
rezin	resin	rinkel	wrinkle
rezistable	resistible	rinocerus	rhinoceros
rezistance	resistance	rinseing	rinsing
reznable	reasonable	riple	ripple
rezolve	resolve	rippen	ripen
rezort	resort	rippof	rip-off
rezult	result	ripublic	republic
rezume	resume	riquire	require
rezurecshun	resurrection	riseing	rising
rhime	rhyme**	riskay	risqué
riaktionary	reactionary	riskchip	risc chip
ribben	ribbon	rist	wrist
ribbuld	ribald	rit	writ
richous	righteous	ritch	rich
richual	ritual	riteful	rightful
rickashay	ricochet	riteoff	write-off

Incorrect	Correct	Incorrect	Correct
riter	**writer**	rooves	**roofs**
rithe	**writhe**	roring	**roaring**
rithem	**rhythm****	rosay	**rosé****
ritowork	**right-to-work**	rosery	**rosary**
ritten	**written**	Rosevelt	**Roosevelt**
riut	**riot**	rosey	**rosy**
rivaluation	**revaluation**	roshes	**rushes**
rivel	**rival**	rost	**roast**
rivishonism	**revisionism**	rotait	**rotate**
rivit	**rivet**	rotery	**rotary**
rize	**rise**	roth	**wroth**
rizome	**rhizome**	rotha	**rather**
roadio	**rodeo**	rotin	**rotten**
roarshock	**Rorschach**	roudy	**rowdy**
robbin	**robin**	roughian	**ruffian**
robery	**robbery**	roveing	**roving**
roche hashanah		royaly	**royally**
	Rosh Hashanah	roze	**rose****
Rockerfellow	**Rockefeller**	rozin	**rosin**
rodeblok	**roadblock**	rubar	**rubber**
rododendrum		rubarb	**rhubarb**
	rhododendron	rubiola	**rubeola**
roebot	**robot**	rubish	**rubbish**
roedent	**rodent**	ruf	**rough****
roeman	**Roman**	ruffneck	**roughneck**
roge	**rogue**	ruge	**rouge**
rogish	**roguish**	rumatism	**rheumatism**
roial	**royal****	rumba	**rhumba**
rokkit	**rocket**	rumbil	**rumble**
rokk n role	**rock and roll**	rumer	**rumor****
roleout	**rollout****	rumije	**rummage**
rollplay	**roleplay**	rumy	**rummy**
rolover	**rollover****	runer	**runner**
romanse	**romance**	runing	**running**
romb	**ROM****	runnaway	**runaway**
rome	**roam****	runne-down	**run down****
rong	**wrong**	runtyen	**Roentgen**
roo	**rue**	rupcher	**rupture**
rooay	**roué**	rurel	**rural**
roobarb	**rhubarb**	rusbelt	**rustbelt**
rood	**rude****	ruset	**russet**
rooler	**ruler**	Rusha	**Russia**
roolet	**roulette**	rusil	**rustle**
roomate	**roommate**	russty	**rusty**
roomatism	**rheumatism**	rustik	**rustic**
roon	**ruin****	rutine	**routine**

Incorrect	Correct	Incorrect	Correct
rutter	**rudder**	ryitus	**riotous**
ruwanda	**Rwanda**	rype	**ripe**
ryenoserus	**rhinocerus**	rythm	**rhythm****

S

Incorrect	Correct	Incorrect	Correct
Sabath	**Sabbath****	sangwin	**sanguine**
sabatical	**sabbatical**	sanktity	**sanctity**
sabature	**saboteur**	sanlot	**sandlot**
sabbotage	**sabotage**	sanstone	**sandstone**
sacarin	**saccharin**	sargent	**sergeant**
sacerment	**sacrament**	sarkastic	**sarcastic**
sacherated	**saturated**	sassage	**sausage**
sacreligous	**sacrilegious**	sassiety	**society**
saffarry	**safari**	sassparilla	**sarsaparilla**
safire	**sapphire**	sasy	**sassy**
safrun	**saffron**	Sataday	**Saturday**
safty	**safety**	satasfactory	**satisfactory**
saif	**safe**	satinism	**Satanism**
saige	**sage**	sattelite	**satellite**
sailsperson	**salesperson**	sattisfaction	**satisfaction**
sakred	**sacred**	saught	**sought**
sakrifice	**sacrifice**	sausidge	**sausage**
saksafone	**saxophone**	saveing	**saving**
salammi	**salami**	savey	**savvy**
salieva	**saliva**	savige	**savage**
sallary	**salary****	sawcy	**saucy**
sallmenela	**salmonella**	sawdfish	**swordfish**
sallvation	**salvation**	sawdof	**sawed-off**
salm	**psalm**	sawdy araby	
saloot	**salute****		**Saudi Arabia**
salser	**salsa**	sawftwear	**software**
salyatation	**salutation**	sayder	**Seder**
samareye	**samurai**	saydist	**sadist**
samitic	**Semitic**	sayed	**said**
sammon	**salmon**	saynt	**saint**
sampel	**sample**	scaresity	**scarcity**
sanatashun	**sanitation**	scarsely	**scarcely**
sanaty	**sanity**	scatebored	**skateboard**
sanbag	**sandbag**	scedule	**schedule**
sandwidge	**sandwich**	sceleton	**skeleton**
sangshun	**sanction**	scenry	**scenery**
sangtimonious		sceptical	**skeptical**
	sanctimonious	schock	**shock**

Incorrect	Correct	Incorrect	Correct
schotch	**scotch**	sekwence	**sequence**
scithe	**scythe**	seldem	**seldom**
scizzers	**scissors**	selebrait	**celebrate**
scolastic	**scholastic**	selerity	**celerity**
scool	**school**	selery	**celery****
scrable	**scrabble**	seleschul	**celestial**
scrach	**scratch**	selfs	**selves**
Scripchure	**Scripture**	self steam	**self-esteem**
scuzzy port	**SCSI port**	selibacy	**celibacy**
seady	**seedy**	seliva	**saliva**
seberb	**suburb****	sellar	**cellar****
seceed	**secede**	sellefane	**cellophane**
secendrate	**second-rate**	sellfdiscipline	
secertery	**secretary**		**self-discipline**
secksism	**sexism**	sellfish	**selfish**
secum	**succumb**	sellibate	**celibate****
seddentary	**sedentary**	sellular	**cellular**
seditive	**sedative**	sellulite	**cellulite**
seduse	**seduce**	selluloid	**celluloid**
see art tea	**CRT**	selser	**seltzer**
seecurities	**securities**	seme	**seem****
seedan	**sedan**	semenary	**seminary**
seedy rom	**CD-ROM**	sement	**cement**
seekretive	**secretive**	semetary	**cemetery****
seekwell	**sequel**	semmester	**semester**
seel	**seal**	semminar	**seminar**
seelect	**select**	semyautomatic	
seenario	**scenario**		**semiautomatic**
seeries	**series**	senceless	**senseless**
seeson	**season**	sene	**scene****
seetbelt	**seatbelt**	seneter	**senator**
seeve	**sieve**	senic	**scenic**
see-y-a	**CYA**	senntence	**sentence**
seeze	**seize****	senota	**sonata**
seffhelp	**self-help**	sensative	**sensitive**
segragate	**segregate**	senser	**sensor**
segwee	**segue**	sentaria	**santeria**
seige	**siege**	sentement	**sentiment**
seing	**seeing**	sentenial	**centennial**
seinse	**science**	sentimeter	**centimeter**
seive	**sieve**	sentury	**century**
sekend	**second**	senyer	**senior****
sekret	**secret**	seperate	**separate**
sekskapade	**sexcapade**	sepport	**support**
sekular	**secular**	sepress	**surpress**
sekurety	**security**	serch	**search**

Incorrect	Correct	Incorrect	Correct
sereal	**cereal****	shantoosee	**chanteuse**
serebrally	**cerebrally**	shaperone	**chaperon**
sereise	**series**	shapo	**chapeau**
serface	**surface**	sharade	**charade**
serfing	**surfing**	shardonay	**chardonnay**
sergery	**surgery**	sharewear	**shareware**
sergical	**surgical**	sharlatin	**charlatan**
serjon	**surgeon**	shartroose	**chartreuse**
sermen	**sermon**	shasee	**chassis**
sermize	**surmise**	shato	**château**
serplus	**surplus****	shawt	**short**
serprize	**surprise**	shecana	**Chicana**
serrendipity	**serendipity**	shef	**chef**
sertificate	**certificate**	sheild	**shield**
servalanse	**surveillance**	sheke	**chic****
servay	**survey**	shelfs	**shelves**
servicable	**serviceable**	shellter	**shelter**
servise	**service**	sheneel	**chenille**
servive	**survive**	shenyon	**chignon**
servix	**cervix**	sheperd	**shepherd**
seseed	**secede**	sherbert	**sherbet**
sesession	**secession**	sherif	**sheriff****
sessemee	**sesame**	sheth	**sheath**
sesspool	**cesspool**	shevron	**chevron**
Setember	**September**	shez	**chaise**
sety	**settee**	Shicago	**Chicago**
seudo	**pseudo**	shicanery	**chicanery**
seudonym	**pseudonym**	shicano	**Chicano**
seveer	**severe**	shiek	**sheik****
sevinth	**seventh**	shiffon	**chiffon**
sevral	**several**	shillaylee	**shillelagh**
sexsy	**sexy**	shineing	**shining**
sez	**says**	shipd	**shipped**
sfardim	**Sephardim**	shippment	**shipment**
sfere	**sphere**	shiskabob	**shish kebab**
sfinx	**sphinx**	shizm	**schism**
shagrin	**chagrin**	shlok	**schlock**
shairwear	**shareware**	shoffer	**chauffeur**
shakk	**shack**	sholders	**shoulders**
shaley	**chalet**	shommus	**shamus**
shameleon	**chameleon**	shoodn't	**shouldn't**
shamise	**chemise**	shoostring	**shoestring**
shampain	**champagne**	shoredhand	**shorthand**
shamy	**chamois**	shott	**shot**
shandaleir	**chandelier**	showvinizm	**chauvinism**
shanker	**chancre**	shreik	**shriek****

Incorrect	Correct	Incorrect	Correct
shrein	**shrine**	simantics	**semantics**
shrubry	**shrubbery**	simbal	**symbol****
shtroodle	**strudel**	simester	**semester**
shud	**should**	simetry	**symmetry****
shudown	**shutdown**	similer	**similar**
shugar	**sugar**	simpathy	**sympathy**
shunn	**shun**	simphony	**symphony**
shure	**sure**	simton	**symptom**
shurt	**shirt****	simyalate	**simulate**
shutel	**shuttle**	sinamin	**cinnamon**
shuttout	**shutout**	sinario	**scenario**
shuv	**shove**	sinch	**cinch**
sibbling	**sibling**	sinder	**cinder**
sibercrud	**cybercrud**	sinderella	**cinderella**
siberculchur	**cyberculture**	sindicate	**syndicate**
sickel	**sickle**	sinema	**cinema**
sicure	**secure**	sinergetics	**synergetics**
sidarm	**sidearm**	singel	**single**
sidds	**SIDS**	sinicure	**sinecure**
side bar	**sidebar**	sinigog	**synagogue**
siedline	**sideline**	sinis	**sinus**
sience	**science**	sinn	**sin**
sieze	**seize****	sinncerly	**sincerely**
si-fi	**sci-fi**	sinnic	**cynic**
sigar	**cigar**	sinonym	**synonym**
sigarette	**cigarette**	sinopsis	**synopsis**
siggnificant	**significant**	sinosure	**cynosure**
sightrack	**sidetrack**	sinse	**since**
signerture	**signature**	sinsere	**sincere**
sikedelic	**psychedelic**	sintacks	**syntax**
sikly	**sickly**	sinthetic	**synthetic**
siko	**psycho**	sintilate	**scintillate**
sikofant	**sycophant**	sipher	**cipher**
sikosomatic		siramics	**ceramics**
	psychosomatic	sircumcision	**circumcision**
silacious	**salacious**	sircumstance	
silacone	**silicone**		**circumstance**
silance	**silence**	sirfit	**surfeit**
silf	**sylph**	sirious	**serious**
silible	**syllable**	sirkit	**circuit**
sillabus	**syllabus**	sirrup	**syrup**
sillverwear	**silverware**	sirynge	**syringe**
sillycon	**silicon**	sisk chip	**cisc chip**
silouette	**silhouette**	sisors	**scissors**
silva	**silver**	siss	**sis**
sim	**SIMM**	sist	**cyst**

Incorrect	Correct	Incorrect	Correct
sistem	**system**	skue	**skew**
sistern	**cistern**	skum	**scum**
sitadel	**citadel**	skurlus	**scurrilous**
sitaplasm	**cytoplasm**	skuttel	**scuttle**
siticosis	**psittacosis**	skwad	**squad**
sitizen	**citizen**	skware	**square**
sittuation	**situation**	skwat	**squat**
sivick	**civic**	skweeze	**squeeze**
sivilisation	**civilization**	slakk	**slack**
sivil rites	**civil rights**	slane	**slain**
sixt	**sixth**	slavry	**slavery**
sizemic	**seismic**	slax	**slacks**
sizle	**sizzle**	slayed	**slain**
sizm	**schism**	slimm	**slim**
sizmograph	**seismograph**	slipry	**slippery**
skab	**scab**	slite	**slight****
skalable	**scalable**	sloap	**slope**
skandal	**scandal**	slodown	**slowdown**
skane	**skein**	slugish	**sluggish**
skanner	**scanner**	smeer	**shmear**
skapegote	**scapegoat**	smuck	**schmuck**
skar	**scar**	smugg	**smug**
skarce	**scarce**	smujj	**smudge**
skare	**scare**	smuther	**smother**
skarf	**scarf**	snaffoo	**snafu**
skavenger	**scavenger**	snakk	**snack**
skedule	**schedule**	snall	**snarl**
skeematic	**schematic**	snapp	**snap**
skeme	**scheme**	snappshot	**snapshot**
skif	**skiff**	snawkle	**snorkel**
skilfill	**skillful**	snawt	**snort**
skism	**schism**	snobird	**snowbird**
sklerosis	**sclerosis**	snomobile	**snowmobile**
skoap	**scope**	snops	**schnaps**
skoflaw	**scofflaw**	sodder	**solder****
skone	**scone**	sodeum	**sodium**
skool	**school**	sofen	**soften**
skoolmate	**schoolmate**	sofer	**sofa**
skooner	**schooner**	sofisticate	**sophisticate**
skout	**scout**	sofwear	**software**
skreme	**scream**	soladarity	**solidarity**
skrole	**scroll**	solem	**solemn**
skrub	**scrub**	soler	**solar**
skrue	**screw**	solinoid	**solenoid**
skruplous	**scrupulous**	solisit	**solicit**
skuba	**scuba**	sollid	**solid**

Incorrect	Correct	Incorrect	Correct
sollis	**solace**	spewmoney	**spumoni**
sollution	**solution**	spifee	**spiffy**
solsoe	**solo**	spinn	**spin**
somba	**samba**	spinnof	**spinoff**
sooper	**super**	spirichule	**spiritual**
sooter	**suitor**	spiril	**spiral**
sopes	**soaps**	spirrit	**spirit**
sophmore	**sophomore**	splach	**splash**
sorce	**source****	sponser	**sponsor**
sord	**sword**	sportkast	**sportscast**
sorisis	**psoriasis**	spotlite	**spotlight**
sorow	**sorrow**	spowsal	**spousal**
sory	**sorry**	spowse	**spouse**
soseology	**sociology**	sprea	**spree**
soshalist	**socialist**	sprily	**spryly**
soshill	**social**	spufe	**spoof**
soshiopath	**sociopath**	spuller	**spooler**
sosiety	**society**	spurm	**sperm**
sotay	**sauté**	spurr	**spur**
sothern	**southern**	spye	**spy**
sourkraut	**sauerkraut**	spyurious	**spurious**
sovrin	**sovereign**	sqallid	**squalid**
sovrinty	**sovereignty**	sqwash	**squash**
sownd	**sound**	sree lanker	**Sri Lanka**
spagetti	**spaghetti**	stabb	**stab**
Spannish	**Spanish**	stabbility	**stability**
sparow	**sparrow**	staflococcus	
spasstic	**spastic**		**staphylococcus**
spatt	**spat**	stail	**stale**
spawtsware	**sportswear**	stakout	**stakeout**
spazm	**spasm**	stammp	**stamp**
speach	**speech**	stampeed	**stampede**
spead	**speed**	stanby	**standby**
specktaculer	**spectacular**	standerd	**standard**
speekafone	**speakerphone**	stanser	**stanza**
speeker	**speaker**	starberd	**starboard**
speeshus	**specious**	stardup	**startup**
spektator	**spectator**	starrk	**stark**
spekticle	**spectacle**	starrship	**starship**
spektrum	**spectrum**	stateing	**stating**
spekulate	**speculate**	statment	**statement**
speler	**speller**	statis	**status**
speshialty	**specialty****	stattic	**static**
speshul	**special****	stattistic	**statistic**
spesify	**specify**	statts	**stats**
spesiman	**specimen**	stawk	**stalk****

Incorrect	Correct	Incorrect	Correct
staytis kwo	**status quo**	subbliminal	**subliminal**
stedy	**steady**	subbsistance	**subsistence**
stelth	**stealth**	subburban	**suburban**
stelthy	**stealthy**	suberb	**suburb****
stensh	**stench**	sublyme	**sublime**
sterotipe	**stereotype**	subordnate	**subordinate**
sterrilize	**sterilize**	subumate	**sublimate**
sterritype	**stereotype**	subvursive	**subversive**
stiggma	**stigma**	succede	**succeed**
stilis	**stylus**	sucsess	**success**
stilleto	**stiletto**	sucum	**succumb**
stimmulus	**stimulus**	sufferage	**suffrage**
stine	**stein**	suffishent	**sufficient**
stiph	**stiff**	sufix	**suffix**
stipyalate	**stipulate**	sugjest	**suggest**
stirio	**stereo**	sujjestion	**suggestion**
stokbroker	**stockbroker**	sukceser	**successor**
stokk	**stock**	suksinct	**succinct**
stomick	**stomach**	sullfur	**sulfur** or **sulphur****
stooper	**stupor**	sumaratan	**Samaritan**
stoped	**stopped**	sumary	**summary**
storege	**storage**	sumbody	**somebody**
storee	**story**	sumins	**summons**
stox	**stocks**	sumit	**summit**
stradle	**straddle**	summarine	**submarine**
strate	**straight****	sumshus	**sumptuous**
strate-jacket	**strait-jacket**	sune	**soon**
strech	**stretch**	supacomputer	
streeker	**streaker**		**supercomputer**
strenth	**strength**	supastitious	**superstitious**
strenyous	**strenuous**	supena	**subpoena**
stricly	**strictly**	supercede	**supersede**
stripteez	**striptease**	supireor	**superior**
stroab	**strobe**	suply	**supply**
stroak	**stroke**	suport	**support**
strugle	**struggle**	supose	**suppose**
strutegic	**strategic**	supperfluous	**superfluous**
stryfe	**strife**	supperman	**superman**
strykbraker	**strikebreaker**	supplys	**supplies**
stuble	**stubble**	supprise	**surprise**
studdy	**study**	supranatural	
studeying	**studying**		**supernatural**
stuf	**stuff**	supravise	**supervise**
stuped	**stupid**	supress	**suppress**
stypend	**stipend**	suprintendent	
subbern	**suborn**		**superintendent**

Incorrect	Correct	Incorrect	Correct
supscribtion	**subscription**	syatica	**sciatica**
suregate	**surrogate**	syberculture	**cyberculture**
surkit	**circuit**	sybernetic	**cybernetic**
suround	**surround**	sybil	**sibil**
survise	**service**	syborg	**cyborg**
suspishon	**suspicion**	sybot	**cybot**
susspect	**suspect**	syche	**psyche**
susspend	**suspend**	sychiatrist	**psychiatrist**
suth	**soothe**	sychic	**psychic**
sutle	**subtle****	sychology	**psychology**
sutract	**subtract**	sychosis	**psychosis**
suvenir	**souvenir**	sycobabble	**psychobabble**
suvvival	**survival**	sycotherepy	
swade	**suede****		**psychotherapy**
swair	**swear**	sydebar	**sidebar**
sware	**swear**	sykopath	**psychopath**
swave	**suave**	symetrical	**symmetrical**
sweaps	**sweeps**	symtom	**symptom**
sweapstakes	**sweepstakes**	syndacation	**syndication**
sweathart	**sweetheart**	synic	**cynic**
swerl	**swirl**	syst	**cyst**
swetshirt	**sweatshirt**	systerhud	**sisterhood**
swetshop	**sweatshop**	sytrack	**sidetrack**

T

Incorrect	Correct	Incorrect	Correct
tabanacle	**tabernacle**	taktill	**tactile**
tabb	**tab**	tallent	**talent**
tabblet	**tablet**	tallmid	**Talmud**
tabbulate	**tabulate**	tamata	**tomato**
tabelspoon	**tablespoon**	tammper	**tamper**
tabloyd	**tabloid****	tammpon	**tampon**
tabu	**taboo**	tanduri	**tandoori**
tacks lean	**tax lien**	tangable	**tangible**
tafeta	**taffeta**	tanjent	**tangent**
tailer	**tailor**	tanntalize	**tantalize**
tailite	**taillight**	tanntrum	**tantrum**
taipworm	**tapeworm**	targit	**target**
takeing	**taking**	tarmigan	**ptarmigan**
takkle	**tackle**	tarrdy	**tardy**
takout	**take-out**	tarrif	**tariff**
takover	**takeover**	tarrnish	**tarnish**
takt	**tact****	tarrow	**tarot****
taktics	**tactics**	tarrter	**tartar****

Incorrect	Correct	Incorrect	Correct
taseless	**tasteless**	teltale	**telltale**
tassit	**tacit**	temmerity	**temerity**
tasteing	**tasting**	temmp	**temp****
tatered	**tattered**	temmplit	**template**
tatle	**tattle**	temperarily	**temporarily**
tatoo	**tattoo**	temperment	**temperament**
taudry	**tawdry**	tempral lobe	
tavren	**tavern**		**temporal lobe**
taxible	**taxable**	temprary	**temporary**
taxxpayer	**taxpayer**	temprature	**temperature**
taynt	**taint****	temprence	**temperance**
tean's	**teens**	temt	**tempt****
teapea	**tepee**	temtation	**temptation**
teara	**tiara**	tenament	**tenement**
teater	**teeter**	tenasity	**tenacity**
techst	**text**	tendafoot	**tenderfoot**
tecksture	**texture**	tendancy	**tendency**
tecnical	**technical**	tenden	**tendon**
tee bills	**T-bills**	tendonitis	**tendinitis**
tee cell	**t-cell**	tenent	**tenant****
teech	**teach**	tener	**tenor****
teemmate	**teammate**	tenible	**tenable**
teemster	**teamster**	tenit	**tenet****
teemwork	**teamwork**	tennacious	**tenacious**
teenadger	**teenager**	tenndenshous	**tendentious**
teer	**tier****	tennderharted	
teerful	**tearful**		**tenderhearted**
teese	**tease****	tennsion	**tension**
teespoon	**teaspoon**	tennuous	**tenuous**
tejious	**tedious**	tenticle	**tentacle**
tekela	**tequila**	tentitive	**tentative**
teknik	**technique**	teppee	**tepee**
teknology	**technology**	teppid	**tepid**
tekstile	**textile**	terakote	**terra cotta**
telacompute	**telecompute**	terane	**terrain**
telagram	**telegram**	teratory	**territory**
tellacast	**telecast**	terbojet	**turbojet**
tellecomunication		tererist	**terrorist**
	telecommunication	terestrial	**terrestrial**
tellephone	**telephone**	terf	**turf**
tellescope	**telescope**	terible	**terrible**
tellethon	**telethon**	terific	**terrific**
tellevision	**television**	terify	**terrify**
tellex	**telex**	teritorial	**territorial**
tellmarketing		terkey	**turkey**
	telemarketing	termoil	**turmoil**

Incorrect	Correct	Incorrect	Correct
terncoate	**turncoat**	theiter	**theater**
terndown	**turndown**	themselfs	**themselves**
terniket	**tourniquet**	therafter	**thereafter**
ternip	**turnip**	theriputic	**therapeutic**
ternover	**turnover**	thermanooklear	
ternpike	**turnpike**		**thermonuclear**
ternround	**turnaround**	thermistat	**thermostat**
terodactil	**pterodactyl**	therrby	**thereby**
terpentine	**turpentine**	thersday	**Thursday**
terpetude	**turpitude**	thersty	**thirsty**
terpitude	**turpitude**	therteen	**thirteen**
terrasore	**pterosaur**	thery	**theory**
terrer	**terror****	thesawris	**thesaurus**
terribally	**terribly**	thesus	**thesis**
terris	**terrace**	theze	**these**
terrorbite	**terabyte**	thiefs	**thieves**
terryackid	**teriyaki**	thikskinned	**thick-skinned**
tesstickle	**testicle**	thimbell	**thimble**
tesstis	**testis**	thimus	**thymus**
tesstosterone	**testosterone**	thingpad	**thinkpad**
testafy	**testify**	thinnsksind	**thin-skinned**
testamony	**testimony**	thiroid	**thyroid**
testiment	**testament**	thogh	**though**
testube	**test tube**	thoro	**thorough**
testube baby		thorrax	**thorax**
	test-tube baby	thousind	**thousand**
tetatet	**tête-à-tête**	thred	**thread**
tetsee	**tsetse**	threshhold	**threshold**
tettrasiklin	**tetracycline**	thret	**threat**
Teusday	**Tuesday**	thriftey	**thrifty**
texbook	**textbook**	thriling	**thrilling**
thallidomide	**thalidomide**	thriveing	**thriving**
thalmus	**thalamus**	thrommbosis	**thrombosis**
thangsgiving		throte	**throat**
	Thanksgiving	thru	**through****
thawt	**thought**	thugg	**thug**
thawtful	**thoughtful**	thum	**thumb**
theem	**theme**	thummtack	**thumbtack**
theeology	**theology**	thunnder	**thunder**
theeretical	**theoretical**	thunnderstorm	
theerum	**theorem**		**thunderstorm**
thef	**theft**	third person	**third person**
theif	**thief**	thurmometer	
theirfore	**therefor****		**thermometer**
their's	**theirs**	thurrowfare	**thoroughfare**
theirselves	**themselves**	thurty	**thirty**

Incorrect	Correct	Incorrect	Correct
thwort	**thwart**	togle kee	**toggle key**
Tibbet	**Tibet**	toilit	**toilet****
tibbia	**tibia**	tokin	**token**
tickel	**tickle**	toksic	**toxic**
tiecoon	**tycoon**	tole	**toll****
tieing	**tying**	tollerant	**tolerant**
tiepist	**typist**	tomagraphy	**tomography**
tietan	**titan**	tomaine	**ptomaine**
tietfisted	**tightfisted**	tomali	**tamale**
tif	**tiff**	tommboy	**tomboy**
tifoid	**typhoid**	tommorow	**tomorrow**
tifus	**typhus**	tonage	**tonnage**
til	**till**	tonnic	**tonic**
timerity	**temerity**	tonnsil	**tonsil**
timmerous	**timorous**	tonsalectomey	
timmid	**timid**		**tonsillectomy**
timtable	**timetable**	toobal	**tubal**
tiney	**tiny****	tooberkulosis	
tingel	**tingle**		**tuberculosis**
tinitis	**tinnitus**	toogether	**together**
tinkture	**tincture**	tooition	**tuition**
tinnsel	**tinsel**	toolip	**tulip**
tipe	**type**	toom	**tomb****
tipical	**typical**	toomer	**tumor**
tipist	**typist**	toomesence	**tumescence**
tipography	**typography****	toomstone	**tombstone**
tippoff	**tip-off**	toonight	**tonight**
tiranical	**tyrannical**	toopay	**toupee****
tirant	**tyrant**	toor	**tour****
tirany	**tyranny**	Toosday	**Tuesday**
tirms	**terms**	toosh	**tush**
tishew	**tissue**	tooshay	**touché**
tite	**tight**	toothe	**tooth**
titel	**title**	tootie frootie	**tutti frutti**
tittalate	**titillate**	tootoo	**tutu**
tittular	**titular**	tootpick	**toothpick**
tobbaco	**tobacco**	toppic	**topic**
tobogun	**toboggan**	tora	**Torah**
tocko	**taco**	torador	**toreador**
to-day	**today**	torchure	**torture**
todey	**toady**	torement	**torment**
todler	**toddler**	torenado	**tornado**
toekinism	**tokenism**	torepedo	**torpedo**
toetalatarian	**totalitarian**	torid	**torrid**
togga	**toga**	torint	**torrent**
toggether	**together**	tork	**torque**

Incorrect	Correct	Incorrect	Correct
torper	**torpor**	treeage	**triage**
torrso	**torso**	treety	**treaty**
totling	**totaling**	treezon	**treason**
tott	**tot****	trekie	**trekkie**
tottem	**totem**	tremmer	**tremor**
tousand	**thousand**	treo	**trio**
towhold	**toehold**	treshure	**treasure**
tractball	**trackball**	tresspas	**trespass**
tradegy	**tragedy**	tressury	**treasury**
tradin	**trade-in**	tresurer	**treasurer**
trafick	**traffic**	trewsew	**trousseau**
traidmark	**trademark**	tribyatery	**tributary**
trakea	**trachea**	triger	**trigger**
traktion	**traction**	trilligy	**trilogy**
tramatic	**traumatic**	trimendous	**tremendous**
tranceparent	**transparent**	trimm	**trim**
trane	**train**	tripplecate	**triplicate**
trankwilizer	**tranquilizer**	trist	**tryst**
trannslait	**translate**	trivvial	**trivial**
trannsmit	**transmit**	trole	**troll**
trannsport	**transport**	troppical	**tropical****
trannsposition		trowma	**trauma**
	transposition	trowsers	**trousers**
transend	**transcend**	truble	**trouble**
transexual	**transsexual**	trudition	**tradition**
transfrence	**transference**	truefully	**truthfully**
transhent	**transient**	truely	**truly**
transkrip	**transcript**	trujectory	**trajectory**
transsfer	**transfer**	trummpet	**trumpet**
tranzaction	**transaction**	tryad	**triad**
tranzcription		tryangle	**triangle**
	transcription	trybe	**tribe**
tranzfusion	**transfusion**	trycicle	**tricycle**
tranzister	**transistor**	tryed	**tried**
tranzit	**transit**	trymester	**trimester**
tranzition	**transition**	tryseps	**triceps**
tranzlater	**translator**	tryumph	**triumph**
tranzplant	**transplant**	tuchdown	**touchdown**
tranzvestite	**transvestite**	tuff	**tough**
traser	**tracer**	tumer	**tumor**
travvesty	**travesty**	tummul	**tumult**
traydname	**trade name**	tumy	**tummy**
trayter	**traitor**	tunell	**tunnel**
trecherus	**treacherous**	tung	**tongue****
trechery	**treachery**	tunnage	**tonnage**
treck	**trek**		

Incorrect	Correct	Incorrect	Correct
turist	**tourist**	tweaser	**tweezer**
turkoise	**turquoise**	tweek	**tweak**
turminate	**terminate**	twich	**twitch**
turminel	**terminal**	twilite	**twilight**
turmite	**termite**	tydings	**tidings**
turms	**terms**	tyin	**tie-in**
turniket	**tourniquet**	tyming	**timing**
turrntable	**turntable**	tympany	**timpani** or
turse	**terse**		**tympani**
tursely	**tersely**	typeriter	**typewriter**
turtiary	**tertiary**	tyrade	**tirade**
tuthepaste	**toothpaste**	tythe	**tithe**
twealth	**twelfth**	tytrope	**tightrope**

U

ubbiquitous	**ubiquitous**	unalatteral	**unilateral**
ubjective	**objective**	unalienable	**inalienable**
ucharist	**Eucharist**	unamed	**unnamed**
uforia	**euphoria**	unamurican	**un-American**
uge	**huge**	unanamus	**unanimous**
ugenics	**eugenics**	unapeeling	**unappealing**
ukalalee	**ukulele**	unason	**unison**
Ukreign	**Ukraine**	Unatarian	**Unitarian****
ulltimite	**ultimate****	unatural	**unnatural**
ulltirior	**ulterior**	unaverse	**universe**
ulogy	**eulogy**	unawganized	**unorganized**
ulser	**ulcer**	unbeelievable	
ultamatum	**ultimatum****		**unbelievable**
ultersound	**ultrasound**	unclowded	**unclouded**
ultervilet	**ultraviolet**	unconshus	**unconscious**
umanatarien		unconsolable	
	humanitarian		**inconsolable**
umane	**humane**	uncumftable	
umanity	**humanity**		**uncomfortable**
umberella	**umbrella**	undadog	**underdog**
umble	**humble****	undagrad	**undergrad**
umbridge	**umbrage**	undaprivilledged	
umid	**humid**		**underprivileged**
umidifer	**humidifier**	undataker	**undertaker**
umility	**humility**	unddress	**undress**
ummbillical	**umbilical**	undegraduate	
ummpire	**umpire****		**undergraduate**
umpopular	**unpopular**	undeground	**underground**

Incorrect	Correct	Incorrect	Correct
underiter	**underwriter**	unkle	**uncle**
underrline	**underline****	unkonditionel	
underware	**underwear**		**unconditional**
undigestible	**indigestible**	unkonscious	**unconscious**
undinyable	**undeniable**	unkonventional	
undisirable	**undesirable**		**unconventional**
undoo	**undue****	unkooth	**uncouth**
undoubtably	**undoubtedly**	unkshus	**unctuous**
unduely	**unduly**	unlode	**unload**
undyeing	**undying**	unlysensed	**unlicensed**
uneek	**unique****	unnacustomed	
uneiform	**uniform**		**unaccustomed**
unempeachible		unnattached	**unattached**
	unimpeachable	unncommon	**uncommon**
unering	**unerring**	unndergo	**undergo**
unerned	**unearned**	unnderhanded	
unerth	**unearth**		**underhanded**
unescapable	**inescapable**	unnderworld	**underworld**
unesessary	**unnecessary**	unneqil	**unequal****
uneversly	**universally**	unnering	**unerring**
unexpensive	**inexpensive**	unnerstand	**understand**
unezy	**uneasy**	unnfavrable	**unfavorable**
unfagetible	**unforgettable**	unnit	**unit**
unfare	**unfair**	Unnited Nashuns	
unferl	**unfurl**		**United Nations**
unfinnished	**unfinished**	unnlawful	**unlawful**
unfitt	**unfit**	unnocupied	**unoccupied**
unfotunate	**unfortunate**	unnowable	**unknowable**
unfrendly	**unfriendly**	unnpregudiced	
unfrequent	**infrequent**		**unprejudiced**
unganely	**ungainly**	unnprincipaled	
ungarded	**unguarded**		**unprincipled**
ungoddly	**ungodly**	unown	**unknown**
ungreatful	**ungrateful**	unparralelled	
unhelthy	**unhealthy**		**unparalleled**
unholey	**unholy**	unperceptibel	
unick	**eunuch****		**imperceptible**
unidulterated		unplesent	**unpleasant**
	unadulterated	unpresidented	
unifey	**unify**		**unprecedented**
uniquivikal	**unequivocal**	unredeemable	
unitey	**unity**		**irredeemable**
Unittid Stats		unrooly	**unruly**
	United States	unsertin	**uncertain**
univercity	**university**	unskryupulous	
unkemp	**unkempt**		**unscrupulous**

Incorrect	Correct	Incorrect	Correct
untill	**until**	uristics	**heuristics**
unumployed	**unemployed**	urocentric	**Eurocentric**
ununhibited	**uninhibited**	urodollar	**Eurodollar**
unuptrusive	**unobtrusive**	uronalisis	**urinalysis**
unutached	**unattached**	Urope	**Europe**
unvale	**unveil**	urranium	**uranium**
unyun	**union****	urvra	**oeuvre**
upers	**uppers**	useable	**usable**
uphology	**ufology**	usefull	**useful**
uppgrade	**upgrade**	useing	**using**
upproar	**uproar**	use to	**used to**
uproute	**uproot**	usige	**usage**
uptical	**optical**	usualy	**usually**
uptite	**uptight**	uther	**other**
uptix	**upticks**	uthinasia	**euthanasia**
upwrite	**upright**	utterus	**uterus**
uranal	**urinal**	uttility	**utility**
Urasian	**Eurasian**	uzenet	**Usenet**
urb	**herb**	uzer frendly	
ureeka	**eureka**		**user-friendly**
uria	**urea**	uzury	**usury**

V

Incorrect	Correct	Incorrect	Correct
vaccilate	**vacillate**	vandel	**vandal**
vaccuous	**vacuous**	vaneer	**veneer**
vacincy	**vacancy**	vanesh	**vanish**
vacinnation	**vaccination**	vangard	**vanguard**
vacume	**vacuum**	vankwish	**vanquish**
vail	**veil**	vannila	**vanilla**
vajina	**vagina**	vanntage	**vantage****
vajinitis	**vaginitis**	vantrillokwist	
vakant	**vacant**		**ventriloquist**
vakation	**vacation****	vaped	**vapid**
valadate	**validate**	varacose	**varicose**
valadictory	**valedictory**	varrnish	**varnish**
valer	**valor****	varyence	**variance****
valintine	**valentine**	varyible	**variable**
vallid	**valid**	vasilate	**vacillate**
vallium	**Valium**	vassectomy	**vasectomy**
valuble	**valuable****	vassel	**vassal****
valv	**valve**	Vatecan	**Vatican**
vammpire	**vampire**	vayper	**vapor**
vanaty	**vanity**	vaze	**vase**

Incorrect	Correct	Incorrect	Correct
vazleen	**vaseline**	verible	**variable**
vear	**veer**	verilaty	**virility**
vecablerry	**vocabulary**	verious	**various**
vecks	**vex**	vermen	**vermin**
vecter	**vector****	vermooth	**vermouth**
vedgetarian	**vegetarian**	Vermount	**Vermont**
veedee	**VD**	versafy	**versify****
veedio	**video**	Versighs	**Versailles**
veel	**veal**	vertabra	**vertebra****
veenel	**venal****	vertabrate	**vertebrate****
veeva	**viva**	vertabril	**vertebral**
vegitable	**vegetable**	verticle	**vertical**
vehimint	**vehement**	vertue	**virtue****
veicle	**vehicle**	vertule realaty	
vejee	**veggie** or **vegie**		**virtual reality**
vellcrow	**velcro**	verufyible	**verifiable**
vellem	**vellum**	vesinety	**vicinity**
vellvet	**velvet**	vesle	**vessel****
velosity	**velocity**	vesst	**vest**
velupchus	**voluptuous**	vestabule	**vestibule**
venchure	**venture**	vestage	**vestige**
vender	**vendor**	vestid	**vested**
Veneetion	**Venetian**	vetaranery	**veterinary**
venella	**vanilla**	Vet Nam	**Viet Nam**
vengance	**vengeance**	vetos	**vetoes**
venim	**venom**	vetrans	**veterans**
venntrikle	**ventricle**	vew	**view**
venorashun	**veneration**	Veyenna	**Vienna**
venorible	**venerable****	vi	**vie**
ventellate	**ventilate**	vibrent	**vibrant**
ventellation	**ventilation**	vicker	**vicar**
venul	**venal****	vicksin	**vixen**
venum	**venom**	victem	**victim**
venumus	**venomous**	victer	**victor****
venus	**venous**	victry	**victory**
venyue	**venue**	vidiocasset	**videocassette**
verafiable	**verifiable**	vieduck	**viaduct**
verafucation	**verification**	vieing	**vying**
verafy	**verify****	vien	**vein****
verassity	**veracity****	vienell	**vinyl**
veraty	**verity****	vigel	**vigil**
verbil	**verbal**	vigelence	**vigilance**
verbily	**verbally**	viger	**vigor**
verchill	**virtual****	vigerous	**vigorous**
vergin	**virgin**	vilage	**village**
veriaty	**variety**	vilense	**violence**

Incorrect	Correct	Incorrect	Correct
vilet	**violet****	voegue	**vogue****
vilinist	**violinist**	voiagere	**voyageur**
villify	**vilify**	voiyer	**voyeur**
villin	**villain**	volentary	**voluntary**
vinager	**vinegar**	voletell	**volatile**
vindacate	**vindicate****	volyum	**volume**
vinear	**veneer**	vomet	**vomit**
vinella	**vanilla**	vosiferus	**vociferous**
vinntner	**vintner**	vowcher	**voucher**
vinyet	**vignette**	vowl	**vowel**
violon	**violin**	voyce	**voice**
vipar	**viper**	voyce male	**voice mail**
viris	**virus**	vudka	**vodka**
virrility	**virility**	vuedue	**voodoo**
virulance	**virulence**	vuepoint	**viewpoint**
virulant	**virulent**	vulchur	**vulture**
vishious	**vicious**	vulger	**vulgar**
visiate	**vitiate**	vuluptuos	**voluptuous**
visige	**visage**	vulver	**vulva**
visinnity	**vicinity**	vuntrilloquist	
viskis	**viscous**		**ventriloquist**
vissera	**viscera**	vurb	**verb**
vissid	**viscid**	vurdict	**verdict**
vissta	**vista**	vurnaculer	**vernacular**
vitaman	**vitamin**	vurs	**verse**
vitel	**vital**	vursatil	**versatile**
vitely	**vitally**	vursion	**version**
vito	**veto**	vursus	**versus****
vittles	**victuals**	vurtigo	**vertigo**
vivod	**vivid**	vusinaty	**vicinity**
vizable	**visible**	vyabel	**viable**
vizhun	**vision**	vyalin	**violin**
vizhunary	**visionary**	vybrater	**vibrator****
vizual	**visual**	vycarious	**vicarious**
vodvil	**vaudeville**	vyoofinder	**viewfinder**

W

Incorrect	Correct	Incorrect	Correct
wafur	**wafer**	waler	**whaler**
waggon	**wagon**	walet	**wallet**
waine	**wane**	wallnut	**walnut**
waitism	**weightism**	walts	**waltz**
waje	**wage**	walup	**wallop**
wakon	**waken**	wantabee	**wannabee**

Incorrect	Correct	Incorrect	Correct
wantin	**wanton****	wership	**worship**
warbel	**warble**	werth	**worth**
wardon	**warden**	westurn	**western**
warent	**warrant**	weteware	**wetware**
warr	**war****	wether	**weather****
warrantee	**warranty**	weylay	**waylay**
warreor	**warrior**	wherehouse	**warehouse**
warrm-bludded		whiggle room	
	warm-blooded		**wiggle room**
warrt	**wart**	whisle	**whistle**
wary	**wary**	wholigram	**hologram**
washdog	**watchdog**	wholistic	**holistic**
wassp	**WASP**	wholography	**holography**
wasteage	**wastage**	whores d'urve	
wastful	**wasteful**		**hors d'oeuvres**
wastline	**waistline**	whoroscope	**horoscope**
watamelon	**watermelon**	widder	**widow**
watever	**whatever**	wierd	**weird**
watsh	**watch**	wiertap	**wiretap**
watterproof	**waterproof**	wifes	**wives**
wawmharted		wijette	**widget**
	warm-hearted	wikked	**wicked**
waylayed	**waylaid**	wildurness	**wilderness**
wearhouse	**warehouse**	wilfull	**willful**
webb	**web**	wimmin	**women**
weding	**wedding**	windsheer	**windshear**
weener	**wiener**	winfall	**windfall**
weighside	**wayside**	winjammer	**windjammer**
weild	**wield****	winndows	**windows**
welch rabid	**welsh rabbit**	winse	**wince****
welhealed	**well-heeled**	winsheeld	**windshield**
wellcome	**welcome**	wiplash	**whiplash**
wellfare	**welfare**	wipperwill	**whippoorwill**
wellter	**welter**	wirkup	**workup**
welnown	**well-known**	Wisconson	**Wisconsin**
welth	**wealth**	wisedom	**wisdom**
Wensday	**Wednesday**	wisk broom	**whisk broom**
weppon	**weapon**	wisky	**whiskey**
werkfair	**workfare**	wisper	**whisper**
werkforse	**workforce**	wissful	**wistful**
werklode	**workload**	wissle	**whistle**
werkstation	**work station**	wissteria	**wisteria**
werld	**world**	wistleblower	
werld wide web			**whistleblower**
	World Wide Web	witdraw	**withdraw**
werm	**worm**	wite	**white**

Incorrect	Correct	Incorrect	Correct
wite coller	**white collar**	worp	**warp**
witewash	**whitewash**	wossel	**wassail**
withold	**withhold**	wot	**what**
withur	**wither****	wreckueum	**requiem**
wittel	**whittle**	wresle	**wrestle**
wittness	**witness**	writeing	**writing**
wiziwig	**WYSIWYG**	wumanizer	**womanizer**
wizkid	**whiz kid**	wun	**won****
wizzard	**wizard**	wund	**wound**
wolfs	**wolves**	wun-man	**one-man**
wonderous	**wondrous**	wurd	**word**
wonliner	**one-liner**	wurkaholic	**workaholic**
wonst	**once**	wurkers compensation	
won-up	**one-up**		**workers' compensation**
wooly	**woolly**	wurld	**world**
woom	**womb**	wurm	**worm**
woosted	**worsted**	wurry	**worry**
workible	**workable**	wurse	**worse**
worning	**warning**	wyre	**wire**

X, Y, Z

Incorrect	Correct	Incorrect	Correct
xlyaphone	**xylophone**	yulogy	**eulogy****
xmass	**Xmas**	yoman	**yeoman**
x-rey	**x-ray**	yondar	**yonder**
yack	**yak**	yoonyun	**union****
y'all	**you all**	yot	**yacht**
yanky	**Yankee****	your's	**yours****
yasheeva	**yeshiva**	youser-frendly	
yat	**yacht**		**user-friendly**
yawho	**yahoo**	you-turn	**U-turn**
yeest	**yeast**	yugenics	**eugenics**
yeild	**yield**	yukka	**yucca**
yeller	**yellow**	yumanatarien	
yenn	**yen****		**humanitarian**
yerself	**yourself**	yumanity	**humanity**
yestaday	**yesterday**	yumid	**humid**
yidish	**Yiddish**	yumidifer	**humidifier**
yocal	**yokel**	yumility	**humility**
yodal	**yodel**	yum kipper	**Yom Kippur**
yogee	**yogi****	yung	**young**
yoger	**yoga****	yungster	**youngster**
yogert	**yogurt** or **yoghurt**	yunisex	**unisex****
		yuppity	**uppity**

Incorrect	Correct	Incorrect	Correct
yupy	**yuppy**	zeroe	**zero**
yurine	**urine**	zerography	**xerography**
yuristics	**heuristics**	zero-kuepon	**zero-coupon**
yurn	**yearn**	zillyon	**zillion**
yurocentric	**Eurocentric**	ziltsh	**zilch**
yurolojist	**urologist**	zink	**zinc****
yuth	**youth**	zippcode	**zip code**
zanee	**zany**	zithur	**zither**
zaping	**zapping**	zodeac	**zodiac**
zar	**czar**	zoftik	**zaftig or zoftig**
Zavier	**Xavier**	zoneing	**zoning**
zeel	**zeal**	zookini	**zucchini**
zeenith	**zenith**	zoolegy	**zoology**
zefir	**zephyr**	zosster	**zoster**
zein	**zine or 'zine**	zume	**zoom**
zellous	**zealous****	Zuse	**Zeus**
zennology	**zenology**	zylophone	**xylophone**
zenofobia	**xenophobia**	zyonist	**Zionist**

aberrant, deviating • **abhor-rent**, detestable

aberration, deviation • **abrasion**, scrape

abject, spiritless • **object**, a material thing; to oppose

abjure, renounce • **adjure**, entreat

ablation, wearing away • **ablution**, washing off

aboard, on a vehicle • **abort**, end prematurely • **abroad**, out of country

abrasion, scrape • **aberration**, deviation

abrogate, repeal • **arrogate**, claim unjustly

abscess, sore • **abscise**, to cut • **abscissa**, math coordinate • **obsess**, to preoccupy

abstract, select, excerpt • **obstruct**, block

accede, agree • **exceed**, go beyond

accent, speech • **ascent**, rise • **assent**, agree

accept, receive • **except**, omit

access, admittance • **excess**, over a limit

accidence, word inflections • **accidents**, unfortunate events

accident, unfortunate event • **Occident**, the Far East

accomplice, crime partner • **accomplish**, achieve

acentric, not centered • **eccentric**, strange

acetic, vinegar • **aesthetic**, appreciative of beauty • **ascetic**, self-denial

acme, peak • **acne**, skin outbreak

activate, rouse • **actuate**, put in motion

acts, to perform on stage, things done • **axe**, tool

actually, really • **actuary**, insurance analyst

ad, advertisement • **add**, to increase

adapt, make fit • **adept**, expert • **adopt**, take in

addable, can be added • **edible**, can be eaten

addition, adding • **edition**, issue

adds, increases • **ads**, advertisements • **adz**, tool

adduce, quote as proof • **deduce**, draw a conclusion

adieu, farewell • **ado**, commotion

adjoin, next to • **adjourn**, put off

adjure, entreat • **abjure**, renounce

ado, commotion • **adieu**, farewell

adverse, against • **averse**, unwilling

advert, pay attention • **avert**, avoid • **overt**, obvious

advice, suggestion • **advise**, to suggest

aerie, eagle's nest • **eerie**, ghostly • **Erie**, the lake

aesthetic, appreciative of beauty • **acetic**, vinegar • **ascetic**, self-denial

afar, distant • **affair**, event • **affaire**, romance

affect, act or influence • **effect**, result of action; to bring about

affective, emotional • **effective**, impressive; actual

affluent, wealthy • **effluent**, liquid waste

Africans, people of Africa • **Afrikaans**, language • **Afrikaners**, S. African natives of Dutch descent

aggression, attack • **egression**, departure

aid, help • **aide**, assistant

aides, assistants • **aids**, helps • **AIDS**, disease

ail, to be ill • **ale**, drink

ailment, illness • **aliment**, food

air, gas • **e'er**, ever • **ere**, before • **err**, do wrong • **heir**, inheritor

aisle, passage • **I'll**, I will • **isle**, island

alimentary, nutritive • **elementary**, primary

all, every • **awl**, tool

allay, calm • **alley**, lane • **alloy**, composed of two metals • **ally**, friend

allege, accuse • **allergy**, sensitivity

allocation, share • **elocution**, speech

allow, permit • **aloe**, plant

allowed, permitted • **aloud**, speak

all ready, completely prepared • **already**, before now

all together, all in one place • **altogether**, totally

all ways, every method • **always**, every time

allude, refer to • **elude**, escape

allusion, reference to • **elusion**, evasion; escape by deception • **illusion**, false impression

allusive, referring to • **elusive**, evasive • **illusive**, deceptive

alms, charity • **arms**, body

altar, church • **alter**, change

alternate, first one, then the other • **alternative**, substitute

altitude, height • **attitude**, point of view

amateur, inexperienced • **armature**, magnet part

ambidextrous, left- and right-handed • **ambisextrous**, sex indistinguishable

amend, change • **emend**, remove errors

amiable, good-natured • **amicable**, friendly

amity, friendship • **enmity**, hostility

amoral, without a sense of moral responsibility • **immoral**, evil

amour, love • **armoire**, wardrobe • **armor**, tanks

ample, enough • **ampule**, bottle

anal, uptight • **annual**, yearly • **annul**, void

analog, electronic • **analogue**, similar

analyst, psychoanalyst • **analyze**, to dissect

anecdote, story • **antedate**, predate • **antidote**, poison cure

angel, heavenly • **angle**, mathematics

anima, feminine side • **animal**, living being

annual, yearly • **anal**, uptight • **annul**, void

anomie, disorientation • **enema**, anal cleansing • **enemy**, foe

ant, insect • **aunt**, relative

ante, before • **anti**, against • **aunty**, relative

antedate, predate • **anecdote**, story • **antidote**, poison cure

anterior, outside • **interior**, inside

antic, a caper • **antique**, anything very old

anus, opening of the alimentary canal • **heinous**, hateful

anyone, any person; people • **any one**, any of several

anyway, in any case • **any way**, one or another way

apatite, mineral • **appetite**, craving

apologia, written defense • **apology**, expression of regret

apostille, marginal note • **apostle**, disciple • **epistle**, religious letter

apposite, appropriate • **opposite**, contrary

apposition, grammatical construction • **opposition**, those opposing

appraise, to judge • **apprise**, inform

aquarium, fish tank • **Aquarius**, Zodiac sign

arc, curved line • **arch**, building • **ark**, vessel

area, portion of land • **aria**, opera selection

armature, magnet part • **amateur**, inexperienced

armoire, wardrobe • **amour**, love • **armor**, tanks

arms, body • **alms**, charity

arose, got up • **arroz**, rice • **arouse**, awaken

arraign, accuse • **arrange**, settle

arrogate, claim unjustly • **abrogate**, repeal

artist, one skilled in fine arts • **artiste**, skilled performer

artistic, relating to the arts • **autistic**, withdrawn

ascent, rise • **accent**, speech • **assent**, agree

ascetic, self-denial • **acetic**, vinegar • **aesthetic**, appreciative of beauty

aspirant, one who seeks • **aspirate**, to draw out • **aspirin**, medication

assay, evaluate • **essay**, composition

assert, to be forceful • **assort**, to classify

assignation, appointment to meet • **assignment**, allotted task

assistance, help • **assistants**, people who help

assurance, certainty • **insurance**, protection

astray, not proper • **estray**, straying

ate, did eat • **eight**, the number

attach, bind • **attaché**, aide • **attack**, assault

attendance, act of attending • **attendants**, helpers

attitude, point of view • **altitude**, height

auger, foretell • **augur**, tool

aught, zero • **ought**, should • **out**, away; unfashionable

aunt, relative • **ant**, insect

aunty, relative • **ante**, before • **anti**, against

aural, hearing • **oral**, verbal

auricle, external ear • **oracle**, person of great wisdom

autarchy, autocratic rule • **autarky**, national economic self-sufficiency

auteur, film director • **hauteur**, haughty

autistic, withdrawn • **artistic**, relating to the arts

autograft, organ transplant • **autograph**, signature

automation, electronics • **automaton**, robot

auxiliary, subordinate • **axillary**, relating to the armpit

averse, unwilling • **adverse**, against

avert, avoid • **advert**, pay attention • **overt**, obvious

avoid, evade • **ovoid**, egg-shaped

awe, fear • **oar**, boat • **o'er**, over • **or**, alternative • **ore**, mineral

awful, terrible • **offal**, garbage

awl, tool • **all**, every

axe, tool • **acts**, performs

axes, tools • **axis**, line

axillary, relating to the armpit • **auxiliary**, subordinate

axle, wheel shaft • **excel**, to be superior

aye, yes • **eye**, see • **I**, me

B

babble, chatter • **bauble**, trifle • **bubble**, thin liquid ball

bach, to live alone • **batch**, a group or number

bad, no good • **bade**, asked

bail, security • **bale**, bundle

bait, a lure • **bate**, lessen

bald, no hair • **balled**, put in ball • **bawled**, cried

ball, round • **bawl**, cry

ballad, song, poem • **ballet**, dance • **ballot**, vote

balm, ointment • **bomb**, explosive

baloney, bunk • **bologna**, sausage

band, ring; orchestra • **banned**, barred

bands, groups • **banns**, marriage • **bans**, prohibits

banquet, feast • **banquette**, bench

banzai, Japanese cheer • **bonsai**, dwarf tree

bard, poet • **barred**, stopped

bare, naked • **bear**, carry; animal

baring, exposing • **bearing**, carriage; support

baron, noble • **barren**, empty

barred, stopped • **bard**, poet

barter, trade • **batter**, to hurt; hitter

base, foundation • **bass**, deep tone

bases, foundations; stations • **basis**, the groundwork

bastard, illegitimate • **basted**, sewed

batch, a group or number • **bach**, to live alone

bate, lessen • **bait**, lure

bath, body soaking • **bathe**, to wash body

bathos, anticlimax • **pathos**, arousing pity

bauble, trifle • **babble**, chatter • **bubble**, thin liquid ball

baud, unit of telegraph signal speed • **bawd**, a procuress

bawl, cry • **ball**, round

bawled, cried • **bald**, no hair • **balled**, put in a ball

bazaar, a fair • **bizarre**, weird

be, exist • **bee**, insect

beach, shore • **beech**, tree

bean, vegetable • **been**, past of be • **bin**, box

bear, carry; animal • **bare**, naked

bearing, carriage; support • **baring**, exposing

beat, strike • **beet**, vegetable

beatify, make happy; religious act • **beautify**, make beautiful

beau, dandy; lover • **bow**, (pron. 'oh'), with arrow

beer, drink • **bier**, coffin

belie, contradict • **belly**, stomach

bell, rings • **belle**, beauty

bellow, pumps air • **below**, under

berry, fruit • **bury**, to cover

berth, place to sleep • **birth**, born

beseech, beg • **besiege**, surround, in war

beside, at the side of • **besides**, in addition to

better, more than good • **bettor**, one who bets

biannual, twice a year • **biennial**, every two years

bib, shield tied under chin • **bibb**, part of mast

bid, request • **bide**, wait

bier, coffin • **beer**, drink

bight, bay • **bite**, to cut • **byte**, computer unit

billed, sent a bill • **build**, construct

bin, box • **bean**, vegetable • **been**, past of be

bite, to cut • **bight**, bay • **byte**, computer unit

bizarre, weird • **bazaar**, a fair

bleep, radio signal; to censor • **blip**, radar image

blew, wind; breath • **blue**, color

bloat, to make fat • **blot**, spot; fault

bloc, political group • **block**, solid piece; prevent

blotch, odd mark • **botch**, poor work

boar, swine • **bore**, drill; dull

board, lumber or climb on • **bored**, weary

boarder, roomer • **border**, edge

body, animal/human structure • **buddy**, pal

bogey, golf • **bogy**, evil • **boogie**, party; dance

bold, daring • **bowled**, did bowl

bolder, braver • **boulder**, big rock

bole, clay; tree trunk • **boll**, weevil • **bowl**, dish; game

bologna, food • **baloney**, bunk

bomb, explosive • **balm**, ointment

bonny, pretty • **bony**, big-boned

bonsai, dwarf tree • **banzai**, Japanese cheer

boom, loud sound • **boon**, blessing

boot, shoe • **bought**, purchased • **bout**, fight

bootie, baby shoe • **booty**, plunder

border, edge • **boarder**, roomer

bore, drill, dull • **boar**, swine

bored, weary • **board**, lumber; climb on

born, given birth • **borne**, carried

borough, town • **burro**, donkey • **burrow**, hole; dig

botch, poor work • **blotch**, odd mark

bough, tree • **bow**, (pron. 'ow') bend; yield

bouillon, soup • **bullion**, gold, silver

bow, (pron. 'oh') with arrow • **beau**, lover

bowl, dish; game • **bole**, clay; tree trunk • **boll**, weevil

bowled, did bowl • **bold**, daring

boy, lad • **buoy**, a float

braes, hillsides • **brays**, utters harsh sounds • **braze**, to solder

Brahman, Hindu caste; cattle • **Brahmin**, cultured person

braid, trim • **brayed**, bellowed

brake, stop • **break**, destroy

brands, marks; product types • **brans**, cereals

brash, reckless • **brass**, metal; chutzpah

breach, break; violation • **breech**, bottom

breaches, breaks • **breeches**, trousers

bread, food • **bred**, raised

breadth, expanse • **breath**, air inhaled • **breathe**, to inhale and exhale

break, destroy • **brake**, stop

breech, bottom • **breach**, break; violation

brewed, liquor • **brood**, offspring; worry

brews, makes liquor • **bruise**, wound

briar, pipe wood • **brier**, thorny bush

bridal, wedding • **bridle**, restrain; horse

Britain, country • **Briton**, person

broach, tool; discuss • **brooch**, a clasp

brows, foreheads • **browse**, read here and there

bruit, rumor • **brute**, savage

bubble, thin liquid ball • **babble**, chatter • **bauble**, trifle

buddy, pal • **body**, animal/ human structure

build, construct • **billed**, sent a bill

bullion, gold, silver • **bouillon**, soup

buoy, support • **boy**, lad

burley, a thin-bodied tobacco • **burly**, large, muscular

burro, donkey • **borough**, town • **burrow**, hole, dig

bursa, body pouches • **bursar**, financial officer

bury, put in ground • **berry**, fruit

bus, vehicle • **buss**, kiss

bussed, sent by bus • **bust**, bosom

but, however • **butt**, end; object

buy, purchase • **by**, near • **bye**, sport

byte, computer unit • **bight**, bay • **bite**, to cut

C

cabal, a secret group • **cable**, wire

cacao, tree of cocoa beans • **cocoa**, chocolate

cache, hiding place • **cash**, money

caddie, golf attendant • **caddy**, tea box

calendar, time • **calender**, machine to press

call, cry out • **caul**, membrane

callous, unfeeling • **callus**, hard skin

calm, quiet • **cam**, machinery part

Calvary, crucifixion • **cavalry**, horse troops

canapé, food • **canopy**, covering

cannon, gun • **canon**, law

cant, dialect • **can't**, cannot

canvas, cloth • **canvass**, to solicit

capital, main; city • **Capitol**, the building

carat, diamond • **caret**, proofreader's mark • **carrot**, vegetable

caries, dental decay • **carries**, conveys; bears

carnal, bodily, fleshly • **channel**, waterway • **charnel**, dead bodies

carousal, orgy • **carousel**, merry-go-round

cash, money • **cache**, hiding place

cask, box • **casque**, helmet

cast, to fling • **caste**, class

caster, swivelled wheel • **castor**, secretion used in medicines

casual, easy going • **causal**, the cause of

cataclasm, breakage, disruption • **cataclysm**, great flood

caught, did catch • **court**, law

caul, membrane • **call**, cry out

causal, producing an effect • **casual**, easygoing

cause, to bring about • **caws**, the sounds made by crows

cavalry, horse troops • **Calvary**, crucifixion

cay, island • **key**, lock opener • **quay**, wharf

cease, stop • **seas**, bodies of water • **sees**, observes • **seize**, grab

cede, give up • **seed**, flower

ceiling, top • **sealing**, closing

celebrate, to honor, be festive • **celibate**, unmarried; sexually inactive

celery, vegetable • **salary**, wage

cell, prison; unit in biology • **sell**, opposite of buy

cellar, basement • **seller**, one who sells

cemetery, graveyard • **symmetry**, proportionate

censer, incense container • **censor**, moral overseer • **censure**, condemn

census, population count • **senses**, sight, touch

cents, money • **scents**, smells • **sense**, judgment; awareness

cereal, food • **serial**, in a row

cession, yielding • **session**, meeting

champagne, wine • **champaign**, a plain

channel, waterway • **carnal**, bodily, fleshly • **charnel**, dead bodies

charted, put on a chart • **chartered**, rented

chased, ran after • **chaste**, pure

chauffeur, driver • **shofar**, ram's horn

cheap, priced low • **cheep**, sound of young birds

check, money • **Czech**, nationality

chert, a rock • **shirt**, garment

chews, eats • **choose**, select

chic, stylish • **sheik**, Arab chief

Chile, country • **chili**, food • **chilly**, cold

choir, singers • **quire**, measure of paper

choler, rage • **collar**, neck band • **collard**, vegetable • **color**, hue

choral, singing • **coral**, sea life • **corral**, animal pen

chord, music • **cord**, rope • **cored**, removed the core

chow, food; dog • **ciao**, goodbye

christen, baptize • **Christian**, a believer in Christ

chute, drop • **shoot**, fire

cite, point out • **sight**, see • **site**, place

clan, family • **klan**, Ku Klux Klan

clause, contract • **claws**, sharp nails

clench, close teeth • **clinch**, to embrace; to conclude a deal

clew, ball • **clue**, hint

click, noise • **clique**, small group

climactic, refers to climax • **climatic**, refers to climate

climb, ascent • **clime**, climate

clique, small group • **click**, noise

clone, copy • **clown**, joker

close, shut • **clothes**, apparel • **cloths**, small fabrics

coal, fire • **koel**, a cuckoo • **kohl**, eye shadow

coarse, rough • **course**, class; passage

coat, garment • **cote**, shelter • **côte**, coast

cockscomb, a garden plant • **cock's comb**, comb of a cock • **coxcomb**, fop

cocoa, chocolate • **cacao**, tree of cocoa beans

cola, a drink • **kola**, a nut or tree

collage, a type of painting • **college**, higher education

collar, neck band • **choler**, rage • **collard**, vegetable • **color**, hue

collision, crash • **collusion**, fraud

cologne, fragrance • **colon**, intestine; punctuation

Colombia, a country in South America • **Columbia**; the university

colonel, officer • **kernel**, seed

coma, sleep • **comma**, punctuation

comedy, humor • **comity**, welfare • **committee**, a group with a definite purpose

comet, celestial body • **commit**, entrust

command, order • **commend**, praise

commendation, praise • **condemnation**, denunciation

complacence, self-satisfaction • **complaisance**, fulfillment of wishes of others

complacent, pleased with oneself • **complaisant**, desirous of pleasing

complement, balance • **compliment**, praise

complementary, completing • **complimentary**, free

comprehensible, understandable • **comprehensive**, inclusive

concur, agree • **conquer**, defeat

condemn, to find guilty • **contemn**, to despise

condemnation, denunciation • **commendation**, praise

confidant, a person confided in • **confident**, certain

confirmer, one who ratifies • **conformer**, one who complies with established customs

congenial, agreeable • **congenital**, dating from birth

conscience, moral sense • **conscientious**, painstaking • **conscious**, aware

conservation, preservation • **conversation**, talk

consul, diplomat • **council**, an assembly • **counsel**, advice

contact, connection • **contract**, legal agreement

contemn, to despise • **condemn**, to find guilty

contend, dispute • **content**, happy

continence, self-restraint • **countenance**, face

continual, repeated again and again • **continuous**, without a break

convection, heat transmission • **conviction**, belief; guilt

convert, changed loyalty • **covert**, secret • **covet**, desire another's property

coolie, laborer • **coolly**, in a cool manner

coral, sea life • **choral**, singing • **corral**, animal pen

cord, rope • **chord**, music • **cored**, removed the core

core, center • **corps**, army • **corpse**, dead body

corespondent, paramour in divorce proceedings • **correspondent**, one party to exchange of letters

corner, intersection • **coroner**, death investigator

corporal, of the body; a soldier • **corporeal**, material; tangible

corps, army group • **core**, center • **corpse**, dead body

cortisone, medicine • **courtesan**, a prostitute

costume, clothes • **custom**, habit

costumer, one who makes costumes • **customer**, buyer

cot, bed • **cut**, wound

cote, shelter • **coat**, garment • **côte**, coast

cough, illness • **cuff**, sleeve's end; handcuff

council, an assembly • **consul**, diplomat • **counsel**, advice

councillor, member of council • **counselor**, advisor; lawyer

countenance, face • **continence**, self-restraint

course, class; passage • **coarse,** rough

court, law • **caught,** did catch

courtesan, a prostitute • **cortisone,** medicine

courtesy, manners • **curtsy,** bow

cousin, a relative • **cozen,** to deceive

covet, desire another's property • **convert,** changed loyalty • **covert,** secret

coward, one who lacks courage • **cowered,** crouched

coxcomb, fop • **cockscomb,** a garden plant • **cock's comb;** comb of a cock

craps, dice • **crepes,** pancakes

creak, noise • **creek,** stream • **crick,** pain in the neck

cream, milk fat • **creme,** liqueur

crease, fold • **kris,** cheese; dagger

credible, believable • **creditable,** praiseworthy

crews, sailors • **cruise,** voyage

critic, one who criticizes • **critique,** criticism

crochet, a kind of knitting • **crotchet,** a quirk; a hook

croquet, a game played with mallets, balls • **croquette,** a fried cake of minced food

crudités, cold vegetables • **crudity,** vulgarity

cruise, voyage • **crews,** sailors

cue, hint; billiards • **queue,** line

cuff, sleeve's end; handcuff • **cough,** illness

culled, picked • **cult,** sect

currant, a berry • **current,** stream of water or events; contemporary

curtsy, bow • **courtesy,** manners

custom, habit • **costume,** clothes

customer, buyer • **costumer,** one who makes costumes

cygnet, a young swan • **signet,** a seal

cymbal, music • **symbol,** sign

D

daily, every day • **dally,** idle • **delay,** put off

dairy, food • **diary,** personal record

dais, platform • **dice,** craps

dam, water • **damn,** curse

days, plural of day • **daze,** confused

deacon, clergy • **decon,** deconstruction

dead, deceased • **deed,** act

dear, loved • **deer,** animal

debauch, to seduce • **debouch,** to march out

deceased, dead • **diseased,** sick

decent, good • **descent,** go down • **dissent,** disagreement

decree, law • **degree,** award from school

deduce, draw a conclusion • **adduce,** quote as proof

deer, animal • **dear,** loved one

defer, postpone • **differ,** disagree

definite, precise • **definitive**, final

defused, without a fuse • **diffused**, filtered or mixed in

degree, school award • **decree**, law

demur, to disagree • **demure**, modest

dependant, the noun: one who relies on • **dependent**, relying on another

dependence, reliance on others • **dependents**, those supported by a given person

depositary, the one receiving a deposit • **depository**, a place where anything is deposited

deposition, testimony in writing • **disposition**, temperament

depraved, evil • **deprived**, taken away

deprecate, express disapproval • **depreciate**, to lessen in value

descendant, offspring • **descendent**, falling; proceeding from an original ancestor

descent, go down • **decent**, good • **dissent**, disagreement

desecrate, act irreverently • **desiccate**, to dry out

desert, dry land • **dessert**, food

desolate, barren • **dissolute**, given to wasteful, pleasure-seeking activities

detract, to take away from • **distract**, to divert

device, a scheme; means • **devise**, invent

dew, moisture • **do**, to act • **due**, owed

diagram, sketch • **diaphragm**, part of body

diary, personal record • **dairy**, food

dice, craps • **dais**, platform

die, death • **dye**, change color

died, passed away • **diet**, food intake

differ, disagree • **defer**, postpone

diffused, filtered or mixed in • **defused**, without a fuse

dilation, widening • **dilution**, watering down

dine, eat • **dyne**, a unit of force in physics

diner, eatery • **dinner**, meal

dinghy, small boat • **dingy**, dirty

disapprove, condemn • **disprove**, prove wrong

disburse, pay out • **disperse**, break up

discomfit, to upset another • **discomfort**, uneasiness

discreet, prudent • **discrete**, separate, disconnected

discus, sport • **discuss**, to talk

diseased, sick • **deceased**, dead

disposition, temperament • **deposition**, testimony in writing

dissent, disagreement • **decent**, good • **descent**, go down

dissolute, given to wasteful, pleasure-seeking activities • **desolate**, barren

distal, away from body's center • **distill**, purify; reduce

distract, to divert • **detract**, to take away from

divers, several • **diverse**, different

do, to act • **dew**, moisture • **due**, owed

doc, short for doctor • **dock**, boat haven

doe, deer • **dough**, bread

doer, one who does • **dour**, severe • **dower**, widow's estate share

does, female deers • **doze**, nap

done, finished • **dun**, ask for payment

draft, plan • **draught**, flow of air

drier, more dry • **dryer**, machine

dual, two • **duel**, fight

dudgeon, anger; resentment • **dungeon**, cell in basement of a prison

due, owing • **dew**, moisture • **do**, act

dully, with dullness • **duly**, as is due

dye, change color • **die**, death

dyeing, changing color • **dying**, death

dyne, a unit of force in physics • **dine**, eat

E

earn, gain • **urn**, vase

eccentric, strange • **acentric**, not centered

edge, border • **etch**, draw; engrave

edible, eatable • **addible**, can be added

edition, published form or number • **addition**, anything added

e'er, ever • **air**, gas • **ere**, before • **err**, do wrong • **heir**, inheritor

eerie, ghostly • **aerie**, eagle's nest • **Erie**, the lake

effect, result; to bring about • **affect**, to cause

effective, impressive; operative • **affective**, emotional

effluent, liquid waste • **affluent**, wealthy

egression, departure • **aggression**, attack

eight, the number • **ate**, did eat

Eire, Ireland • **IRA**, Individual Retirement Account • **ire**, wrath

either, one of two • **ether**, gas

elder, n: an older person • **older**, adj. lived longer

elegy, poem; lament • **eulogy**, praise

element, part • **ailment**, illness • **aliment**, food

elementary, primary • **alimentary**, nutritive

elicit, draw out • **illicit**, illegal

eliminate, wipe out • **illuminate**, shed light on

elocution, speech • **allocation**, share

elude, evade • **allude**, refer to • **illude**, cheat

elusion, evasion; escape by deception • **allusion**, reference to • **illusion**, false impression

elusive, evasive • **allusive**, referring to • **illusive**, deceptive

emasculate, castrate • **immaculate**, pure

emend, remove errors • **amend**, change

emerge, to come out • **immerge**, to plunge into

emersed, standing above • **immersed**, plunged in liquid

emigrant, leaves country • **immigrant**, enters country

eminent, distinguished • **immanent**, inherent • **imminent**, impending

emit, to send out • **immit**, to send in

emollient, softening • **emolument**, profit; salary; fee

empire, dominion • **umpire**, referee

enable, to make able • **unable**, not able

endogenous, from within • **indigenous**, native

enema, anal cleansing • **anomie**, disorientation • **enemy**, foe

enervate, to deprive of nerve or strength • **innervate**, to invigorate

enfold, to wrap • **unfold**, to lay open

enmity, hostility • **amity**, friendship

enroll, join • **unroll**, to display

ensure, to make sure or secure • **insure**, to obtain insurance; guarantee

enter, to go in • **inter**, to bury

entitled, deserving • **untitled**, lacking a title

entomology, study of insects • **etymology**, study of words

envelop, to surround • **envelope**, stationery

enwrap, wrap around • **unwrap**, uncover

epic, narrative • **epoch**, era

epigraph, motto • **epitaph**, inscription • **epithet**, curse

epistle, religious letter • **apostil**, marginal note • **apostle**, disciple

equable, not varying; even-tempered • **equitable**, fair

era, age • **error**, mistake

ere, before • **air**, gas • **e'er**, ever • **err**, do wrong • **heir**, inheritor

erect, to build • **eruct**, to belch; cast forth

Erie, the lake • **aerie**, eagle's nest • **eerie**, ghostly

erotic, sexy • **erratic**, uneven

errand, trip • **errant**, roving

error, mistake • **era**, age, period

eruption, a bursting out • **irruption**, a bursting in

especial, exceptional, preeminent • **special**, particular, specific

essay, composition • **assay**, evaluate

estray, straying • **astray**, not proper

etch, draw; engrave • **edge**, border

etching, drawing • **itching**, tickling

ether, drug • **either**, one of two

ethnology, study of human groups • **ethology**, animal behavior

etymology, study of words • **entomology**, study of insects

eulogy, praise • **elegy**, lament; poem

eunuch, sexless • **unique**, sole

eunuchs, emasculated men • **unix**, computer operating system

everyone, all persons • **every one**, each one, considered separately, one after the other

everything, the entire situation, viewed as one total mass • **every thing,** each item in the given situation

ewe, sheep • **yew,** tree • **you,** person

exalt, glorify • **exult,** rejoice

exceed, go beyond • **accede,** agree

excel, to be superior • **axle,** wheel shaft

except, leave out • **accept,** agree

exceptionable, objectionable • **exceptional,** out of the ordinary

excess, too much • **access,** get to

exciting, rousing strong feelings • **exiting,** leaving

exercise, practice • **exorcise,** drive away evil spirits

exists, is real • **exits,** doors; departures

expansive, capable of stretching • **expensive,** costly

expiation, making amends • **expiration,** termination; air expulsion

expose, to uncover • **exposé,** an account of scandalous facts or shameful deeds

extant, still done • **extent,** width

eye, see • **aye,** yes • **I,** me

F

face-ism, discrimination by looks • **fascism,** dictatorial movement

faces, front parts of head • **facies,** appearance • **feces,** excrement

facet, side • **faucet,** water flow control

facility, skill • **felicity,** happiness

facts, actual occurrences • **FAQS,** frequently asked questions • **fax,** facsimile

faerie, fairies' abode • **fairy,** sprite • **ferry,** boat

fain, gladly • **feign,** pretend

faint, weak • **feint,** movement to deceive

fair, just • **fare,** pay for travel

faker, fraud • **fakir,** holy man

fantasy, a far-fetched imaginary idea • **phantasm,** ghost; illusion

farther, refers to physical distance • **father,** parent • **further,** refers to extent or degree

fascism, dictatorial movement • **face-ism,** discrimination by looks

fatal, deathly • **fateful,** of very great importance

fate, destiny • **fete,** festival

faucet, water • **facet,** side

faun, rural deity • **fawn,** servile; young deer

fays, fairies • **faze,** worry • **phase,** stage

feast, meal • **fest,** celebration

feat, act • **feet,** body

feint, pretend • **faint,** weak

felicity, happiness • **facility**, skill

ferment, yeast • **foment**, incite

ferry, boat • **faerie**, fairies' abode • **fairy**, imaginary being

fetch, get and return • **fetish**, magical object

fete, festival • **fate**, destiny

fiancé, engaged • **finance**, money

fiend, monster • **friend**, companion

file, holder • **phial**, tube

filing, putting in order • **filling**, to make full

finale, the end • **finally**, at last • **finely**, excellently

finch, bird • **flinch**, wince

find, locate • **fined**, penalty

fineness, being fine • **finesse**, subtlety, skill

fir, tree • **fur**, hair of animal

fiscal, money • **physical**, body

fisher, one who fishes • **fissure**, split

flagrant, glaring • **fragrant**, nice odor

flair, aptitude • **flare**, burn

flaunt, ostentatious display • **flout**, reject contemptuously

flaw, fault • **floor**, room surface

flea, insect • **flee**, run away

flèche, a spire • **flesh**, meat

flecks, spots • **flex**, bend

flew, did fly • **flu**, influenza • **flue**, chimney

flock, number of animals • **flog**, whip

floe, ice • **flow**, pour

florescence, flowering • **fluorescence**, giving light

florid, ornate • **fluoride**, chemical

flour, food • **flower**, plant

flout, reject contemptuously • **flaunt**, ostentatious display

foggy, blurred • **fogy**, conservative

foment, incite • **ferment**, yeast

fond, affectionate • **font**, typeface

fondling, caressing • **foundling**, deserted infant

for, in behalf of • **fore**, golf • **four**, number

forego, precede • **forgo**, do without

foreword, introduction • **forward**, move ahead

form, shape • **forum**, public discussion

formally, conventionally • **formerly**, before now

formication, prickly sensation • **fornication**, intercourse

fort, military • **forte**, strong point

forth, forward • **fourth**, number

foul, dirty, unfair • **fowl**, bird

found, located • **fount**, a spring; a source

foundling, deserted infant • **fondling**, caressing

four, number • **for**, on behalf of • **fore**, golf

fractions, math numbers • **fractious**, quarrelsome

fragrant, nice odor • **flagrant**, glaring

franc, French money • **frank**, blunt

frays, battles • **phrase**, words

freak, abnormal being • **phreak**, illegal phone user

frees, sets free • **freeze**, cold • **frieze**, cloth or ornament

friar, monk • **fryer**, fowl

friend, companion • **fiend**, monster

funeral, a ceremony for the dead • **funereal**, mournful

fur, hair of animal • **fir**, tree

furry, having fur • **fury**, anger

further, refers to extent or degree • **farther**, refers to physical distance • **father**, parent

fuss, bother • **fuzz**, sparse hair; slang for police

G

GAAP, generally accepted accounting principles • **gap**, an opening

gabble, talk • **gable**, roof • **gobble**, swallow hastily

gaff, hook • **gaffe**, mistake

gage, security • **gauge**, measure

gaggle, flock; group • **gargle**, rinse throat

gait, walk • **gate**, opening

galleon, ship • **gallon**, measure

gallstone, gall bladder mass • **goldstone**, spangled glass

gamble, bet • **gambol**, frolic

gamete, sexual cell • **gamut**, full range

gamin, a street urchin • **gammon**, a deceitful trick

gantlet, narrowing of two railroad tracks; punishment • **gauntlet**, glove

gap, an opening • **GAAP**, generally accepted accounting principles

gat, channel • **ghat**, mountain pass

gate, door • **gait**, walk

GATT, trade agreement • **get**, to obtain

gauche, naive • **gouache**, art

gauge, measure • **gage**, security

gaunt, thin • **jaunt**, trip

gauze, thin wrapping • **gays**, homosexuals • **gaze**, look

gel, colloid • **jell**, to congeal

genes, heredity • **jeans**, clothing

genius, brilliant • **genus**, subdivision

genteel, polite • **gentile**, non-Jew or non-Mormon • **gentle**, tame

German, of Germany • **germane**, relevant

gesture, movement • **jester**, clown

get, to obtain • **GATT**, trade agreement

ghoul, demon • **goal**, aim

gibe, to sneer at • **jibe**, to agree; to swing from side to side

gild, gold cover • **guild**, association

gilt, gold • **guilt**, blame

gin, liquor • **jinn**, a spirit

glacier, iceberg • **glazier**, glass maker

glitch, misfunction • **glitz**, showiness

glitterati, celebrities • **literati**, people of letters

gloom, a sad, dismal atmosphere • **glume**, grass

gluten, substance found in flour of wheat and other grains • **glutton**, one who eats to excess

glutenous, like gluten • **glutinous**, like glue • **gluttonous**, greedy

gnu, animal • **knew**, did know • **new**, not old

goal, aim • **ghoul**, demon

gobble, swallow hastily • **gabble**, talk • **gable**, roof

gofer, servant • **gopher**, animal

goldstone, spangled glass • **gallstone**, gall bladder mass

golf, game • **gulf**, bay

gorilla, ape • **guerrilla**, war

grate, bars; grind • **great**, large

grease, oil or unctuous matter • **Greece**, a nation in Europe

grill, to broil • **grille**, a grating

grip, grasp • **gripe**, complain • **grippe**, disease

grisly, ghastly • **gristly**, containing cartilage • **grizzly**, black

gristle, cartilage • **grizzle**, grumble

groan, moan • **grown**, mature

groove, indentation • **grove**, orchard

guarantee, to secure • **guaranty**, assure debt repayment

guerrilla, warfare • **gorilla**, ape

guessed, did guess • **guest**, visitor

guild, association • **gild**, gold cover

guilt, blame • **gilt**, gold

gulf, bay • **golf**, game

gurney, stretcher • **journey**, trip

H

habitant, inhabitant • **habitat**, natural environment

hail, salute; ice • **hale**, hearty

hair, on head • **hare**, rabbit

haircut, the process of cutting hair • **haricot**, bean; stew

hall, room • **haul**, pull in

hallow, to make holy • **halo**, circle of light around head • **holler**, to shout • **hollow**, empty inside

halve, divide in two • **have**, possess

handmade, made by hand • **handmaid**, servant

handsome, attractive • **hansom**, cab

hangar, shelter • **hanger**, clothes holder

hangup, inhibition • **hang up**, to end conversation

hardly, barely • **heartily**, warmly

hardy, strong • **hearty**, vigorous

hare, rabbit • **hair**, strands on body

hart, stag • **heart**, body

hassle, trouble; bother • **hustle**, hurry; scam

hatched, gave birth • **hatchet,** chopping instrument

hatful, a filled hat • **hateful,** malicious

haul, pull in • **hall,** room

haunch, buttocks • **hunch,** conjecture

hauteur, haughty • **auteur,** film director

have, possess • **halve,** divide in two

haven, refuge • **heaven,** abode of God

hay, dried grass eaten by cattle • **hey!,** an exclamation

heal, mend • **heel,** of foot • **hell,** Hades • **he'll,** he will

hear, listen • **here,** this place

heard, did hear • **herd,** animals

hearing, ability to hear • **herring,** fish

heart, vital organ • **hart,** stag

hearty, vigorous • **hardy,** strong

heaume, helmet • **home,** a house

heaven, abode of God • **haven,** refuge

he'd, he would • **heed,** obey

heel, of foot • **heal,** mend • **hell,** Hades • **he'll,** he will

heinous, hateful • **anus,** opening of the alimentary canal

heir, inheritor • **air,** gas • **e'er,** ever • **ere,** before • **err,** do wrong

hence, from this time or place • **whence,** from which time or place • **wince,** to flinch

here, this place • **hear,** detect sound

heroin, drug • **heroine,** female hero

hew, chop • **hue,** color

hey!, an exclamation • **hay,** dried grass eaten by cattle

higher, taller • **hire,** employ

him, he • **hymn,** song

ho, exclamation • **hoe,** tool

hoard, collect • **horde,** mob

hoarse, harsh • **horse,** animal

hoary, old • **whorey,** wanton

hobby, recreation • **hubby,** husband

hockey, ice sport • **hooky,** unexcused absence

hoes, digs • **hose,** stockings

hoist, raised • **host,** person who receives guests

hole, opening • **whole,** complete

hold-up, robbery • **holed up,** taken refuge

holey, having holes • **holy,** religious • **wholly,** fully

holiday, a day of exemption from work • **holy day,** a religious feast day

holler, to shout • **hallow,** to make holy • **halo,** circle of light around head to show saintliness • **hollow,** empty inside

home, a house • **heaume,** helmet

homogeneous, of the same character, essentially alike • **homogenous,** of common origin

honk, sound of horn or geese • **hunk,** well-built male

hoop, circle • **whoop,** holler

horde, mob • **hoard,** saved treasure

horse, animal • **hoarse,** rough sound

hose, stockings; tubing • **hoes,** tools

hospitable, friendly • **hospital,** treats the sick

hostel, lodging • **hostile,** antagonistic

hour, time • **our,** belongs to us

hubby, husband • **hobby,** recreation

hue, color • **hew,** chop

human, of people • **humane,** kind

humble, modest • **umbel,** flower cluster

humerus, bone • **humorous,** funny

hunch, conjecture • **haunch,** buttocks

Hungary, the country • **hungry,** ravenous

hunk, well-built male • **honk,** sound of horn or geese

hunter, one who hunts • **junta,** coup leaders

hurdle, barrier • **hurtle,** to rush

hymn, song • **him,** he

hypercritical, over-critical • **hypocritical,** pretending to be what one is not

---

I

I, me • **aye,** yes • **eye,** see

idle, inactive • **idol,** statue • **idyll,** simple pastoral scene

I'll, I will • **aisle,** passage • **isle,** island

illegible, unreadable • **ineligible,** unqualified

illicit, illegal • **elicit,** draw out

illude, cheat • **allude,** refer to

illuminate, shed light on • **eliminate,** wipe out

illusion, false impression • **allusion,** reference to • **elusion,** evasion; escape by deception

illusive, deceptive • **allusive,** referring to • **elusive,** evasive

imbrue, moisten, especially with blood • **imbue,** permeate; color deeply

immanent, inherent • **imminent,** impending • **eminent,** distinguished

immerge, to plunge into • **emerge,** to come out

immersed, plunged into; absorbed • **emersed,** standing out

immigrant, enters country • **emigrant,** leaves country

imminent, about to happen • **eminent,** well-known

immit, to send in • **emit,** to send out

immoral, evil • **amoral,** without a sense of moral responsibility

immunity, exemption from duty; power to resist disease • **impunity,** exemption from punishment or harm

impassable, closed • **impassible,** incapable of being hurt • **impossible,** not possible

impostor, pretender • **imposture,** deception

imprudent, unwise • **impudent,** impertinent

impute, ascribe • **input,** to enter; to provide information

in, [prep.] on the inside • **inn**, hotel

inane, pointless • **insane**, mad

inapt, unqualified • **inept**, unskilled

incest, sex between relatives • **insects**, bugs • **insists**, demands

incidence, rate of occurrence • **incidents**, happenings

incipient, beginning to exist • **insipient**, unwise

incite, stir up • **insight**, keen understanding

indict, charge with a crime • **indite**, to compose

indigenous, native • **endogenous**, from within

indiscreet, unwise • **indiscrete**, unseparated

indivisible, can't be divided • **invisible**, can't be seen

ineligible, not qualified • **illegible**, unreadable

inept, unskilled • **inapt**, unqualified

inequity, injustice • **iniquity**, wickedness

infect, contaminate • **infest**, swarm • **invest**, to put in money

infirmary, clinic • **infirmity**, physical weakness

ingenious, original • **ingenuous**, innocent

inn, hotel • **in**, [prep.] on the inside

innervate, to invigorate • **enervate**, to deprive of strength

input, to enter; to provide information • **impute**, ascribe

insane, mad • **inane**, pointless

insert, to put in • **inset**, that which is set in

insight, keen understanding • **incite**, stir up

insipient, unwise • **incipient**, beginning to exist

insolate, to expose to the sun • **insulate**, to protect; isolate

installation, being put in place • **instillation**, inserting eye drops

insurance, protection • **assurance**, certainty

insure, guarantee; take insurance • **ensure**, to make sure or secure

intense, in an extreme degree • **intents**, purpose

inter, to bury • **enter**, to go in

intercession, petition for another • **intersession**, between semesters

interior, inside • **anterior**, outside

interjection, inserted remark • **introjection**, unconscious ideas

interment, burial • **internment**, state of being detained or held

intern, hospital assistant doctor • **inturn**, an inward turn or bend

interpellate, to question a minister or executive officer • **interpolate**, to alter or insert new matter

interstate, between states • **intestate**, without a will • **intrastate**, within state

intimate, having close relations • **intimidate**, to frighten

inturn, an inward turn or bend • **intern**, hospital assistant doctor

invisible, can't be seen • **indivisible**, can't be divided

ion, particle • **iron**, metal

IRA, Individual Retirement Account • **Eire**, Ireland • **ire**, wrath

irrelevant, not pertinent • **irreverent**, disrespectful

irruption, a bursting in • **eruption**, a bursting out

isle, island • **aisle**, passage • **I'll**, I will

itching, tickling • **etching**, drawing

its, belonging to it • **it's**, it is

I've, I have • **IV**, intravenous • **ivy**, plant

J

jab, hit lightly • **job**, employment

jam, to squeeze; a sweet spread • **jamb**, side of door

jaunt, trip • **gaunt**, thin

jealous, envious • **zealous**, enthusiastic

jeans, clothing • **genes**, heredity

jejune, childish • **jejunum**, part of small intestine

jell, to congeal • **gel**, colloid

jester, clown • **gesture**, movement

jewel, cut gem • **joule**, energy unit • **jowl**, jaw

Jewry, Jewish people • **jury**, court

Jews, people of Jewish descent • **juice**, drink

jibe, to agree; to swing from side to side • **gibe**, to sneer at

jinks, pranks • **jinx**, bad luck

jinn, a spirit • **gin**, liquor

jog, run • **jug**, liquid holder

joggle, shake lightly • **juggle**, handle several objects together

joule, energy unit • **jewel**, cut gem

journey, trip • **gurney**, stretcher

joust, to join battle • **just**, equitable

juggler, one who juggles • **jugular**, throat

junta, coup leaders • **hunter**, one who hunts

jury, court • **Jewry**, the Jewish people

just, equitable • **joust**, to join battle

jut, stick out • **jute**, fiber

K

Kaddish, Hebrew prayer for dead • **Kiddush**, prayer for wine

ken, to know • **kin**, relatives

kernel, seed • **colonel**, officer

ketch, boat • **catch**, take hold of

key, lock opener • **quay**, wharf • **cay**, island

kibbutz, Israeli commune • **kibitz**, offer advice

kid, child • **kit**, equipment • **kite**, flying toy • **kith**, relatives

kill, murder • **kiln**, oven

killed, did kill • **kilt**, Scottish skirt worn by men

kinesics, body movements • **kinetics**, caused by movement

Klan, Ku Klux Klan • **clan**, family

knave, rogue • **nave**, part of church

knead, to press • **need**, must have

kneel, to rest on the knees • **knell**, to ring, as for death

knew, did know • **gnu**, animal • **new**, not old

knight, feudal rank • **night**, opposite of day

knit, fabric • **nit**, insect

knob, protuberance • **nob**, head

knock, to strike • **nock**, notch of an arrow

knot, what you tie • **not**, denial

know, to understand • **no**, opposite of yes

knowable, can be known • **noble**, lordly; fine character • **Nobel**, prize

knows, understands • **noes**, negatives • **nose**, on face

kohl, eye shadow • **coal**, fire • **koel**, a cuckoo

kola, a nut or tree • **cola**, a drink

kris, cheese; dagger • **crease**, fold

L

lade, to load • **laid**, placed

Ladino, Sephardic language • **Latina**, Hispanic woman • **Latino**, Hispanic male

lager, beer • **logger**, tree cutter

lain, did lie • **lane**, path

lair, den • **layer**, a thickness; fold

lam, run away • **lamb**, young sheep

lama, monk • **llama**, animal

lame, can't walk • **lamé**, gold fabric

lanced, pricked • **lancet**, surgical knife

language, words and usage • **languish**, to live in misery

larva, insect • **lava**, volcano

laser, a beam of coherent light • **lazar**, a leper

lass, girl • **last**, the end one

later, afterwards • **latter**, the last one of two

lath, strip of wood • **lathe**, a machine tool

laud, praise • **lord**, a noble

law, rule • **lore**, learning

laws, rules • **loss**, amount that is lost • **lost**, past tense of lose

lay, to deposit • **lei**, a wreath

layer, thickness; fold • **lair**, den

lea, meadow • **lee**, shelter

leach, dissolve • **leech**, bloodsucker

lead, metal; to guide • **led**, did guide

leaf, tree • **leave**, depart • **lief**, gladly

leak, crack • **leek**, vegetable

lean, thin • **lien**, legal charge

least, smallest • **lest**, unless

lei, wreath • **lay**, put down

lentil, pea • **lintel**, beam

lessee, tenant • **lesser**, smaller • **lessor**, one who leases

lessen, to decrease • **lesson**, instruction

letter, written message • **litter**, garbage

levee, dike • **levy**, fine; tax

liable, obligated • **libel**, slander

liar, tells lies • **lyre**, musical instrument

libido, sexual drive • **livedo**, skin discoloration

lichen, plant • **liken**, to compare

lickerish, eager, craving • **licorice**, a flavoring

lie, falsehood • **lye**, chemical

lief, gladly • **leaf**, tree • **leave**, depart

lien, claim • **lean**, thin

lightening, making lighter; relieving • **lightning**, flash in sky

lighter, not as heavy • **liter**, liquid measure • **litter**, strewn things

limb, leg or arm • **lime**, a caustic; fruit • **limn**, draw or outline • **Lyme**, disease

linage, number of lines • **lineage**, ancestry

lineal, of descendants • **linear**, in a line

lineament, detail • **liniment**, a thin ointment

links, joins • **lynx**, animal

lintel, beam • **lentil**, pea

liqueur, sweet liquor • **liquor**, alcoholic drink

literati, people of letters • **glitterati**, celebrities

lived, did live • **livid**, enraged

llama, animal • **lama**, monk

lo!, exclamation • **low**, down; base

load, burden • **lode**, ore

loan, lending • **lone**, alone

loath, reluctant • **loathe**, despise

local, not widespread • **locale**, a place

loch, lake • **lock**, fastening

locks, fastenings • **lox**, salmon

locus, locality • **locust**, insect

lode, mineral • **load**, burden

lodge, cabin • **loge**, theater

logger, tree cutter • **lager**, beer

lone, alone • **loan**, lending

loop, closed circuit • **loupe**, magnifier

loose, not tight • **lose**, fail

loot, booty • **lute**, musical instrument

lord, noble • **laud**, praise

lore, learning • **law**, rule

loss, amount that is lost • **laws**, rules • **lost**, past tense of lose

low, down; base • **lo!**, exclamation

lox, smoked salmon • **locks**, fastenings

lumbar, part of body • **lumber**, wood

luxuriance, state of being luxurious • **luxuriant**, exceedingly fertile • **luxurious**, sumptuous

lye, chemical • **lie**, falsehood

Lyme, disease • **limb**, leg or arm • **lime**, chemical; fruit • **limn**, draw or outline

lynx, animal • **links**, joins
lyre, musical instrument • **liar**, tells lies

M

made, did make • **maid**, servant

magma, rock • **magna**, great

magnate, prominent person • **magnet**, attracts iron

mail, letters • **male**, man

main, principal • **mane**, hair of animal

maize, corn • **maze**, confusing paths

Malay, the people • **melée**, confused struggle

malt, used in brewing • **molt**, to shed

manner, method • **manor**, estate

mantel, shelf at fireplace • **mantle**, cloak

marc, refuse remaining after pressing seeds, fruits • **mark**, sign

marital, in marriage • **marshal**, official • **martial**, warlike

marriage, wedding • **mirage**, illusion

marry, wed • **merry**, gay

marshal, official • **marital**, in marriage • **martial**, warlike

mascle, a steel plate • **muscle**, body tissue • **mussel**, shellfish

mason, bricklayer • **meson**, a particle

massed, assembled • **mast**, on boat

massif, mountain • **massive**, large

mastication, chewing • **masturbation**, sexual self-stimulation

maybe, perhaps • **may be**, may happen

maze, confusing paths • **maize**, corn

mean, nasty • **mien**, bearing

meat, food • **meet**, encounter

medal, award • **meddle**, interfere • **metal**, material • **mettle**, spirit

meddler, one who interferes • **medlar**, tree

melée, confused struggle • **Malay**, the people

Mensa, genius's organization • **menses**, menstrual blood

merry, gay • **marry**, wed

meson, in physics, a particle • **mason**, bricklayer

meteor, solar particles • **métier**, one's calling

meteorology, study of atmosphere • **metrology**, system of weights and measures

mews, cat's sound; row of stables • **muse**, think

mien, bearing • **mean**, nasty

might, strength; may • **mite**, small insect; small child

mil, unit of measure • **mill**, grinding machine; factory

militate, have an effect • **mitigate**, make less severe

millenary, a thousand • **millinery**, hats

milligram, 1/1,000 of a gram • **myelogram**, spinal x-ray

mime, silent comic • **mine**, belongs to me

mince, to cut into small pieces • **mints**, places where money is made; candies

mind, brain • **mined**, dug

miner, one who mines • **minor**, below legal age; unimportant

minion, subordinate official • **minyan**, quorum

minks, animals • **minx**, pert girl

mirage, illusion • **marriage**, wedding

Miss, single woman • **Mrs.**, married woman • **Ms.**, single or married woman • **mss.**, manuscripts

missal, book for Mass • **missile**, weapon

missed, failed • **mist**, haze

misses, fails to hit • **missus**, wife

mite, small insect or child • **might**, strength; may

mitigate, make less severe • **militate**, have an effect

mnemonic, of memory • **pneumonic**, of the lungs

moat, ditch • **mote**, speck

modal, relating to mode • **model**, example

mode, manner • **mowed**, cut down

molt, to shed • **malt**, used in brewing

moor, tie up • **Moor**, the people • **more**, additional

moose, deer-like animal • **mouse**, rodent • **mousse**, pudding

moot, debatable • **mute**, silent

moral, ethical • **morale**, spirit

morays, eels • **mores**, customs

more, additional • **moor**, tie up • **Moor**, the people

morn, morning • **mourn**, grieve

morning, A.M. • **mourning**, grieving

mother, a female parent • **mudder**, a horse

motif, theme • **motive**, reason

mouse, rodent • **moose**, deer-like animal • **mousse**, pudding

mouton, sheepskin • **mutton**, meat of sheep

mowed, cut down • **mode**, manner

Mrs., married woman • **Miss**, single woman • **Ms.**, any woman • **mss.**, manuscripts

muscle, body tissue • **mascle**, a steel plate • **mussel**, shellfish

muse, think • **mews**, cat's sound; row of stables

musical, of music • **musicale**, gathering

Muslim, religion • **muslin**, cloth

mustard, spice • **mustered**, summoned

mute, silent • **moot**, debatable

myelogram, spinal x-ray • **milligram**, 1/1000 of a gram

N

NAFTA, trade agreement • **naphtha**, chemical

naught, nothing • **naughty**, mischievous

naval, navy • **navel**, body part

nave, part of church • **knave**, rogue

nay, no • **né**, original name • **née**, maiden name • **neigh**, cry of horse

need, lack • **knead**, to press

neither, nor • **nether**, below

new, not old • **gnu**, animal • **knew**, did know

news, information • **noose**, rope for hanging

nibble, bite gently • **nybble**, half a byte

niche, suitable role or position • **nick**, cut lightly

night, opposite of day • **knight**, feudal rank

nimbly, quickly • **NIMBY**, not in my backyard

nit, insect • **knit**, stitch

no, opposite of yes • **know**, to understand

nob, head • **knob**, protuberance

noble, lordly; fine character • **knowable**, can be known • **Nobel**, the prize

nock, arrow notch • **knock**, strike

nocturn, a midnight prayer • **nocturne**, musical composition

nod, head movement • **node**, small swelling • **note**, short written piece

nodule, small lump • **noodle**, pasta

noes, negatives • **knows**, understands • **nose**, on face

none, not one • **nun**, religious order

nook, secluded corner • **nuke**, to bomb

not, no • **knot**, what you tie

nougat, candy • **nugget**, lump

nozzle, spout • **nuzzle**, to snuggle

nybble, half a byte • **nibble**, bite gently

O

oar, boat • **awe**, fear • **o'er**, over • **or**, alternative • **ore**, mineral

oat, cereal • **oath**, legal pledge

obit, obituary • **orbit**, movement around a body

object, a material thing; to oppose • **abject**, spiritless

oblique, slanting; indirect • **obloquy**, shame; censure

oblivious, unaware • **obvious**, evident

obsess, to preoccupy • **abscess**, sore • **abscise**, to cut • **abscissa**, math coordinate

obstruct, block • **abstract**, select, excerpt

Occident, the Far East • **accident**, unfortunate event

ocher, pale yellow • **occur**, to happen • **okra**, vegetable

ode, poem • **owed**, did owe

of, belonging to • **off**, away from

offal, garbage • **awful**, terrible

office, work location • **orifice**, opening

oh, surprise • **ow**, cry of pain • **owe**, debt

older, refers to age only • **elder**, refers to age and wisdom gained

once, one time • **ounce**, 1/16th of a pound

one, single • **wan**, pale • **won**, did win

onion, vegetable • **union**, workers' group

op. cit., in work previously quoted • **opposite**, facing

opera, musical drama • **opry**, short for Grand Old Opry

opposite, other side • **apposite**, suitable

opposition, those opposing • **apposition**, grammatical construction

opt, choose • **upped**, increased

or, alternative • **awe**, fear • **oar**, boat • **o'er**, over • **ore**, mineral

oracle, person of great wisdom • **auricle**, ear

oral, verbal • **aural**, hearing

ordinance, law • **ordnance**, military supply

organ, part of body; musical instrument • **origin**, source

organism, living being • **orgasm**, sexual climax

oscillate, vibrate • **osculate**, kiss

ought, should • **aught**, zero • **out**, away; unfashionable

our, belongs to us • **hour**, time

overdo, overindulge • **overdue**, late

overlie, lie over • **overly**, excessively

overt, obvious • **advert**, pay attention • **avert**, avoid

ovoid, egg-shaped • **avoid**, evade

owed, did owe • **ode**, poem

P

packed, bundled • **pact**, agreement

pad, cushion; slang: to overcharge • **paid**, did pay

paddy, rice field • **pâté**, paste • **patty**, small pie

paean, hymn of joy • **peon**, peasant

pail, bucket • **pale**, enclosure; lacking color

pain, ache • **pane**, window

pair, two • **pare**, shave • **pear**, fruit

palate, taste • **palette**, artist's board • **pallet**, bed

pall, covering; gloomy effect • **Paul**, name

pall-mall, game • **pell-mell**, haste

paltry, few • **poultry**, fowl

panda, animal • **pander**, pimp

parish, diocese • **perish**, die

parity, equality • **parody**, witty imitation

parlay, bet • **parley**, talk

parole, prison • **payroll**, pay

partition, divider • **petition**, plea

passable, capable of being passed • **possible**, capable of feeling

passed, did pass • **past**, former time

pastor, clergyman • **pasture**, land for grazing

pastoral, rural • **pastorale**, music

pathos, tender • **bathos**, anti-climax

patience, forebearance • **patients**, under doctor's care

patty, small pie • **paddy**, rice field • **pâté**, paste

Paul, saint • **pall**, covering; gloomy effect

pause, delay • **paws**, touch clumsily; feet • **pores**, openings

paw, foot • **pore**, opening • **pour**, make flow

peace, no war • **piece**, portion

peak, top • **peek**, look • **pique**, anger

peaked, thin • **peeked**, looked • **piqued**, aroused

peal, bell • **peel**, strip

pear, fruit • **pair**, two • **pare**, shave

pearl, gem • **purl**, knitting

pecks, strikes; kisses • **pecs**, slang for pectoral muscles • **picks**, chooses

pedal, foot lever • **peddle**, sell

peer, look; equal • **pier**, dock

pellet, ball • **palette**, artist's board • **pallet**, bed

pell-mell, haste • **pall-mall**, game

pen, writing instrument • **pin**, thin metal piece

penal, prison • **penile**, relating to the penis

penance, religious • **pennants**, sports

pendant, ornament • **pendent**, suspended

penne, pasta • **penny**, cent

penned, written • **pent**, shut in

peon, peasant • **paean**, hymn of joy

per, for each • **purr**, cat's sound

perfect, exact • **prefect**, high official

perish, die • **parish**, diocese

persecute, to hound • **prosecute**, enforce law

personal, private • **personnel**, employees

perspective, vision • **prospective**, future

perverse, contrary • **preserve**, save

petition, plea • **partition**, divider

phantasm, ghost; illusion • **fantasy**, a far-fetched imaginary idea

phase, stage • **fays**, fairies • **faze**, worry

phial, tube • **file**, holder

philter, love potion • **filter**, purifier

phrase, words • **frays**, battles

phreak, illegal phone user • **freak**, abnormal being

physic, a remedy • **physique**, body

physical, body • **fiscal**, money

pi, Greek letter • **pie**, food

pica, printing measure • **piker**, cheapskate

picaresque, rascal • **picturesque**, colorful

picture, image • **pitcher**, vessel; baseball

pidgin, the jargon used as a language between foreigners and the Chinese • **pigeon**, a bird • **piggin**, wooden pail

piece, portion • **peace**, no war

pier, dock • **peer**, look; equal

piker, cheapskate • **pica**, printing measure

pillar, column • **pillow**, head cushion

pinnacle, peak • **pinochle**, game of cards

pious, religious • **Pius**, name of a Pope

pique, anger • **peak**, top • **peek**, look

pistil, flower • **pistol**, gun

pitcher, vessel; baseball player • **picture**, image

plague, deadly disease • **plaque**, award; tooth film

plain, simple • **plane**, smooth; airplane

plaintiff, one who sues • **plaintive**, sad

plait, braid • **plate**, dish

planed, smoothed • **planet**, heavenly body • **planned**, organized • **plant**, to put into soil

playa, desert basin • **player**, one who plays

pleas, requests • **please**, to satisfy

plod, trudge • **plot**, scheme; burial place

plum, fruit • **plumb**, line

pneumonic, of the lungs • **mnemonic**, of memory

pogrom, violent attack on Jews • **program**, plan; performance

poker, cards • **polka**, dance

pole, stick • **poll**, vote

polygamy, more than one mate at one time • **polygyny**, more than one female mate at one time

pool, swimming area; combination • **pull**, draw towards one

poplar, tree • **popular**, well-known

populace, the masses • **populous**, thickly inhabited

pore, opening • **paw**, foot • **pour**, cause to flow

pores, openings • **pause**, hesitate • **paws**, feet

porpoise, mammal • **purpose**, aim

portable, can be carried • **potable**, can be drunk

portend, foretell • **pretend**, make believe

portion, share • **potion**, dose

poultry, fowl • **paltry**, few

practice, the business of a doctor • **practise**, to repeat a performance

pray, say prayers • **prey**, victim; hunt

precede, go before • **proceed**, advance

precedence, priority of rank • **precedents**, previous decisions • **presidents**, chief officials

precedent, going before • **president**, chief official

précis, resume • **precise**, accurate

precisian, a precise person • **precision,** accuracy

prefect, high official • **perfect,** exact

prefer, choose • **proffer,** offer

premier, best; high official • **premiere,** cultural opening • **primer,** basic text

preposition, grammar • **proposition,** offer

prescribe, give directions • **proscribe,** to outlaw

prescription, something ordered • **proscription,** an imposed restriction

presence, being present • **presents,** gives; gifts

presentiment, premonition • **presentment,** presentation

preserve, save • **perverse,** contrary

president, chief official • **precedent,** going before

presidents, chief officials • **precedence,** priority of rank • **precedents,** previous decisions

pretend, make-believe • **portend,** foretell

prey, victim • **pray,** to entreat

pries, opens • **prize,** award

prince, a title of nobility • **prints,** marks made by pressure

principal, main; head • **principle,** strong belief

proceed, advance • **precede,** go before

prod, stimulate • **proud,** self-respect • **prude,** excessive propriety

prodigy, young genius • **protégé,** under care

proffer, offer • **prefer,** choose

profit, gain • **prophet,** seer

program, plan; performance • **pogrom,** violent attack on Jews

pronounce, speak, enunciate • **pronouns,** substitutes for nouns

property, possessions • **proprietary,** by one firm • **propriety,** correctness

prophecy, prediction • **prophesy,** to predict

prophylactic, disease preventive object • **prophylaxis,** preventive measures against disease, dangers

proposition, offer • **preposition,** grammar: to, of, by, etc.

proscribe, outlaw • **prescribe,** give directions

proscription, an imposed restriction • **prescription,** something ordered

prosecute, enforce law • **persecute,** to harass

prospective, future • **perspective,** vision

prostate, gland • **prostrate,** horizontal; overcome

protégé, one helped by senior • **prodigy,** young genius

pubic, region of body • **public,** people

puisne, a junior • **puny,** slight

punned, told a joke based on words • **punt,** kick; boat

pupal, development stage of larva • **pupil,** student

pure, unmixed • **purée,** food

purl, knitting • **pearl,** gem

purpose, aim • **porpoise,** mammal

pus, body fluid • **puss,** cat

put, place • **putt,** golf

Q

quack, incompetent doctor • **quark**, physical particle • **quirk**, odd behavior

quadrille, square dance • **quadrillion**, a million billions

quadruped, four-footed animal • **quadruple**, times four • **quadruplet**, one of four children born together

quality, excellence • **quantity**, amount

quarry, prey; excavation • **query**, question

quarts, 32 ounces • **quartz**, a mineral

quasi, seeming • **queasy**, ill

quaver, tremble • **quiver**, shake; arrow holder

quay, wharf • **cay**, island • **key**, lock opener

quean, female cat; an immoral person • **queen**, female sovereign

queerest, strangest • **querist**, questioner

queue, line • **cue**, hint; billiards

quiet, still • **quite**, completely; very

quietude, peace; quiet • **quietus**, death

quince, fruit • **quinsy**, throat infection • **quints**, quintuplets

quire, 24 sheets of paper • **choir**, singers

quota, number • **quote**, saying

R

rabbis, Jewish religious leaders • **rabies**, viral disease

rabbit, animal • **rabid**, intense • **rarebit**, food

raga, Indian music • **ragout**, stew • **reggae**, Caribbean music

rain, water • **reign**, rule • **rein**, guides horse

raise, lift • **rays**, light beams • **raze**, demolish

RAM, random access memory • **ROM**, read only memory

rap, knock • **wrap**, fold

rapped, knocked • **rapt**, absorbed • **wrapped**, packed

rational, having reason • **rationale**, explanation

raw, uncooked • **roar**, noise

read, book • **red**, color • **reed**, grass

real, actual • **reel**, wind in; stagger

realize, understand • **relies**, counts on

rebait, rehook • **rebate**, deduction

rebound, to spring back • **redound**, to accrue

recede, move back • **reseed**, seed again

recent, not long past • **rescind**, take back • **resend**, send again • **resent**, feel annoyance

recluse, loner • **recuse**, challenge to judge or juror

reek, smell • **wreak**, inflict • **wreck**, destroy

referee, arbitrator • **reverie**, dream

regal, royal • **regale**, feast

reign, rule • **rain**, water • **rein**, on horse

relic, souvenir of the past • **relict**, a widow

relies, counts on • **realize**, understand

replay, to play again; to view again • **reply**, respond

respectfully, with esteem • **respectively**, in the order given

rest, repose • **wrest**, pull away

retch, to vomit • **wretch**, unfortunate person

reveille, signal to awake • **revelry**, gaiety

reverend, minister • **reverent**, respectful

review, survey • **revue**, theater

rheum, watery discharge • **room**, space

rhyme, poetry • **rhythm**, meter, beat • **rime**, frost

riffle, to thumb through • **rifle**, gun

right, correct • **rite**, ceremony • **wright**, workman • **write**, put words on paper

ring, circle; bell • **wring**, squeeze

road, path • **rode**, did ride • **rowed**, pulled boat

roam, wander • **Rome**, city

roar, noise • **raw**, uncooked

robber, crook • **rubber**, elastic

roc, fabled bird • **rock**, stone; sway

roe, fish eggs • **row**, to oar

roil, to stir up • **royal**, crown

role, part • **roll**, turn around; bread

rollout, football play • **roll out**, to get out of bed

rollover, act of deferring payment • **roll over**, to defer payment

ROM, read only memory • **RAM**, random access memory

room, space • **rheum**, watery discharge

roomer, one who rooms • **rumor**, gossip

root, plant • **route**, way

rose, flower • **rosé**, wine • **rows**, lines

rote, mechanical repetition • **wrote**, did write

rough, coarse • **ruff**, collar; fish; bluster

rouse, awaken • **rows**, quarrels

row, to pull boat with oars • **roe**, fish eggs

rowed, pulled boat • **road**, path • **rode**, did ride

rude, lacking refinement • **rued**, regretted

ruin, destroy • **rune**, letter

rumor, gossip • **roomer**, one who rooms

rundown, summary • **run-down**, worn out • **run down**, to chase; to decline

rung, step; did ring • **wrung**, squeezed

rye, grain; alcohol • **wry**, distorted

S

Sabbat, witch's assembly • **Sabbath**, day of rest

sac, animal or plant pouch • **sack**, bag

sachet, bag • **sashay**, trip

sail, on boat • **sale**, sell at low price

sake, end; purpose • **saki**, liquor

salary, wage • **celery**, vegetable

salon, room • **saloon**, barroom

salud, Sp. for to your health • **salute**, greeting

salvage, to save from wreckage • **selvage**, the edge of woven fabric

sane, not mad • **seine**, fishing net

sanitary, hygienic • **sanitory**, conducive to health

Satan, devil • **sateen**, cotton fabric resembling satin • **satin**, fabric

satire, irony • **satyr**, a sylvan deity

sauce, liquid • **source**, origin

saver, one who saves • **savor**, taste

savior, one who saves • **Saviour**, Christ

saw, cut • **soar**, rise • **sore**, hurt

scam, crooked trick • **scan**, look over

scene, place • **seen**, viewed

scents, smells • **cents**, money • **sense**, brains

scrip, money • **script**, story

sculptor, one who carves • **sculpture**, work of sculptor

sea, water • **see**, look

sealing, closing • **ceiling**, top of room

seam, join • **seem**, appear

seamen, sailors • **semen**, male fluid

sear, burn • **seer**, prophet

seas, bodies of water • **sees**, observes • **seize**, grab

sects, people with unique views • **sex**, intimacy

seed, flower • **cede**, give up

seen, did see • **scene**, place

seine, fishing net • **sane**, not mad

sell, opposite of buy • **cell**, prison; in biology

seller, one who sells • **cellar**, basement

selvage, the edge of woven fabric • **salvage**, to save from wreckage

senior, older • **señor**, mister

sense, brains • **cents**, money • **scents**, smells

senses, sight, touch • **census**, population count

serf, slave • **surf**, sea

serge, fabric • **surge**, sudden increase

serial, in a row • **cereal**, food

session, meeting • **cession**, yielding

settler, colonist • **settlor**, one who makes a legal settlement

sew, stitch • **so**, like this • **sow**, plant

shanty, hut • **chantey**, song

sharif, Arab prince • **sheriff**, county officer

shear, clip • **sheer**, transparent

shed, hut • **she'd**, she would

sheik, Arab chief • **chic**, stylish

shirt, garment • **chert**, a rock

shoe, foot • **shoo**, send away

shofar, ram's horn • **chauffeur**, driver

shone, did shine • **shown**, did show

shoot, fire a gun • **chute**, drop

shriek, cry out • **shrike**, bird

shtick, comedy routine • **stick**, rod

sic, thus • **sick**, ill

side, next to • **sighed**, did sigh

sighs, sound • **size**, bigness

sight, see • **cite**, point out • **site**, place

sign, symbol; put name on • **sine**, mathematics

signet, a seal • **cygnet**, a young swan

singeing, burning • **singing**, song

size, bigness • **sighs**, sounds

skull, head • **scull**, boat

Slav, Eastern European • **slave**, one who has lost his freedom

slay, kill • **sleigh**, sled

sleight, trick • **slight**, small; snub

sloe, plum • **slow**, not fast

so, like this • **sew**, stitch • **sow**, plant

soar, rise • **saw**, cut • **sore**, hurt

sodality, a fellowship • **solidarity**, union

sold, did sell • **soled**, put on a sole

solder, to fuse • **soldier**, military

sole, shoe • **soul**, spirit

some, a few • **sum**, total

someone, some person • **some one**, one of several

son, child • **sun**, sky

source, origin • **sauce**, liquid

spear, weapon • **sphere**, round

special, particular, specific • **especial**, exceptional, pre-eminent

speciality, quality of being special • **specialty**, an employment limited to one kind of work

specie, coin • **species**, class

staff, employees • **staph**, bacterium

staid, sober • **stayed**, remained

stair, to climb • **stare**, look steadily

stake, post or gamble • **steak**, food

stalk, stem of plant; walk stealthily • **stork**, bird

stationary, fixed • **stationery**, paper supplies

statue, likeness • **stature**, height • **statute**, law

stayed, remained • **staid**, sober

steal, rob • **steel**, metal

step, pace • **steppe**, plain

stile, step • **style**, fashion

stodgy, uninteresting • **stogie**, cigar • **stooge**, comedian's aide

straight, direct • **strait**, body of water

stricture, binding • **structure**, form

subtile, fine • **subtitle**, movie translation • **subtle**, hard to sense

suburb, near city • **superb**, very good

succor, help • **sucker**, fool

sued, did bring legal action • **suede**, fabric • **swayed**, influenced

suit, clothes • **suite**, rooms • **sweet**, sugary

sulfa, drug • **sulphur**, mineral

sum, total • **some**, a few

summary, wrap-up • **summery**, fit for summer

sun, sky • **son**, child

sundae, ice-cream • **Sunday**, Sabbath

surf, sea • **serf**, slave

surge, sudden increase • **serge**, fabric

surplice, vestment • **surplus**, excess

symbol, sign • **cymbal**, music

symmetry, even; pleasing proportion • **cemetery**, graveyard

---

T

tableau, picture • **tabloid**, newspaper

tacked, fastened • **tact**, consideration

tacks, fasteners • **tax**, money paid government

tail, end • **tale**, story

taint, bad element • **taunt**, make fun of • **tint**, shade

talc, powder • **talk**, speak

tape, recording or measuring device • **taupe**, gray-brown

taper, candle; narrow • **tapir**, animal

tarantella, dance • **tarantula**, spider

tare, weight • **tear**, rip

taro, food • **tarot**, cards

tartar, on teeth; chemical • **Tartar**, a people • **tartare**, sauce • **Tatar**, a people

taught, did teach • **taut**, tense

tea, beverage • **tee**, golf peg

team, group • **teem**, swarm

tear, (pron. like 'ear') crying • **tier**, layer

tear, (pron. like 'air') rip • **tare**, weight

teas, drinks • **tease**, annoy

technics, technical rules • **techniques**, manners of performance

teeth, plural of tooth • **teethe**, to grow teeth

temp, temporary worker • **tempt**, induce wrongdoing

tempera, art technique • **tempura**, Japanese food

tenant, renter • **tenet**, belief

tenor, singer • **tenure**, duration

tern, bird • **turn**, rotate

terra, earth • **terror**, great fear

than, comparative: as in "greater than" • **then**, at that time

their, belongs to them • **there**, that place • **they're**, they are

therefor, for that, for it, for them, etc. • **therefore**, for this reason

thong, strap • **tong**, implement • **Tong**, Chinese gang • **tongue**, mouth

thrash, to swing or strike • **thresh**, to beat out grain

threw, tossed • **through**, penetrated; finished

throe, pang • **throw**, hurl

throne, king • **thrown**, tossed

thyme, herb • **time**, duration • **tine**, fork prong

tic, twitching • **tick**, pillow; clock

tide, ocean • **tied**, connected

tier, layer • **tear**, (pron. like 'ear') crying

timber, wood • **timbre**, tone

tinny, like tin • **tiny**, small

to, toward • **too**, also • **two**, number

tocsin, alarm • **toxin**, poison

toe, foot • **tow**, pull

toil, labor • **toile**, fabric

toiled, worked • **told**, said

toilet, bathroom • **toilette**, grooming, attire

tole, metalware • **toll**, fee; to sound

tomb, grave • **tome**, book

tong, implement • **Tong**, Chinese gang • **tongue**, mouth • **thong**, strap

topee, sun-helmet • **toupee**, hairpiece for men

topical, timely • **tropical**, hot climate

topography, maps, charts • **typography**, printing

tortious, legal term referring to tort • **tortuous**, twisting • **torturous**, painful

tot, child • **tote**, carrying bag

tour, trip • **tower**, building

toxin, poison • **tocsin**, alarm

track, path • **tract**, region

trail, path • **trial**, court

travail, toil • **travel**, journey

tray, food carrier • **trey**, three in cards or dice

treaties, agreements • **treatise**, account

troop, company of soldiers • **troupe**, company of actors

trustee, administrator • **trusty**, reliable convict

tuba, musical instrument • **tuber**, root of plant

turban, hat • **turbine**, power

turn, rotate • **tern**, bird

two, number • **to**, toward • **too**, also

typography, printing • **topography**, maps, charts

U

udder, milk gland • **utter**, speak

ultimate, final • **ultimatum**, final demand

umbel, flower cluster • **humble**, modest

umpire, referee • **empire**, dominion

unable, not able • **enable**, to make able

unaware, not aware • **unawares**, unexpectedly

underlay, a support • **underlie**, be the basis • **underline**, draw a line under

undo, reverse • **undue**, excessive

unequal, not the same • **unequaled**, unparalleled; exceptional

unexceptionable, unimpeachable • **unexceptional**, ordinary

unfold, to lay open • **enfold**, to wrap

ungird, unbind • **ungirt**, slack

unintelligent, not smart • **unintelligible**, can't be read

union, workers' organization • **onion**, vegetable

unique, sole • **eunuch**, sexless

unisex, sex not evident • **unsex**, take away sexual power

unitary, whole; relates to a unit • **Unitarian**, religious faith

universal, covering all • **universe**, cosmos; everything

Unix, computer operating system • **eunuchs**, emasculated men

unlike, not like • **unlikely**, improbable

unread, not read • **unready**, not ready

unreal, imaginary • **unreel**, unwind from a reel

unroll, to display • **enroll**, join

untidy, sloppy • **untied**, unbound

untitled, lacking a title • **entitled**, deserving

unwanted, not wanted • **unwonted**, rare

unwrap, uncover • **enwrap**, wrap around

upped, increased • **opt**, choose

urban, of a city • **urbane**, polished

urn, vase • **earn**, gain; to receive a salary

usurious, lending at exorbitant rates • **uxorious**, submits to wife

utter, speak • **udder**, milk gland

V

vacation, rest • **vocation**, job

vague, imprecise • **vogue**, fashionable

vain, proud • **vane**, weather • **vein**, blood vessel

valance, drapery • **valence**, in chemistry, degree of combining power

vale, valley • **veil**, face covering

valet, personal aide • **valley**, low area

valor, bravery • **velour**, fabric

valuable, of much worth • **voluble**, talkative

vantage, higher position • **vintage**, old

variance, conflicting • **variants**, slight differences

vary, to alter • **very**, extremely

vassal, serf • **vessel**, container; ship

vector, directed quantity; line • **victor**, winner

venal, mercenary • **venial**, pardonable

venerable, respected • **venereal**, disease

veracious, truthful • **voracious**, greedy

veracity, truth • **voracity**, hunger

verify, confirm • **versify**, write poetry

verity, truth • **vérité**, cinéma vérité: realism

verses, poetry • **versus**, against

vertebra, bone in backbone • **vertebrate**, animal with backbone

vial, glass • **vile**, loathsome • **viol**, music

vibrant, energetic • **vibrate**, move rapidly

vibrato, vibrating musical tone • **vibrator**, exerciser

vice, depravity • **vise**, clamp

victor, winner • **vector**, directed quantity; line

vigilant, alert • **vigilante**, self-appointed crimebusters

villa, estate • **viola**, string instrument • **voilà**, behold

vindicate, absolve • **vindictive**, revengeful

violate, disregard; break • **violent**, injurious; furious • **violet**, color

violation, transgression • **volition**, choice

viral, of a virus • **virile**, manly

virtual, acting in effect • **virtue**, goodness

virtuoso, exceptional performer • **virtuous**, moral

visa, travel permit • **viz.**, for example; namely

visor, sunshade • **vizier**, Muslim official

vocable, word form • **vocal**, expressive

vocation, job • **vacation**, rest

voilà, behold • **villa**, estate • **viola**, string instrument

Volga, Russian river • **vulgar**, crude, impolite

volition, choice • **violation**, transgression

voracious, greedy • **veracious**, truthful

voracity, hunger • **veracity**, truth

voyager, traveler • **voyageur**, expert guide

W

wade, walk through water • **weighed**, did weigh

wail, cry • **whale**, mammal

waist, body • **waste**, to squander

wait, stay for • **weight**, heaviness

waive, give up • **wave**, water; gesture

waiver, surrender claim • **waver**, falter

wan, pale • **one**, single • **won**, did win

wander, roam • **wonder**, speculate

wanton, sensual • **wonton**, dumpling

war, combat • **wore**, past tense of wear

ward, division • **warred**, fought

ware, goods • **wear**, clothes • **where**, which place?

wary, cautious • **weary**, tired

waste, to squander • **waist**, body

WATS, telephone • **watts**, units of electrical power • **what's**, what is wax, sticky substance • **whacks**, hits

way, direction • **weigh**, to measure heaviness; to consider • **whey**, milk

we, us • **wee**, tiny

weak, feeble • **week**, 7 days

weal, state • **we'll**, we will • **wheel**, round body

weather, atmosphere • **whether**, if

wed, marry • **we'd**, we would • **weed**, unwanted plant

weighed, did weigh • **wade**, walk through water

weight, heaviness • **wait**, stay for

welch, cheat • **Welsh**, from Wales

wen, cyst • **when**, what time

were, past of to be • **we're**, we are • **whir**, buzzing sound • **whirl**, spin

wet, water • **whet**, appetite

whale, mammal • **wail**, cry

what's, what is • **WATS**, telephone • **watts**, units of electrical power

whence, from which place • **hence**, from this time or place • **wince**, to flinch

where, which place? • **ware**, goods • **wear**, clothes

which, what one? • **witch**, hag

Whig, political party • **wig**, hair cover

while, during • **wile**, trick

whiled, passed time away • **wield**, to hold • **wild**, uncontrolled

whine, complain • **wine**, drink

whit, smallest bit • **wit**, cleverness

whither, where • **wither**, decay

whole, complete • **hole**, opening

wholly, fully • **holey**, having holes • **holy**, religious

whoop, holler • **hoop**, circle

whore, prostitute • **who're**, who are

whorey, wanton • **hoary**, old

who's, who is • **whose**, to whom

wile, trick • **while**, during

wince, to flinch • **hence**, from this time or place • **whence**, from where

wine, drink • **whine**, complain

wit, cleverness • **whit**, smallest bit

won, did win • **wan**, pale • **one**, single

wonder, speculate • **wander**, roam

wont, habit • **won't**, will not

wonton, dumpling • **wanton**, sensual

wood, lumber • **would**, might

wore, did wear • **war**, combat

worst, least good • **wurst**, sausage

wrap, fold • **rap**, knock

wrapped, packed • **rapped**, knocked • **rapt**, absorbed

wreak, inflict • **wreck**, destroy • **reek**, smell

wrest, pull away • **rest**, repose

wretch, unfortunate person • **retch**, to vomit

wright, workman • **right**, correct • **rite**, ceremony • **write**, put words on paper

wring, squeeze • **ring**, circle; bell

wrote, did write • **rote**, mechanical repetition

wrung, squeezed • **rung**, step; did ring

wry, distorted • **rye**, grain; alcohol

Y, Z

y'all, you all • **yawl**, sailboat • **yowl**, loud cry

yang, masculine principle • **yank**, pull

Yankee, New Englander; northerner • **Yanqui**, Spanish for U.S. citizen

yawl, sailboat • **y'all**, you all • **yowl**, loud cry

yaws, tropical disease • **yours**, belonging to you

ye, religious: you • **yea**, yes

yen, desire; Japanese money • **yin**, feminine principle

yew, tree • **ewe**, sheep • **you**, person

yoga, Hindu philosophy • **yogi**, yoga practitioner

yoke, frame for animals • **yolk**, egg

yore, olden times • **your**, belongs to you • **you're**, you are

you'll, you will • **Yule**, Christmas

yours, belonging to you • **yaws**, tropical disease

yowl, loud cry • **y'all**, you all • **yawl**, sailboat

zealous, enthusiastic • **jealous**, envious

zinc, metal • **zing**, vigor

Quick List of Correct Spellings

abandon	abstinence	acerb	adapt**
abate	abstract**	acetic**	add**
abatement	absurd	acetone	addable**
abbey	abuse	ache	addenda
abbot	abyss	achieve	addict
abbreviate	academic	Achilles heel	addiction
abdomen	academy	acid	addition**
abduct	accede**	acidosis	address
aberrant**	accelerate	acknowledge	adds**
aberration**	accent**	acknowledg-	adduce**
abet	accept**	ment	adenoma
abhor	access**	acme**	adept**
abhorrent**	accessory	acne**	adequate
ability	accidence**	acolyte	adequately
abject**	accident**	acoustics	adhere
abjure**	accidentally	acquaint-	adhesion
ablation**	accidents**	ance	adieu**
ablaze	acclaim	acquire	adjacent
able	acclimate	acquisition	adjoin**
abled	accommo-	acquit	adjourn**
ableism	date	acquittal	adjudication
ablution**	accompani-	acquitted	adjure**
ably	ment	acre	adjustable
aboard**	accompany	acreage	adjutant
abode	accom-	acrobat	administra-
abolition	plice**	across	tion
aborigine	accom-	acrostic	administra-
abort**	plish**	activate**	tor
abortion	accord	active	admirable
about	according	activist	admiral
abrade	accordion	actor	admissible
abrasion**	accost	acts**	admission
abrasive	account	actual	admit
abroad**	accountant	actually**	admittance
abrogate**	accredit	actuary**	admonish
abrupt	accredita-	actuate**	admonition
abscess**	tion	acumen	ado**
abscise**	accrue	acupuncture	adobe
abscissa**	accumulate	acute	adolescence
absence	accuracy	ad**	adolescent
absent	accurate	adage	adopt**
absolutely	accuse	adamant	adorable
absorb	accustom	Adam's	adore
absorption	acentric**	apple	adrenal

ads**
adult
advance
advantage
advanta-
geous
adventitious
adverse**
advert**
advertise
advertise-
ment
advice**
advisable
advise**
adviser
advisory
advocate
adz**
aegis
aerial
aerie**
aerobic
aerobics
aerodynam-
ics
aeronautics
aerosol
aesthetic**
afar**
affable
affair**
affaire**
affect**
affective**
affidavit
affiliate
affinity
affirm
affirmative
affix
afflict
affluence
affluent**
afford
affront
Afghan

afire
afraid
Africa
Africans**
Afrikaans**
Afrikan-
ers**
Afrocentric
aftercare
afternoon
afterwards
against
aged
ageism
agencies
agency
agenda
aggrandize
aggravate
aggregate
aggression**
aggressive
aggrieved
aghast
agile
agility
aging
ago
agonize
agony
agoraphobia
agrarian
agree
agreeable
agreed
agreeing
agriculture
aground
ague
aid**
aide**
aides**
AIDS**
aids**
ail**
ailment**
air**
airbag

airplane
airwaves
aisle**
à la carte
Al-anon
albino
albumin
alchemy
alcohol
alcoholic
alcoholism
al dente
ale**
alert
algae
algorithm
alias
alibi
alien
alienation
align
aliment**
alimen-
tary**
alimony
all**
allay**
allege**
allegiance
allegro
allergic
allergy**
alleviate
alley**
alliance
allocate
allocation**
allot
allotment
allow**
allowance
allowed**
alloy**
all ready**
all right
all to-
gether**
allude**

allure
allusion**
allusive**
all ways**
ally**
alma mater
almanac
almighty
almond
almost
alms**
aloe**
alone
aloof
aloud**
alpha
alphabet
alphanu-
meric
already**
also
also ran
altar**
alter**
alter ego
alternate**
alterna-
tive**
although
altitude**
alto
altogether**
altruism
aluminum
always**
amalgam
amal-
gamated
amateur**
ambassador
ambiance
ambidex-
trous**
ambience
ambiguous
ambisex-
trous**
ambition

ambulance
ameliorate
amen
amenable
amend**
amendment
amenorrhea
American
AMEX
amiable**
amicable**
amity**
ammonia
ammunition
amnesia
amniocente-
    sis
amoeba
amok
among
amoral**
amorous
amount
amour**
amp
ampere
ampheta-
    mine
amphithea-
    ter
ample**
amplifica-
    tion
amplifier
amplify
ampule**
amputate
amputation
amputee
Amtrak
amuse
amusement
anabolic
anal**
analgesic
analog**
analogous
analogue**

analogy
analyses
analysis
analyst**
analytic
analytical
analyze**
anatomy
ancestor
ancestry
anchor
anchorman
anchovy
ancient
android
anecdotal
anecdote**
anemic
anent
anesthetic
aneurism
aneurysm
anew
angary
angel**
anger
angina
angiocardio-
    gram
angioma
angle**
angora
angry
angst
anguish
anima**
animal**
animus
ankh
ankle
annex
annihilate
anniversary
annotate
announce-
    ment
annoyance
annual**
annually

annuity
annul**
annulled
anoint
anomaly
anomie**
anonymous
anorexia
anorexia ner-
    vosa
another
answer
ant**
antacid
antagonist
antarctic
Antarctica
ante**
antecede
antecedent
antedate**
antenna
anterior**
anthrax
anti**
anti-
    American
antibiotic
antibody
antic**
anticipate
antidepres-
    sant
antidote**
antihista-
    mine
antique**
antiseptic
antitoxin
anus**
anxiety
anxious
any
anyone**
any one**
any time
anyway**
any way**

anywhere
aorta
apartheid
apartment
apatite**
apex
aphorism
aplomb
apnea
apocryphal
apogee
apologia**
apologies
apologize
apology**
apostil**
apostle**
apostrophe
apotheosis
appall
appalled
apparatus
apparel
apparent
apparently
appeal
appear
appearance
appease
appellate
append
appendec-
    tomy
appendicitis
appendix
appetite**
applaud
apple
appliance
applicant
application
applicator
applies
apply
appoint
appointee
appointment
apposite**

157

apposi- tion**	Arkansas	ascetic**	assure
appraisal	armature**	ASCII	asthma
appraise**	armful	ashamed	astigmatism
appreciable	armistice	ashen	astonish
appreciate	armoire**	ashore	astray**
apprehend	armor**	Asia	astringent
apprentice	arms**	Asian	astronaut
apprise**	arose**	asinine	astronomy
approach	around	askance	astute
appropriate	arouse**	asked	asylum
approve	arraign**	asparagus	atavism
approximate	arrange**	asphalt	ate**
apricot	arrangement	asphyxia	atheist
apron	array	aspirant**	athlete
apropos	arrears	aspirate**	athletic
apt	arrest	aspiration	atmosphere
aptitude	arrested	aspire	atom
aquarium**	arrhythmia	aspirin**	atone
Aquarius**	arrival	assail	atrium
arabesque	arrive	assailant	atrocity
arbitrary	arrogance	assassin	atrophy
arbitrate	arrogant	assassinate	attach**
arbitrator	arrogate**	assault**	attaché**
arbor	arrow	assay**	attack**
arc**	arroz**	assemble	attacked
arcade	arsenic	assent**	attain
arch**	art	assert**	attempt
archaic	art deco	assertive	attend
archangel	arteriosclero- sis	assess	attend- ance**
archeology	artery	assessed	attendant
archetype	arthritis	asset	attendants**
architect	article	assign	attention
archive	artifact	assigna- tion**	attenuate
archives	artificial	assign- ment**	attest
arctic	artillery	assimilable	attic
area**	artist**	assimilation- ist	attire
arena	artiste**	assist	attitude**
areola	artistic**	assistance**	attorney
argot	artistically	assistant	attract
argue	arts	assistants**	attribute
argument	artware	associate	attrition
aria**	arty	association	auction
arise	arugula	assort**	audacious
arising	asbestos	assume	audible
aristocrat	ascend	assurance**	audience
arithmetic	ascent**		audio
ark**	ascertain		audiophile

audit
auditorium
auger**
aught**
augur**
August
aunt**
aunty**
au pair
aura
aural**
au revoir
auricle**
austere
autarchy**
autarky**
auteur**
authentic
author
authority
authorize
autism
autistic**
autobiogra-
    phy
autofocus
autograft**
autograph**
autoim-
    munity
automatic
automati-
    cally
automa-
    tion**
automa-
    ton**
automobile
autopilot
autumn
auxiliary**
available
avalanche
avant-garde
avenue
average
averse**
aversion

avert**
aviary
aviator
avid
avocado
avoid**
avoidable
await
aware
awe**
awesome
awful**
awhile**
awkward
awl**
awry
axe**
axes**
axillary**
axis**
axle**
aye**

B
babble**
baby
babysit
bacchanal
bach**
bachelor
bacitracin
backbone
background
backlog
backstabber
backtrack
backward
bacon
bacteria
bad**
bade**
badge
bagel
baggage
bagged
bags
bail**

bailiwick
bailout
bait**
balance
balcony
bald**
bale**
balk
ball**
ballad**
balled**
ballerina
ballet**
ballistics
balloon
ballot**
ballpoint
balm**
balmy
baloney**
bamboo
banana
band**
bandage
bandana
bandit
bands**
bandwagon
banish
banister
banjos
bankrupt
bankruptcy
banned**
banner
banns**
banquet**
banquette**
bans**
banzai**
Baptist
baptize
barbarian
barbecue
barbiturate
bard**
bare**
barefaced

bargain
baring**
barley
Bar Mitzvah
barn
barometer
baron**
barracks
barracuda
barrage
barred**
barrel
barren**
barricade
barrier
barter**
basal
base**
baseball
basement
bases**
bash
basic
basically
basin
basis**
bask
basketball
Bas Mitzvah
Basque
bass**
bastard**
baste
basted**
batch**
bate**
bath**
bathe**
bathos**
baton
battalion
batten
batter**
battered
    baby
battered
    wife

battered women
battery
bauble**
baud**
baud rate
bawd**
bawl**
bawled**
bay
bayou
bazaar**
bazooka
BBS
be**
beach**
beacon
bean**
beanball
bear**
bearing**
bearish
beast
beat**
beatify**
beau**
beautician
beautiful
beautify**
beauty
beaver
because
become
becoming
bedbug
bedmate
bedspread
bee**
beech**
been**
beep
beer**
beet**
beetle
before
befriend
began
beggar

begin
beginner
beginning
behalf
behavior
behemoth
beige
Beijing
belfry
belie**
belief
believe
belittle
bell**
belladonna
belle**
bellicose
belligerent
bellow**
bellwether
belly**
below**
Beltway
benchmark
bends
beneath
beneficial
beneficiary
benefit
benefited
benevolent
benign
bent
benzocaine
bequeath
berate
bereaved
bereft
beret
beriberi
berry**
berserk
berth**
beseech**
beside**
besides**
besiege**
bestial

beta
betray
better**
bettor**
beverage
beware
bewilder
bey
beyond
bialy
biannual**
bias
bib**
bibb**
Bible
biceps
bicultural
bicuspid
bicycle
bid**
bide**
biennial**
bier**
bifocal
bigamy
biggest
bight**
bigot
big shot
bigwig
bile
bilingual
bilious
billboard
billed**
billet
billiard
billion
billionaire
bill of fare
billow**
bimbo
bin**
binary
binoculars
biocentrism
biochemistry
biofeedback

biography
biology
bionics
biopsy
bipolar
birch
bird
birdie
birth**
birthmark
birthmother
birthright
birthstone
biscuit
bisect
bisque
bissync
bistro
bitch
bite**
bitten
bitter
bivouac
bivouacked
biz
bizarre**
blackboard
blackguard
blackhead
blackmail
bladder
blameless
blanch
blanket
blare
blasé
blasphemy
blast
blaster
blatant
bleach
bleak
bled
bleed
bleep**
blessed
blew**
blight

blind
blintz
blip**
blister
blithe
blitz
blizzard
bloat**
bloated
blob
bloc**
block**
blockade
blond
blood
bloodbath
blossom
blot**
blotch**
blotter
blouse
bludgeon
blue**
blue baby
blueberry
blueblood
blueprint
blues
bluff
blunder
blunt
blur
blurb
B'nai B'rith
B.O.
boar**
board**
boarder**
boast
boats
boatswain
bod
bodice-
ripper
body**
bodyguard
bogey**
bogon

bogosity
bogus
bogy**
boiler plate
boisterous
bold**
bolder**
bole**
boll**
bologna**
bolster
bomb**
bombshell
BOMFOG
bone
boned
bones
bonfire
bonnet
bonny**
bonsai**
bon soir
bonus
bon vivant
bony**
boogie**
book
bookkeeping
Boolean
boom**
boombox
boon**
boos
boot**
bootie**
booty**
booze
border**
borderline
bore**
bored**
born**
borne**
borough**
borrow
borscht
bosom
bossa nova

bossy
botch**
bottle
bottleneck
bottom
bottomless
botulism
boudoir
bough**
bought**
bouillon**
boulder**
boulevard
boundary
bouquet
bourbon
bourgeois
bout**
boutique
bow**
bowel**
bowl**
bowled**
boy**
boycott
bozo
bra
brace
bracelet
braces
braes**
braggart
Brahman**
Brahmin**
braid**
Braille
brain
brainstorm
braise**
brake**
brand-new
brands**
brandy
brans**
brash**
brass**
brassiere
bravado

bravery
brawl
brayed**
brays**
braze**
brazen
breach**
breaches**
bread**
breadth**
break**
breakable
break-even
breakfast
breakout
break-
through
breakup
breast
breath**
breathe**
bred**
breech**
breeches**
breed
breeze
brethren
brew
brewed**
brews**
briar**
bribe
bridal**
bridegroom
bridge
bridle**
brief
briefcase
brier**
brigadier
bright
brilliant
bristle
Britain**
Britannica
Briton**
brittle
bro'

161

broach*
Broadway
broccoli
brochure
broke
broken
brokerage
bronchial
bronchitis
brooch**
brood**
brook
brothers
brownstone
brows**
browse**
bruise**
bruit**
brusque
brute**
bubble**
bubo
buck
bucket
buckle
bucks
Buddha
buddy**
budge
budget
buffalo
buffer
buffet
buffoon
bug
bugged
bugle
build**
built
bulimia
bulge
bulldozer
bullet
bulletin
bullion**
bully
bulwark
bumblebee

bummer
bumper
bundle
bungalow
bunion
buns
buoy**
buoyant
burden
bureau
burger
burglar
burglary
burial
burlap
burlesque
burley**
burly**
burnout
burnt
burro**
burrow**
bursa**
bursar**
bursitis
burst
bury**
bus**
busily
business
buss**
bussed**
bust**
busted
bustier
bustle
busy
busybody
but**
butcher
butt**
button
buxom
buy**
buy-in
buy-out
buzz
buzzwords

by**
bye**
byline
bypass
byproduct
byte**

C
cabal**
cabbage
cabinet
cable**
cacao**
cache**
cacophony
cactus
caddie**
caddy**
cadenza
cadet
café
café au lait
cafeteria
caffeine
cagey
cahoots
Cajan
Cajun
calamity
calcium
calculate
calculus
calendar**
calender**
calf
caliber
calico
California
calisthenics
call**
callous**
callus**
calm**
calorie
Calvary**
calves
calypso

cam**
camaraderie
camcorder
camel
camellia
Camelot
cameo
camera
camouflage
campaign
camphor
campus
Canada
canal
canapé*
canard
cancel
cancer
candidate
candle
candor
canine
canister
canker
cannabis
canneloni
cannery
cannibal
cannon**
canoe
canon**
canopy**
cant**
can't**
cantaloupe
cantilever
canvas**
canvass**
canyon
cap
capable
capacious
capacity
capillary
capital**
capitation
    fee
Capitol**

capitulate
capped
cappucino
caprice
capricious
capsule
captain
caption
captive
capture
carafe
caramel
carat**
caravan
carbohy-
drate
carbon
carbon diox-
ide
carbon
monoxide
carbuncle
carburetor
carcass
carcinogen
carcinoma
cardboard
cardiac
cardinal
career
careful
caress
caret**
caretaker
careworn
Caribbean
caricature
caries**
caring
carjack
carnage
carnal**
carnival
carotene
carotid
carousal**
carouse
carousel**

carpal
carriage
carried
carries**
carrot**
carrying
carte
  blanche
cartel
cartilage
carton
cartoon
cartridge
Casanova
cascade
casement
cash**
cashew
cashier
cashmere
casino
cask**
casket
casque**
casserole
cassette
cassock
cast**
castanet
caste**
caster**
castigate
castle
castor**
castrate
casual**
casualty
cataclasm**
cataclysm**
catacomb
catalog
catapult
cataract
catarrh
catastrophe
catatonic
catch
category

caterpillar
catfish
cathedral
catheter
Catholic
catlike
CAT scan
catty**
Caucasian
caucus
caught**
caul**
cauliflower
caulk
causal**
cause**
cause
  célèbre
caustic
caution
cavalcade
cavalier
cavalry**
caveat
caveat emp-
  tor
cavel
cavernous
cavity
caws**
cay**
CD-ROM
cease**
cedar
cede**
ceiling**
celebrate**
celebrity
celerity
celery**
celestial
celibacy
celibate**
cell**
cellar**
cello
cellophane
cellular

cellulite
cellulitis
celluloid
cellulose
Celtic
cement
cemetery**
censer**
censor**
censure**
census**
centennial
center
centigrade
centimeter
central
centrifugal
cents**
century
CEO
ceramics
cereal**
cerebellum
cerebral
cerebrally
ceremony
certain
certificate
cervix
cession**
cesspool
chafe
chagrin
chagrined
chain
chair
chaise
chalet
chalk
chalk talk
challenge
chameleon
chamois
cham-
  pagne**
cham-
  paign**
champion

chancre	chert**	chosen	citrus
chandelier	cherub	chow**	civic
changeable	chestnut	chowder	civil
channel**	chevron	chow mein	civilization
chanteuse	chews**	christen**	civil rights
Chanukah	chic**	Christian**	clairvoyance
chaos	Chicago	Christmas	clairvoyant
chapeau	Chicana	chrome	clamor
chapel	chicanery	chronic	clan**
chaperon	Chicano	chronology	clandestine
chaplain	chicken pox	chrysanthe-	clannish
character	chief	mum	claque
charade	chieftain	chubby	classified
charcoal	chiffon	chuck	classify
chardonnay	chignon	chummy	clause**
chariot	children	Chunnel	claws**
charisma	Chile**	chupah	cleanse
charitable	chili**	church	cleanser
charity	chilly**	churning	clear
charlatan	chimney	chute**	clearance
charnel**	Chinatown	chutzpah	cleavage
charted**	chintz	ciao**	clench**
charter	chip	cider	clerical
chartered**	Chippendale	cigar	clew**
chartreuse	chiropody	cigarette	cliché
chase	chiropractor	cinch	click**
chased**	chisel	Cincinnati	client
chasm	chivalrous	cinder	clientele
chassis	chivalry	Cinderella	climactic**
chaste**	chlamydia	cinema	climate
chastity	chloral hy-	cinnamon	climatic**
chat	drate	cipher	climax
château	chlorine	circle	climb**
chatter	chloroform	circuit	clime**
chauffeur**	chocolate	circular	clinch**
chauvinism	choice	circumcise	clinic
cheap**	choir**	circumcision	clinker
cheat	choler**	circumfer-	clipper
check**	cholera	ence	clique**
cheddar	cholesterol	circum-	clitoris
cheep**	choose**	stance	cloak
cheese	chopper	circumvent	clobber
chef	choral**	cisc chip	cloche
chemical	chord**	cistern	clock
chemise	choreogra-	citadel	cloister
chemist	phy	citation	clone**
chenille	chortle	cite**	close**
cherish	chorus	citizen	closeout

164

closet
closing
closure
clothes**
cloths**
clown**
cloy
cloze**
club
clubby
clue**
clumsy
clutch
coach
coagulate
coal**
coalition
coarse**
coat**
cobbler
cobol
cocaine
cockamamie
cockpit
cockroach
cock's
  comb**
cocks-
  comb**
cocktail
cocoa**
coconut
code
codeine
coerce
coercion
coffee
coffin
cogitate
cognac
cognitive
coherent
coiffure
coincidence
coitus
coke
cola**
colander

cold
cold-
  blooded
coleslaw
colic
coliseum
colitis
collaborate
collage**
collapse
collapsible
collar**
collard**
collateral
colleague
collect
collector
college**
collegiate
collision**
colloquial
collusion**
cologne**
Colombia**
colon**
colonel**
colonic
colonnade
color**
coloratura
colossal
Colosseum
colostomy
Columbia**
column
columnist
coma**
comb
comedian
comedy**
comet**
comfortable
comic
coming
comity**
comma**
command**

commemo-
  rate
commence
commend**
commend-
  able
commenda-
  tion**
commensu-
  rate
commerce
commercial
commission
commit**
committed
committee**
commodity
common
commotion
commune
communi-
  cate
communism
communist
community
commute
commuter
compact
companion
comparable
comparative
compass
compatible
compel
compelled
compen-
  dium
compensa-
  tion
compete
competence
competent
competition
compla-
  cence**
compla-
  cent**

complai-
  sance**
complai-
  sant**
comple-
  ment**
complemen-
  tary**
complexion
compliance
complicate
compli-
  ment**
complimen-
  tary**
compose
composition
compound
comprehend
comprehensi-
  ble**
comprehen-
  sion
comprehen-
  sive**
compressed
compression
compromise
comptroller
compulsory
compute
computer
comrade
conceal
concede
conceit
conceive
concentrate
concentra-
  tion
concentric
concept
concert
concession
concierge
conciliate
concise
conclave

conclude
conclusion
concoct
concourse
concrete
concur**
concurrence
concussion
condemn**
condemna-
tion**
condensa-
tion
condescend
condiment
condition
condo
condom
condomin-
ium
condone
conduct
confection-
ary
confederate
confer
conference
conferred
confess
confidant**
confidence
confident**
confinement
confirm
confirmer**
confiscate
conflagra-
tion
conformer**
Confucius
congeal
congenial**
congenital**
conglomer-
ate
congratulate
congrega-
tion

congress
congressio-
nal
congruous
conjecture
conjugal
conjugate
conjunction
conjunctivi-
tis
conjure
connect
Connecticut
connection
connoisseur
connotation
connote
connubial
conquer**
conscience**
conscien-
tious**
conscious**
consensus
consequence
conserva-
tion**
conservative
conserva-
tory
consider
considerable
consignment
consistent
console
consolidate
consonant
conspicuous
conspiracy
constable
constant
constellation
constitute
constitution
construct
construction
consul**
consult

consultant
consume
consummate
consump-
tion
contact**
contagious
contain
contaminate
contemn**
contemplate
contempo-
rary
contempt
contempti-
ble
contend**
content**
contest
conti-
nence**
continent
continual**
continually
continu-
ous**
contour
contracep-
tion
contracep-
tive
contract**
contractual
contralto
contraption
contrariwise
contrary
contrast
contretemps
contribute
contrive
control
controlled
controver-
sial
controversy
convalesce
convalescent

convec-
tion**
convenient
convent
convention
converge
conversa-
tion**
converse
convert**
convertible
convict
conviction**
convolute
convulse
cookery
cookie
cookie cut-
ter
cookie jar
cool
coolie**
coolly**
cooperate
coordination
copious
copper
copyright
copywriter
coral**
cord**
cordial
cordless
corduroy
core**
cored**
core dump
corespond-
ent**
coriander
cornea
corned beef
corner**
cornice
corny
corona
coronary
coroner**

166

corporal**
corporation
corporeal**
corps**
corpse**
corpuscle
corral**
corralled
correct
correctness
correlate
correlation
corre-
    spond**
correspon-
    dent**
corridor
corroborate
corrugated
corrupt
corsage
corset
cortisone**
cosmic
cosmonaut
cosmopoli-
    tan
Cossack
costume**
costumer**
cot**
côte**
cote**
cotillion
cottage
cotton
couch po-
    tato
cough**
could
couldn't
council**
councillor**
counsel**
counselor**
countdown
counte-
    nance**

counterfeit
countess
country
coup de
    grâce
coup d'état
coupé
couple
coupon
courage
course**
court**
courteous
courtesan**
courtesy**
courtmartial
cousin**
couture
covenant
cover
coverage
covert**
covet**
coward**
cowboy
cowered**
cowhide
coxcomb**
coyly
coyote
cozen**
cozy
crabby
crack
crackle
cradle
craft
crafty
cram
cranberry
crane
cranium
craps**
crawl
crayon
creak**

cream**
crease**
creation
creature
crèche
credence
credential
credible**
credit
creditable**
creditor
credulous
creek**
creep
crème**
crème de la
    crème
crepes**
crescendo
crescent
Cretan**
cretin**
crew
crews**
crick**
cricket
cried
criminal
crimson
cripple
critic**
critical
criticize
critique**
crochet**
crocodile
crone
croquet**
croquette**
cross-exam-
    ine
cross-
    purposes
cross-
    reference
crossroad
cross section

crotchet**
crouch
croup
croupier
crowd
crowned
CRT
crucial
crude
crudités**
crudity**
cruel
cruelly
cruelty
cruelty free
cruet
cruise**
cruiser
crumb
crusade
crusty
crutch
crypt
cryptic
cryptogra-
    pher
cryptology
crystallize
Cuba
cubic
cubicle
cubism
cuckoo
cudgel
cue**
cuff**
cuisine
cul de sac
culinary
culled**
cult**
cultivate
culture
cumin
cunning
cupboard
cupidity

curare
curettage
curfew
curiosity
curious
curly
currant**
currency
current**
curriculum
curry
cursed
cursor
curtain
curtsy**
curvaceous
curve
cusp
cuspy
custard
custody
custom**
customer**
cut**
cutting edge
cutup
CYA
cybercrud
cyberculture
cybernetics
cyberspace
cyborg
cybot
cyclamate
cycle
cyclone
cygnet**
cylinder
cymbal**
cynic
cynosure
cyst
cystitis
cystoscopy
cytoplasm
czar
Czech**

D
dabble
dachshund
dacron
Dada
daffodil
dagger
dahlia
daily**
daiquiri
dairy**
dais**
daisy-wheel
dally**
dam**
damage
damn**
dandelion
dandruff
dangerous
data
data base
date rape
daughter
dawdle
dawn
days**
daze**
dazzle
deacon**
dead**
deadline
deadlock
deaf
deal
dealt
dear**
dearth
death
debate
debauch**
debauchery
debonair
debouch**
debris
debt
debtor
debug

debut
decade
decease
deceased**
deceit
deceive
December
decency
decent**
deception
decibel
decided
deciduous
decimal
decipher
decision
declaration
decline
deco
décolleté
decomposed
decompres-
 sion
decon**
deconges-
 tant
deconstruct
decor
decorate
decrease
decree**
decryption
dedicate
deduce**
deductible
deed**
deer**
de facto
default
defeat
defecate
defendant
defense
defensible
defensive
defer**
deference
deferred

defiance
defibrillate
deficient
deficit
defied
definite**
definitely
definition
definitive**
deflate
deflation
defused**
defy
degree**
dehydrate
deign
deity
delay**
delegate
delete
deletion
deli
deliberate
delicacy
delicatessen
delicious
delight
delinquent
delivery
deluge
delusion
deluxe
delve
demagogue
demean
demeaning
demented
dementia
 praecox
demi-tasse
democracy
democrat
demography
demolish
demonstra-
 ble
demonstrate
demur**

demure**
denial
dense
dental
dental dam
dentifrice
dentine
dentist
deny
deodorant
departure
dependable
dependant**
depen-
  dence**
dependent**
depen-
  dents**
depilatory
deplete
depo-
  provera
deposit
depositary**
deposition**
deposi-
  tory**
depot
depraved
deprecate**
depreciate**
depreciation
depressant
depression
deprivation
deprive
deprived**
depths
deputy
derby
derelict
derivative
derive
derma
dermatitis
derogatory
derrick
descend

descend-
  ant**
descend-
  ent**
descent**
describe
description
desecrate**
desegregate
desensitize
desert**
desertion
desiccant
desiccate**
design
desirable
desktop
desolate**
despair
desperate
despicable
dessert**
destination
destroy
destruct
destruction
destructive
detached
detail
detect
detergent
deteriorate
determine
deterrent
detestable
detour
detox
detoxifica-
  tion
detract**
detritus
deuce
devastate
develop
deviant
deviate
deviation
device**

devil
devious
devise**
devoid
devotion
devour
dew**
dextrous
diabetes
diagnose
diagonal
diagram**
dial
dial-a-
  prayer
dialect
dialogue
diamond
diaper
dia-
  phragm**
diarrhea
diary**
diaspora
dice**
dicey
dichotomy
dictionary
didn't
die**
died**
diehard
diesel
diet**
dietary
dietitian
differ**
difference
differential
difficult
diffuse
diffused**
digest
digestible
digging
digital
digitalis
dignity

digress
digs
dilapidate
dilation**
dilemma
dilettante
diligent
dilute
dilution**
dimension
diminish
diminutive
dimwit
dine**
diner**
dinette
dinghy**
dingy**
dining
dinner**
dinosaur
diocese
dioxin
diphtheria
diploma
dire
direction
dirge
dirty
disability
disabled
disadvan-
  taged
disagree
disagree-
  ment
disallow
disappear
disappoint
disapproba-
  tion
disap-
  prove**
disarray
disaster
disastrous
disburse**

169

disbursement
disc
discard
discern
discharge
disciple
discipline
disclosure
disco
discomfit**
discomfort**
disconcert
disconsolate
discount
discourse
discourteous
discover
discreet**
discrepancy
discrete**
discretion
discretionary
discriminate
discus**
discuss**
discussion
disdain
disease
diseased**
disembowel
disguise
dish
disheveled
dishonest
dishwasher
disillusion
disinfect
disinflation
disinformation
disinter
disk
diskette
dismantle
dismiss

dismissal
dismount
Disney
disparage
dispensary
disperse**
displacement
display
disposable
disposal
disposition**
dispossess
disproportion
disprove**
dispute
disqualify
disreputable
disrespect
disrupt
diss
dissatisfy
dissect
disseminate
dissent**
dissident
dissimilar
dissipate
dissociate
dissolute**
dissolution
dissolve
dissonant
dissuade
distaff
distal**
distance
distasteful
distemper
distill**
distillation
distinct
distinguish
distract**
distraction

distraught
distress
distribute
district
disturb
ditto
diuretic
diva
divan
dive
diver
diverge
divers**
diverse**
diversity
divert
diverticulosis
divest
divestiture
divide
dividend
divine
division
divorce
divulge
Dixie
dizzy
do**
doable
doc**
docile
dock**
doctor
doctrinaire
docudrama
document
documentary
dodge
doe**
doer**
does**
dog
dogged
doggerel
doldrums

dole
dollar
dolphin
dome
domed
domestic
domicile
dominant
domineer
dominion
domino
don**
donate
done**
donkey
donor
don't
doom
door
dopamine
dork
dormant
dormitory
dosage
dose**
dossier
dot
double
double bind
double-blind
double-digit
double-dipper
doubt
douche
dough**
doughnut
dour**
dove
dovetail
Dow
dowager
dowdy
dower**
downer
downfall
downgrade

downpour	due**	**E**	eerie**
downside	duel**	eager	efface
downsize	due process	eagle	effect**
downstairs	dulcet	earache	effective**
downtime	dully**	eardrum	effeminate
downtown	duly**	earl	effervescent
downzoning	dumb	earlier	efficacious
dowry	dumbfound	early	efficiency
doze**	dummy	earn**	efficient
dozen	dump	earnest	effluent**
dozens	dumpy	earring	effort
draft**	dun**	earth	effrontery
dragon	dunce	earwax	eggplant
drainage	dune**	easement	ego
drama	dungaree	easily	egocentric
draught**	dungeon**	east	egression**
drawback	duo	Easter	Eiffel
drawn	duodenum	easy	eight**
dread	duplex	eau de co-	eighteen
dream	duplicate	logne	eighth
dreary	duplicity	eavesdrop	Eire**
dredge	durable	ebony	either**
dried	duration	ebullient	ejaculate
drier**	duress	eccentric**	eject
driftwood	during	ecclesiastical	elaborate
drive	dust-up	echo	elastic
drive-by	dusty	éclair	elation
drive-in	Dutch	eclampsia	elbow
driven	dutiful	eclectic	elder**
driveway	duty	eclipse	elect
drizzle	dwarf	ecology	election
droid	dweeb	economic	electorate
droll	DWEM	economical	electricity
droop	dybbuk	economy	electrocardi-
dropping	dye**	ecstasy	ogram
drowned	dyeing**	ecumenical	electron
drowse	dying**	eczema	electronic
drudgery	dynamic	edema	electronics
druggist	dynamite	edge**	elegance
drugstore	dyne**	edible**	elegant
drumstick	dysentery	edit	elegy**
drunkenness	dysfunction	edition**	element**
dryer**	dysfunc-	editor	elemen-
dual**	tional	editorial	tary**
dub	dyslexia	educable	elephant
dubious	dyspeptic	educate	elephantiasis
dudgeon**	dystrophy	eel	elevate
		e'er**	elevation

171

elevator	emigrant**	enervate**	entrée
eleven	eminence	enfold**	entrepreneur
elf	eminent**	enforce	entry
elicit**	emissary	enforceable	enunciate
eligible	emit**	engagement	enuresis
eliminate**	emollient**	engine	envelop**
elite	emolu-	engineer	envelope**
elitist	ment**	England	enviable
elixir	emotion	English	envious
ellipse	empathy	engrave	environment
ellipsis	emperor	enhance	envy
elliptical	emphasis	enhance-	enwrap**
elm	emphysema	ment	enzyme
el Niño	empire**	enjoyment	ephedrine
elocution**	employee	enlighten	epic**
eloquent	empower	enliven	epicine
elucidate	emptiness	en masse	epicure
elude**	empty	enmesh	epidemic
elusion**	enable**	enmity**	epidermis
elusive**	enamel	ennoble	epigraph**
elves	enamored	ennui	epilepsy
E-mail	encephalitis	enormous	episode
emanate	enchant	enough	epistle**
emascu-	enchilada	enquire	epitaph**
late**	encircle	enrage	epithet**
emascula-	enclosure	enrich	epoch**
tion	encode	enroll**	equable**
embalm	encompass	en route	equally
embark	encore	ensemble	equator
embarrassed	ensure**	ensign	equilibrium
embedded	encounter	ensure**	equinox
embellish	encourage	entail	equipped
embezzle	encroach	entangle	equitable**
embezzler	encrypt	enter**	equity
emblem	encryption	enterprise	equivalent
embolism	encyclopedia	entertain	era**
emboss	endear	enthrall	erase
embrace	endeavor	enthusiasm	ere**
embroider	endoge-	enthusiastic	erect**
embryo	nous**	entice	erection
emend**	endomorph	entire	ergo
emerald	endorsement	entitled**	ergonomics
emerge**	endow	entomol-	Erie**
emergency	endowment	ogy**	ERISA
emerging	endurance	entourage	ermine
emeritus	enema**	entrance	erode
emersed**	enemy**	entrap	erosion
emetic	energetic	entreat	erotic**

172

err**
errand**
errant**
erratic**
erroneous
error**
ersatz
eruct**
erudite
eruption**
erythromy-
cin
escalator
escape
escarole
escort
Eskimo
ESOP
esophagus
esoteric
especial**
espionage
espousal
espresso
esquire
essay**
essence
essential
establish
estate
esteem
esteemed
estimate
estimation
estrange-
ment
estray**
estrogen
et cetera
etch**
etching**
eternity
ether**
Ethernet
ethical
ethnocentric
ethnology**
ethology**

ethos
etiology
etiquette
etymology**
Eucharist
eugenics
eulogy**
eunuch**
eunuchs**
euphemism
euphoria
Eurasian
eureka
Eurocentric
Eurodollar
Europe
European
euthanasia
evacuate
evaluate
evaluation
evaporate
evening
event
eventual
eventually
every
everyone**
every one**
everything**
every
    thing**
everywhere
evict
eviction
evidence
evil
eviscerate
evocative
evoke
evolution
evolve
ewe**
ex
exact
exactly
exaggerate
exalt**

examination
example
exasperate
exceed**
excel**
excellent
except**
exception-
able**
excep-
tional**
excerpt
excess**
excessive
exchange
excise
excitable
excite
excitement
exciting**
exclude
exclusive
excoriate
excrete
excruciate
excursion
exec
execute
executive
exempt
exercise**
exert
exhale
exhaust
exhibit
exhilarate
exhort
exhume
exile
Eximbank
exist
existence
exists**
exit
exiting**
exits**
exodus
exomorph

exonerate
exorbitant
exorcise**
exotic
expansion
expansive**
ex parte
expedite
expedition
expel
expelled
expendable
expense
expensive**
experience
experiment
expert
expertise
expiation**
expiration**
expire
explanation
expletive
explicit
exploit
explore
export
expose**
exposé**
exposure
express
expressway
exquisite
extant**
extempora-
neous
extend
extension
extent**
exterminate
extermina-
tion
external
extinct
extirpate
extol
extoll
extort

extortion
extra
extract
extracurricular
extraordinary
extrapolate
extrasensory
extraterritorial
extravagant
extreme
extricate
extrovert
exult**
eye**
eyebrow
eyelash
eyesight
eyestrain
eyewitness
ezine

F
fable
fabric
fabricate
fabulous
façade
face
face-ism**
faceless
face-lift
face-off
faces**
facesaving
facet**
facetious
facial
facies**
facile
facilitate
facility**
facing
facsimile
fact

faction
factious
factor
factory
facts**
factual
faculty
fad
fade
faerie**
Fahrenheit
fail
faille
failsafe
failure
fain**
faint**
fair**
fairly
fairy**
faith
faker**
fakir**
falcon
fall
fallacious
fallacy
fallback
fallible
fallopian
    tube
false
falsehood
falsetto
falsies
falsify
falter
fame
familiar
familiarize
family
famine
famished
famous
fanatic
fanciful
fancy
fantasize

fantastic
fantasy**
FAQS**
far
farce
fare**
farfetched
farm
farmer
faro
farsighted
farther**
fascinate
fascism**
fascist
fashion
fashionable
fasten
fastidious
fatal**
fatality
fate**
fateful**
father**
fathom
fatigue
fatten
fatty
fatuous
faucet**
fault
faun**
faux pas
favorable
favorite
fawn**
fax**
fays**
faze**
fear
feasibility
feasible
feast**
feat**
feather
feature
February
feces**

federal
Federales
fedora
Fed, the
feebly
feed
feedback
feeder
feeling
feet**
feeze**
feign**
feint**
feisty
felicitate
felicity**
feline
fellow
felony
felt
female
feminine
feminism
femur
fence
fender
ferment**
ferocious
ferret
ferry**
fertile
fertilize
fervor
fest**
fester
festival
fetal**
fetch**
fete**
fetish**
fetter
fettle
fetus
feud
feudal
fever
few
fiancé**

fiasco	finger	flavor	fluctuate
fiberglass	fingerprint	flaw**	fluctuation
fiber-optic	fingertip	flea**	flue**
fibrillation	finite	fleabag	fluent
fibroid	fir**	fleche**	fluid
fibrous	firebug	flecks**	fluke
fickle	firefighter	fledgling	fluores-
fiction	firetrap	flee**	cence**
fictitious	firing	fleece	fluorescent
fiddle	firm	fleet	fluoride**
fidelity	first	flesh**	fluorine
fidget	first aid	flew**	fluoroscope
field	first-rate	flex**	flurry
fiend**	fiscal**	flexible	flute
fierce	fisher**	flextime	flutter
fiery	fishnet	flicker	flux
fiesta	fission	flicks**	fly
FIFO	fissure**	flies	foam
fifth	fitting	flight	fob
fight	fix	flimsy	focal
figurative	fixation	flinch**	focus
figure	fjord	flip	foe
figurehead	flabbergast	flippant	foggy**
file**	flabber-	flirt	fogy**
filet	gasted	flirtatious	foible
filial	flaccid	float	fold
filibuster	flagellation	flock**	foliage
filigree	flagging	floe**	folio
filing**	flagrant**	flog**	folk
Filipino	flagship	flood	folks
filling**	flail	floor**	follicle
film	flair**	floppy	follow
filter	flake	flores-	folly
filthy	flaky	cence**	foment**
finagle	flambé	florid**	fond**
final	flamboyant	Florida	fondle
finale**	flame	florist	fondling**
finalize	flamenco	flounce	fondue
finally**	flammable	flounder	font**
finance**	flap	flour**	football
financial	flapper	flourish	footloose
finch**	flare**	flout**	for**
find**	flatfoot	flow**	forbid
fined**	flatten	flowchart	force
finely**	flatter	flower**	forceful
fineness**	flattery	flown	forceps
finesse**	flatulent	flu**	forcible
finest**	flaunt**	flub	ford

175

fore**
forecast
forecastle
foreclose
foreclosure
forego**
foregone
forehead
foreign
foreman
foremost
forensic
foreperson
foresee
foresight
foreskin
forest
forestall
forever
foreword**
forfeit
forge
forgery
forget
forgive
forgo**
fork
forklift
form**
formal
formalde-
  hyde
formalism
formally**
format
former
formerly**
formica-
  tion**
formidable
formula
fornica-
  tion**
forsake
forsythia
fort**
forte**
forth**

forthright
forties
fortitude
fortuitous
fortunately
fortune
forty
forum**
forward**
fossil
foster
fought
foul**
found**
foundation
foundling**
fount**
fountain
four**
fourteen
fourth**
fowl**
fox
foxy
fracas
fractions**
fractious**
fracture
fragile
fragment
fragrance
fragrant**
frail
frame
frame-up
framework
franc**
franchise
frank**
frankfurter
fraternal
fraud
fraudulent
fraught
frays**
freak**
freckle
Freddie Mac

free agent
freebie
freedom
freelance
freeload
frees**
freeway
freeze**
freeze-dry
freight
frenetic
frenzy
frequency
freshen
Freud
Freudian
friar**
fricassee
friction
Friday
friend**
friendship
frieze**
fright
frill
fringe
fritter
frivolous
frock
frolic
frontal
front-end
frontiersman
frontispiece
frown
frozen
frugal
fruitful
frustrate
fryer**
fuchsia
fudge
fugitive
fugue
fulfill
fulfillment
fullback
full-time

fumble
fume
function
functional
fundamental
fundamental-
  ist
funeral**
funereal**
fungus
funnel
funny
fur**
furious
furlough
furnish
furniture
furor
furry**
further**
furthermore
fury**
fuselage
fuss**
futile
future
fuzz**

G

GAAP**
gabardine
gabble**
gable**
gadfly
gadget
Gaelic
gaff**
gaffe**
gage**
gaggle**
gait**
galaxy
gale
gall
gallant
gallbladder
galleon**

gallery
galley
gallon**
gallop
gallows
gallstone**
galvanize
gamble**
gambol**
game
gamete**
gamin**
gamma
gamma glob-
  ulin
gammon**
gamut**
gamy
gander
gangrene
gantlet**
gap**
garage
garbage
garden
gardener
gargle**
garish
garlic
garnishee
garret
garrulous
garter
gas
gaseous
gasket
gasoline
gastritis
gat**
gate**
gatekeeper
GATT**
gauche**
gaudy
gauge**
gaunt**
gauntlet**
gauss

gauze**
gavel
gawk
gays**
gaze**
gazelle
gazette
gear
geezer
gefilte fish
Geiger
  counter
geisha
gel**
gelatine
gelding
gellato
gem
gendarme
gender
genealogy
generally
generate
generation
generator
generic
generous
genes**
genesis
genetic
genial
genital**
genitalia
genius**
geniuses
genocide
genotype
genre
genteel**
gentile**
gentle**
gentleman
gently
genuflect
genuine
genus**
geodesic
geography

geology
geometry
geriatrics
German**
germane**
germicide
gerontology
gerrymander
gerund
gestalt
gestation
gesture**
gesundheit
get**
getaway
geyser
ghastly
ghat**
ghetto
ghost
ghoul**
giant
gibe**
giddy
gig
gigabit
gigabyte
gigahertz
gigantic
gigantism
giggle
GIGO
gigolo
gild**
gilt**
gimmick
gin**
ginger
gingham
gingiva
gingivitis
Ginnie Mae
Ginny Maes
giraffe
gird
girder
girdle
girl

girlfriend
girlie
giveaway
giveback
gizmo
glacial
glacier**
glamorous
glamour
glance
glare
glass ceiling
glaucoma
glaze
glazier**
gleam
glider
glimmer
glimpse
glitch**
glitter
glitterati**
glitz**
global
gloom**
glorify
glossary
glossies
glossy
glottis
glucose
glue
glume**
gluten**
glutenous**
glutinous**
glutton**
glutton-
  ous**
glycerin
gnarled
gnash
gnat
gnaw
gneiss
gnocci
gnome

177

gnosis
gnu**
goad
goal**
goat
goatee
gobble**
goblet
gocart
goddess
godless
gofer**
goggles
go-go
goiter
goldbrick
golden parachute
goldstone**
golf**
gonad
gondola
gone
gonorrhea
goodlooking
goodwill
goof
goofy
goose
gopher**
gore
gorge
gorgeous
gorilla**
gospel
gossamer
gossip
gotten
gouache**
gouge
goulash
gourd
gourmet
government
governor
gown
grab

grabber
graceful
gracious
grade
gradual
graduate
graduation
graffiti
grain
gram
grammar
Grammy
granddaughter
grandeur
grandfather
grand mal
grandmother
granny
grantsmanship
granule
grapefruit
graph
graphic
graphics
graphology
grasp
grate**
grateful
gratis
gratitude
gratuitous
gratuity
grave
gravel
gravity
grease**
great**
Greece**
greedy
green
greenhouse
greenmail
greet
greeting

gregarious
gremlin
grenade
greyhound
gridiron
gridlock
grief
grievance
grieve
grievous
grill**
grille**
grimace
grime
grin
grind
gringo
grip**
gripe**
grippe**
grisly**
grist
gristle**
gristly**
grit
grits
grizzle**
grizzly**
groan**
grocery
groin
groom
groove**
groovy
grope
gross
grotesque
grouch
ground
groundwork
group
groupie
grove**
grovel
grown**
grown-up
growth

grudge
gruesome
grumpy
grunge
G-string
guacamole
guarantee**
guaranty**
guard
guardian
guerrilla**
guess
guessed**
guest**
guidance
guide
guild**
guile
guileless
guillotine
guilt**
guilty
guinea
guise
guitar
gulag
gulf**
gullible
gunner
gurgle
gurney**
guru
gusto
Gutenberg
guts
gutter
guttural
gymnasium
gymnast
gymnastics
gynecology
gynophobia
gyp
gypsum
gypsy
gyrate
gyroscope

H

habeas corpus
habilitate
habit
habitant**
habitat**
habitual
habituate
hacienda
hack
hacker
hackneyed
haddock
haggard
haggle
hail**
Hail Mary
hair**
haircut**
hairdo
hairdresser
hairy
Haiti
halcyon
hale**
half
halfway
halitosis
hall**
hallelujah
hallmark
hallow**
Halloween
hallucinate
hallucination
hallucinogen
halo**
halve**
halves
hamburger
hamlet
hammer
hammer toe
hamstring
handbag
handbook

handcuffs
handful
handicap
handicraft
handiwork
handkerchief
handle
handmade**
handmaid**
hand-me-down
handsome**
handwriting
hangar**
hanger**
hangover
hang-up**
hang up**
hansom**
Hanukah
happen
happily
harangue
harass
harassment
harbor
hardboiled
hard disk
hardening
hardly**
hardship
hardware
hardy**
hare**
harebrained
Hare Krishna
harelip
harem
haricot**
harlequin
harmless
harmonic
harmonica
harmonious
harness
harp**

harpy**
harridan
harried
harsh
hart**
harvest
has-been
hashish
Hasidim
hassle**
hasten
hatch
hatched**
hatchet**
hate
hateful**
hatful**
hatred
haughty
haul**
haunch**
haunt
haute couture
hauteur**
have**
haven**
havoc
Hawaii
hay**
hazard
hazel
hazy
head**
headache
headdress
headhunter
headlight
headline
head-on
headquarters
heady
heal**
healer
health
heap
hear**

heard**
hearing**
hearsay
hearse
heart**
hearth
heartily**
hearty**
heat
heathen
heatstroke
heaume**
heave
heaven**
heavy
heavyweight
Hebrew
heckle
hectic
he'd**
hedge
hedonist
heed**
heel**
hegemony
heifer
height
Heimlich maneuver
heinous**
heir**
heir apparent
heiress
heirloom
heist
helicopter
hell**
he'll**
heller**
hellion
hellish
hello
helm
helmet
helpful
helpless
hem

179

hematoma
hemisphere
hemoglobin
hemophilia
hemorrhage
hemorrhoids
hence**
henceforth
henna
heparin
hepatitis
herald
herb
herbaceous
herd**
here**
hereafter
hereby
hereditary
heredity
hereon
heresy
heretofore
heritage
hermaphro-
    dite
hermitage
hernia
hero
heroes
heroic
heroin**
heroine**
heroism
herpes
herring**
hers
hesitate
heteroge-
    neous
heterosexual
heuristics
hew**
hexagon
hey!**
hi**
hiatus
hibernate

hiccough
hiccup
hickory
hidden
hideous
hie**
hierarchical
    file
hierarchy
hieroglyphic
high
highball
highbrow
high density
higher**
higher-up
high fidelity
high fre-
    quency
high-handed
high-level
highness
high resolu-
    tion
high-rise
high school
high-strung
high-tech
highway
hijack
hilarious
him**
himself
hindrance
hindsight
Hindu
hinge
hiphop
Hippocratic
    oath
hippopota-
    mus
hippy
hire**
hireling
hirsute
Hispanic
histamine

history
hitch
HIV
HMO
ho**
hoard**
hoarse**
hoary**
hoax
hobble
hobby**
Hobson's
    choice
hockey**
hodgepodge
hoe**
hoes**
hoi polloi
hoist**
holdings
holdout
hold-up
hole**
holed up**
holey**
holiday**
holiness
holistic
hollandaise
holler**
hollow**
holocaust
hologram
holography
holy**
holy day**
homage
home**
homeboy
homeless
homely
homemaker
homesick
homestead
homework
homicide
homogene-
    ous**

homoge-
    nous**
homonym
homophobia
homosexual
honcho
honest
honey
honeydew
honeymoon
honk**
honor
honorable
honorary
hood
hoof
hook
hookworm
hooky**
hoop**
hoot
hope
hopeful
hopeless
hoping
horde**
horizon
horizontal
hormone
hornet
horny
horoscope
horrendous
horrible
horrified
horror
hors
    d'oeuvres
horse**
horsepower
horseshoe
horsy
horticulture
hose**
hosiery
hospice
hospitable**
hospital**

hospitality
host**
hostage
hostel**
hostile**
hotbed
hotdog
hotel
hotelier
hotheaded
hothouse
hound
hour**
hourglass
hour hand
house-
  breaker
household
housekeeper
houses
housewife
housing
hovel
hover
however
howl
hub
hubbub
hubby**
hubcap
hubris
huckleberry
huckster
HUD
huddle
hue**
huge
human**
humane**
humanitar-
  ian
humanities
humanity
humble**
humerus**
humid
humidifier
humiliate

humility
humming
humongous
humor
humorous**
hump
hunch**
hundred
Hungary**
hunger
hungry**
hunk**
hunter**
hunting
hurdle**
hurl
hurray
hurricane
hurry
hurt
hurtle**
husband
hussy
hustle**
hustler
hybrid
hydrangea
hydrant
hydraulic
hydrochloric
  acid
hydrofoil
hydrogen
hydro-
  phobia
hyena
hygiene
hymen
hymn**
hymnal
hyper
hyperactive
hyperbole
hypercriti-
  cal**
hypersensi-
  tive
hypertension

hypertext
hyperther-
  mia
hyphen
hypnosis
hypnotist
hypocrisy
hypocrite
hypocriti-
  cal**
hypodermic
hypoglyce-
  mia
hypotenuse
hypothesis
hypothetical
hysterec-
  tomy
hysteria
hysterical

I
I**
iatrogenic
ibuprofen
iceberg
ichthyology
icing
icon
iconoclast
icy
id
idea
ideal
identical
identify
ideology
idiom
idiosyncrasy
idiot
idle**
idol**
idolater
idyll**
idyllic
iffy
ignite

ignition
ignominious
ignominy
ignorant
ignore
iguana
ikon
ileitis
Iliad
I'll**
illegal
illegible**
illegitimate
illicit**
Illinois
illiterate
illness
illogical
illtempered
illude**
illuminate**
illusion**
illusive**
illustrate
illustrious
image
imagery
imagination
imagine
imbalance
imbecile
imbibe
imbroglio
imbrue**
imbue**
imitation
immaculate
immanent**
immaterial
immature
immeasura-
  ble
immediate
immediately
immemora-
  ble
immense
immensely

immerge**
immerse
immersed**
immigrant**
immigration
imminent**
immit**
immobile
immodest
immolate
immoral**
immortal
immune
immunity**
impact
impair
impale
impartial
impassa-
ble**
impasse
impassible**
impassioned
impatient
impeach
impeccable
impecunious
impede
impediment
impel
impenetra-
ble
impenitent
imperative
impercepti-
ble
imperfect
imperial
imperialism
impersonal
impersonate
impertinent
imperturb-
able
impetigo
impetus
impiety
impinge

impious
implacable
implant
implausible
implement
implicit
implore
imply
impolite
import
importance
imposition
impossibility
impossible**
impostor**
imposture**
impotence
impotent
impractical
impregnable
impregnate
impresario
impress
impression
impression-
ism
imprinting
imprison
improbable
impromptu
improper
impropriety
improve-
ment
improvident
improvise
imprudent**
impudent**
impugn
impulse
impulsive
impunity**
impurity
impute**
in**
inability
in absentia
inaccessible

inaccurate
inadequate
inadmissible
inadvertent
inalienable
inane**
inappropri-
ate
inapt**
inarticulate
inasmuch as
inaudible
inaugurate
inauspicious
incalculable
incandescent
incapable
incapacitate
incarcerate
incarnate
incendiary
incense
incentive
incessant
incest**
incidence**
incident
incidentally
incidents**
incinerator
incipient**
incise
incision
incisive
incisor
incite**
inclement
inclination
incline
inclined
include
inclusive
incognito
incoherent
income
incom-
municado

incompara-
ble
incompati-
ble
incompetent
incompre-
hensible
inconceiv-
able
inconclusive
incongruous
inconsolable
inconspicu-
ous
incontinent
inconvenient
incorporate
incorrigible
incorrupt-
ible
increase
incredible
incredulous
increment
incriminate
incriminator
incubator
incumbent
incurable
incurred
incurring
indebted
indecent
indecisive
indefensible
indelible
indemnity
indent
indenture
independent
indescrib-
able
index
Indian
indicative
indict**
indictment
indifferent

indige-
nous**
indigent
indigestible
indigestion
indignant
indigo
indiscreet**
indiscrete**
indiscrimi-
nate
indispens-
able
indisposed
indistin-
guishable
indite**
individually
indivisible**
indoctrinate
indolent
indomitable
indoors
induce
inducement
induction
inductive
indulge
industrial
industry
inebriate
inedible
ineffable
ineffective
inefficient
ineligible**
inept**
inequality
inequity**
inert
inertia
inescapable
inevitable
inexcusable
inexorable
inexpensive
inex-
perienced

inexplicable
infallible
infamous
infancy
infant
infantile
infantry
infarction
infect**
infection
infectious
infer
inference
inferior
inferiority
infertility
infest**
infidel
infidelity
infiltrate
infinite
infinitely
infinitive
infinity
infirm
infirmary**
infirmity**
inflammable
inflamma-
tion
inflate
inflation
inflection
inflexible
influence
influenza
influx
infomercial
informal
informant
information
informercial
infraction
infrared
infrastruc-
ture
infrequent

infringe
infuriate
infuse
infusion
ingenious**
ingenuous**
ingestion
ingrate
ingratiate
ingredient
inhabit
inhabitant
inhale
inherit
inhibition
inhospitable
inhuman
iniquity**
initial
initialize
initiate
initiation
initiative
inject
injection
injunction
injury
injustice
in-law
inlay
inn**
innate
ineffective
inner
innervate**
innocence
innocuous
innovate
innuendo
innuendoes
innumerable
inoculate
inordinate
input**
inquest
inquire
inquiry

inquisitive
in rem
insane**
insanity
inscription
inscrutable
insect
insecticide
insects**
insecure
inseminate
inseparable
insert**
insertion
inset**
inside
insidious
insight**
insignia
insignificant
insincere
insipid
insipient**
insist
insistent
insists**
insolate**
insolent
insoluble
insolvent
insomnia
inspection
inspiration
instability
installa-
tion**
installment
instance
instan-
taneous
instead
instigate
instill
instilla-
tion**
instinct
institute
institution

institutional-
ization
instruct
instruction
instrument
insubordi-
nate
insufferable
insulate**
insulin
insult
insurance**
insure**
insurgent
intangible
integral
integrate
integration
integrity
integument
intellectual
intelligence
intemperate
intense**
intensify
intention
intents**
inter**
interactive
intercede
intercept
interces-
sion**
intercom
intercourse
interdepen-
dent
interdict
interdiscipli-
nary
interest
interesting
interface
interfere
interference
interferon
interior**

interjec-
tion**
interlude
intermarry
intermediary
intermediate
interment**
intern**
internal
international
Internet
intern-
ment**
interpel-
late**
interper-
sonal
interpo-
late**
interpret
interracial
interrogate
interrupt
intersect
interses-
sion**
interstate**
interval
intervene
intervention
interview
intestate**
intestine
intimacy
intimate**
intimidate**
intolerance
intolerant
intoxicate
intractable
intramural
intransigent
intrastate**
intrauterine
intravenous
intricacy

intrigue
intrinsic
introduce
introjec-
tion**
introspec-
tion
introvert
intrude
intruder
intrusion
intuition
inturn**
Inuit
invade
invalid
invaluable
invariably
invasion
invective
inveigh
inveigle
inventor
inventory
invertebrate
invest**
investigate
investigation
investment
inveterate
invidious
invigorate
invisible**
invitation
in vitro
invoice
invoke
involuntary
involve
invulnerable
inward
iodine
ion**
ipecac
IRA**
irascible
ire**

iridescence
iridescent
iris
irk
iron**
irony
irradiation
irrational
irreconcila-
ble
irredeemable
irredentist
irrefutable
irregular
irrelevance
irrelevant**
irresistible
irresponsible
irreverent**
irrevocable
irrigate
irritable
irruption**
Islam
island
isle**
isolate
isometric
isotope
Israel
issuance
issue
isthmus
Italian
Italy
itch
itching**
item
itemize
itinerary
its**
it's**
IUD
IV**
I've**
ivory
ivy**

J

jab**
jack
jackal
jackass
jacket
jackknife
jackpot
jacuzzi
jade
jag
jagged
jaguar
jail
jailbreak
jalopy
jam**
Jamaica
jamb**
jambalaya
jamboree
jangle
janitor
January
Japanese
jargon
jasmine
jaundice
jaunt**
java
javelin
jaws
Jaycee
jaywalk
jazz
jazzy
jealous**
jeans**
jeep
jeer
Jeffersonian
jejune**
jejunum**
Jekyll and
  Hyde
jell**
jellies
jelly

jeopardy
jeremiad
jerk
jersey
Jerusalem
jester**
Jesuit
jet
jet lag
jetsam
jet set
jettison
jetty
jewel**
jewels
jewelry
jewels
Jewish
Jewry**
Jews**
jib**
jibe**
jiffy
jiffybag
jig
jigger
jiggle
jigsaw
jihad
jimmy
jingle
jingo
jinks**
jinn**
jinx**
jitney
jitters
jive
job**
jobber
jockey
jockstrap
jocular
jocund
jodphurs
jog**
joggle**
joi de vivre

join
joinder
joint
joist
joke
joker
jolly
jolt
jostle
jotting
joule**
jounce
journal
journalist
journey**
joust**
jovial
jowl**
joyful
joyous
joyride
jubilant
jubilee
Judaica
Judaism
Judas
judge
judgment
judicial
judiciary
judo
jug**
juggernaut
juggle**
juggler**
jugular**
juice**
juicy
jujitsu
juju
jukebox
julep
July
jumble
jump
junction
juncture
June

jungle
junior
junk
junk bond
junket
junkie
junky
junta**
jurisdiction
jurist
jury**
just**
justice
justify
jut**
jute**
juvenile
juxtapose

K

Kaddish**
kaffee-
  klatsch
Kafkaesque
kale
kaleidoscope
kamikazi
kangaroo
kapok
Kaposi's sar-
  coma
kaput
karate
karma
kayak
kayo
kazoo
kebob
keel
keen
keep
keeper
keg
kelp
ken**
Kennedy
kennel

185

Keogh plan	kindly	knot**	lair**
kept	kindness	knotted	laissez-faire
kerchief	kindred	know**	lam**
kernel**	kinescope	knowable**	lama**
kerosene	kinesics**	knowledge	lamb**
ketch**	kinetic	knows**	lambaste
ketchup	kinetics**	knuckle	lambskin
ketone	kingdom	K.O.	lame**
ketosis	kingpin	Koel**	lamé**
kettle	kiosk	kohl**	lame duck
kewpie	kipper	kola**	lamentable
key**	kirsch	kosher	lamentation
keyboard	kissed	kris**	laminate
Keynesian	kit**	kummel	LAN
keynote	kitchen	kwashiorkor	lance
keypunch	kite**		lanced**
keystone	kith**		lancet**
khaki	kitten	**L**	landlady
kibble	kiwi	lab	landlocked
kibbutz**	Klan**	label	landlord
kibitz**	kleenex	labor	landmark
kibitzer	kleptomania	laboratory	landscape
kibosh	kludge	labyrinth	lane**
kickback	klutzy	lace	language**
kickoff	knack	lacerate	languish**
kid**	knapsack	laceration	languor
Kiddush**	knave**	lachrymose	lanolin
kidnap	knead**	lackadaisical	lantern
kidney	knee	lackey	laparoscope
kielbasa	kneecap	laconic	lapel
kill**	kneed**	lacquer	lapse
killed**	kneel**	lactation	larceny
killer	knell**	lactose	large
killjoy	knew**	lacuna	largesse
kiln**	knickknack	ladder	larva**
kilo	knife	lade**	laryngitis
kilobaud	knight**	ladies	larynx
kilobyte	knight er-	Ladino**	lascivious
kilocycle	rant	ladle	laser**
kilogram	knish	laetrile	lass**
kilohertz	knit**	lag	lassitude
kilometer	knitting	lager**	lasso
kilowatt	knives	laggard	last**
kilt**	knob**	lagging	latch
kimono	knock**	lagniappe	latchkey kid
kin**	knock-knee	lagoon	late
kindergarten	knockoffs	laid**	lately
kindle	knoll	lain**	latent

186

later**	leakage	lese majesty	liege
lateral	lean**	lesion	lien**
latest	leaped	lessee**	lieu
latex	learn	lessen**	lieutenant
lath**	lease	lesser**	lifeboat
lathe**	leased**	lesson**	lifeguard
Latin	least**	lessor**	lifetime
Latina**	leather	lest**	liftoff
Latino**	leave**	lethal	ligament
latitude	leaven	lethargy	ligature
latter**	leaves	let's	light
latticework	lechery	letter**	lightening**
laud**	lecithin	lettered	lighter**
laudable	lecture	letterhead	lighthearted
laudanum	led**	lettuce	lightning**
laughable	ledger	letup	light pen
laughter	lee**	leukemia	lightweight
launch	leech**	levee**	likely
launder	leek**	level	liken**
laundry	left	leveler	likeness
laurel	left-handed	lever	likewise
lava**	leftovers	leverage	lilac
lavaliere	legacy	levitation	lily
lavatory	legal	levy**	limb**
lavender	legalize	lewd	limber
lavish	legend	lexicon	limbic
law**	legerdemain	liability	limbo
lawn**	legible	liable**	lime**
laws**	legion	liaison	limelight
lawsuit	legionnaires'	liar**	limit
lawyer	disease	libel**	limn**
lax	legislature	liberal	limousine
laxative	legitimate	liberalism	limps
lay**	lei**	libertarian	linage**
layaway	leisure	liberty	linchpin
layer**	leisurely	libidinous	Lincoln
layoff	leitmotiv	libido	lineage**
lazar**	lemon	libido**	lineal**
laziness	lemonade	LIBOR	lineament**
l'chaim	length	library	linear**
L-dopa	lenient	libretto	lineman
lea**	lens	license	linen
leach**	lent	licentious	lineup
lead**	lentil**	lichen**	linger
leader	leopard	lickerish**	lingerie
leaf**	leprechaun	licorice**	linguine
league	leprosy	lie**	linguist
leak**	lesbian	lief**	liniment**

187

linkage	loathsome	loot**	lumpectomy
linked	lobby	loquacious	lunacy
links**	lobe	lord**	lunar
linoleum	lobotomy	lore**	lunatic
lint	lobster	lorgnette	luncheon
lintel**	lobster shift	lose**	luncheonette
lion	local**	loser	lung
lipstick	locale**	loss**	lupus
lip-sync	localize	lost**	lurch
liquefy	locate	lotion	lure
liqueur**	location	lottery	lurk
liquid	loch**	lotto	luscious
liquidate	lock**	loud	luster
liquor**	locket	loudspeaker	lustrous
lissome	lockjaw	lounge	lute**
list	lockout	loupe**	luxuriance**
listen	locks**	lousy	luxuriant**
litany	locomotive	lout	luxurious**
liter**	locus**	louver	luxury
literacy	locust**	Louvre	lydocaine
literal	lode**	lovable	lye**
literary	lodge**	love	lying
literati**	loft	lovely	Lyme**
literature	lofty	loving	Lyme dis-
lithium	logarithm	low**	ease
litigious	loge**	lowball	lymph
litmus	logger**	lowbrow	lymphoma
litter**	logic	low-cal	lynx**
litterbug	logo	lox**	lyre**
little	log-off	loyal	lyric
liturgical	log-on	lozenge	lysergic acid
lived**	loiter	luau	
livedo**	loload	lubricate	**M**
livelihood	lone**	lucid	
lively	loneliness	luck	macabre
livery	lonely	lucrative	macadam
lives	lonesome	lucre	macaroni
livestock	longevity	ludicrous	macaroon
livid**	longhand	lues**	mace
lizard	longitude	luftmensch	machete
llama**	long-winded	luge	Machiavel-
lo!**	loofah	luggage	lian
load**	lookism	lukewarm	machinery
loafer	lookout	lullaby	machismo
loan**	loony	lulu	macho
loanshark	loop**	lumbar**	mackerel
loath**	loophole	lumber**	mackintosh
loathe**	loose**	luminescent	macro

macrobiotic
mad
madame
made**
mademoiselle
Madonna
madras
maelstrom
maestro
Mafia
magazine
maggot
magic
magistrate
magma**
magna**
magnanimous
magnate**
magnesium
magnificence
magnitude
maharajah
mahogany
maid**
maidenly
mail**
mailbox
mailman
maim
main**
mainframe
mainland
mainstream
maintain
maintenance
maitre d'
maize**
majesty
major
majority
makeup
making
maladjusted
malady
malaise

malaprop-ism
malaria
Malay**
male**
malediction
malfeasance
malforma-tion
malice
malicious
malign
malignant
malinger
malleable
malnutrition
malocclu-sion
malpractice
malt**
mambo
mammal
mammary
mammo-gram
mammoth
manacle
manageable
manager
mañana
mandatory
mandible
mane**
maneuver
manganese
mange
manger
mangle
mania
maniac
manic de-pressive
manicotti
manicure
manifesto
manifold
manipula-tive

mankind
manned
mannequin
manner**
manor**
mansion
mantel**
mantelpiece
mantle**
manual
manufacture
manure
manuscript
many
maple
maraschino
marathon
marauder
marble
marc**
Mardi Gras
margarine
margin
marijuana
marine
marital**
maritime
mark**
markdown
market
markup
marmalade
maroon
marquis
marquise
Marrano
marriage**
marriage-able
married
marrow
marry**
marsala
marshal**
martial**
martini
martyr
marvelous

Marxism
Mary**
Maryland
mascara
mascle**
masculine
masochism
masochist
mason**
masonry
masquerade
Massachu-setts
massacre
massage
massed**
masseur
masseuse
massif**
massive**
mast**
mastectomy
master
mastermind
masterpiece
masticate
mastica-tion**
mastoid
masturbate
masturba-tion**
material
maternal
maternity
mathematics
matinée
matriarch
matriculate
matrimony
matrix
matronly
matter
mattress
maturation
mature
matza
matzoh

maudlin	megabyte	meringue	microorgan-
mausoleum	megaloma-	merit	ism
maven	nia	meritocracy	microphone
maverick	megillah	merrily	microproces-
maxi	melancholy	merry**	sor
maximum	mélange	mesa	microscope
maybe**	melanin	mescaline	microsur-
may be**	melanoma	mesmerize	gery
mayonnaise	melée**	meson**	microwave
mayor	mellow	messenger	midday
maze**	melodious	messing	middle
mazeltov	melodrama	messy	midnight
mazuma	melon	metabolism	midst**
mea culpa	meltdown	metal**	midterm
meadow	member	metallic	midwife
meager	membrane	metamor-	mien**
mean**	memento	phosis	might**
meanness	memoir	metaphor	mighty**
meant	memorable	metaphysics	migraine
measles	memoran-	metastasis	migrate
measure	dum	meteor**	mike
meat**	memorial	meteoro-	mil**
meat market	memory	logy**	mile**
mecca	menace	meth	mileage
Mecca	ménage à	methadone	milieu
mechanic	trois	methamphet-	military
mechanize	menagerie	amine	militate**
meclizine	menial	method	militia
medal**	meningitis	Methodist	mill**
medallion	menopause	meticulous	millenary**
meddle**	menorah	métier**	millennium
meddler**	Mensa**	metric	milligram**
media	mensch	metro	millimeter
mediate	menses**	metrology**	millinery**
mediation	menstruate	metropoli-	millionaire
Medicaid	menstrua-	tan	mime**
Medicare	tion	mettle**	mimosa
medicine	mental	mews**	mince**
medieval	mention	Mexican	mind**
mediocre	menu	Mexico	mine**
mediocrity	mercenary	mezzanine	mined**
meditate	merchandise	miasma	miner**
Mediterra-	merchant	Michigan	mineral
nean	mercury	micro	mingle
medium	mercy	microbi-	mini
medlar**	merely	ology	miniature
medley	merge	microchip	minicom-
meet**	merger	microfilm	puter

minimize
minimum
minion**
miniseries
minister
minks**
Minnesota
minor**
minority
minoxidil
mints**
minus
minuscule
minute
minutia
minx**
minyan**
miracle
mirage**
Mirandize
mirror
mirth
misanthrope
misappropri-
ate
miscarriage
miscast
miscella-
neous
mischief
mischievous
misconcep-
tion
misconduct
misde-
meanor
miser
miserable
misery
misfit
misfortune
misgiving
mishap
mislaid
misogyny
Miss**
missal**
missed**

misses**
missile**
missing
mission
missionary
Mississippi
Missouri
misspell
misstate
misstep
missus**
mist**
mistake
mister
mistress
mistrial
misunder-
stand
mite**
mitigate**
mitomycin
C
mitosis
mitten
mixture
mnemonic
moan
moat**
mob
mobbed
mobile
mobilize
moccasin
mocha
mockery
mockup
modal**
modality
mode**
model**
modem
moderate
modern
modernism
modest
modifier
modulate

modus ope-
randi
mogul
moisture
molar
molasses
mole
molecule
molestation
mollify
molt**
momentous
momentum
mommy
track
monarch
monastery
Monday
monetary
money
monitor
monk
monkey
mono-
chrome
monogamist
monolith
monologue
monopoly
monorail
monotone
monotonous
monsieur
monster
monstrous
montage
month
monument
moor**
Moor**
moose**
moot**
mope
moral**
morale**
morality
morass
morays**

morbid
morbidity
more**
moreover
mores**
morgue
moribund
Mormon
morn**
morning**
Morocco
moron
morphine
morsel
mortal**
mortality
mortally
mortar
mortgage
mortify
mortuary
mosaic
mosh
mosque
mosquito
mossy
most
mote**
mother**
motif**
motion
motivate
motive**
motor
motorcycle
mottled
motto
mountain
mourn**
mournful
mourning**
mouse**
mousse**
mouthpiece
mouthwash
mouton**
movement
movie

mowed** | muscular | naïveté | nectarine
moxie | dystrophy | naked | née**
mozzarella | muse** | nameless | need**
Mrs.** | museum | nanny | needle
Ms** | mushroom | nanosecond | needy
mss.** | music | naphtha | nefarious
mucilage | musical** | naphtha** | negate
mucous | musicale** | narcissist | negative
mucus | Muslim** | narcissistic | neglect
mudder** | muslin** | narcolepsy | negligee
muddy | mussel** | narcotics | negligence
muff | mustache | narration | negotiate
muffin | mustard** | narrative | Negro
mug | muster | narrow | Negroes
mugger | mustered** | narrowband | neigh**
Muhamma- | mustn't | narrow- | neighbor
dan | mutant | minded | neighbor-
mulatto | mutation | nasal | hood
mulish | mute** | nascent | neither**
mullah | mutiny | NASDAQ | nemesis
mul- | mutton** | nastiness | neo
ligatawny | mutual | nasturtium | neologism
multicul- | muumuu | national | neonatal
tural | muzzle | native | nephew
multimedia | myasthenia | nativity | nephritis
multimillion- | gravis | natty | nepotism
aire | myelo- | naturally | nerd
multina- | gram** | nature | nerve
tional | myeloma | naturopathy | nervous
multiple scle- | myopia | naught** | nestle
rosis | myopic | naughty** | nether**
multiplex | myrtle | nausea | network
multiplier | mysterious | nauseous | neural
multiply | mystery | naval** | neuralgia
multitasking | mystic | nave** | neuritis
multitude | mysticism | navel** | neurologist
mumble | mystify | navigable | neuron
mundane | myth | navy | neurosis
muni | mythical | nay** | neurotic
municipal | | né** | neuter
mural | | Neanderthal | neutral
murder | **N** | nearsighted | neutralize
murderer | nab | neat | neutron
murky | nadir | nebulous | new**
murmur | NAFTA** | necessary | news**
Murphy's | nagged | necessity | newscaster
Law | nail | necrology | newspaper
muscle** | naïve | necromancy | newspeak

newt
next
nexus
Niagara
nibble**
nice
nicely
niche**
nick**
nickel
nickname
nicotine
niece
Nielsen's
night**
nightclub
nightfall
nightmare
nihilism
nil
nimble
nimbly**
NIMBY**
nineteen
ninety
ninth
nipple
nirvana
nit**
nitrogen
no**
nob**
Nobel**
noble**
noblesse
  oblige
nock**
nocturn**
nocturnal
nocturne**
nod**
node**
nodule**
noes**
no-fault
no-frills
no-hitter
noise

no-knock
noload
nomad
nom de
  plume
nominal
nominate
nonchalant
noncom
nondeduct-
  ible
none**
nonentity
nonexempt
nonfat
nonpareil
nonplus
nonprofit
nonsectarian
nonsense
non sequitur
nonsizist
nonsupport
non-U
nonviolence
noodle**
nook**
noose**
norm
normal
norming
north
northerly
nose**
nosebleed
nosegay
no-show
nostalgic
nostril
nosy
not**
notable
notary
notation
notch
note**
notebook
noteworthy

nothing
notice
noticeable
notify
notion
notorious
nougat**
noun
nourish
nouveau
  riche
novel
November
novice
Novocaine
nowhere
noxious
nozzle**
nubile
nuclear
nucleus
nudge
nudist
nudity
nugget**
nuisance
nuke**
nullification
numb
number
numeral
numeric
numerical
numerous
numskull
nun**
nunnery
nuptial
nurse
nursemaid
nursery
nurture
nutrition
nutty
nuzzle**
nybble**
nymph

nymphoma-
  niac
NYSE

O

oaf**
oar**
oasis
oat**
oath**
obbligato
obdurate
obedience
obeisance
obese
obesity
obey
obfuscate
obit**
obiter dic-
  tum
obituary
object**
objection
objection-
  able
objective
objet d'art
obligation
obligatory
oblige
oblique
obliterate
oblivious**
oblong
obloquy**
obnoxious
oboe
obscene
obscuran-
  tism
obscure
obsequies
obsequious
observance
observation
observatory

observe
obsess**
obsession
obsolescent
obsolete
obstacle
obstetrician
obstinate
obstreperous
obstruct**
obstruction
obtain
obtrusive
obtuse
obverse
obviate
obvious**
occasion
occasional
Occident**
occlusion
occult
occupancy
occupant
occupation
occupied
occur**
occurred
occurrence
ocean
oceanogra-
   phy
ocher**
o'clock
octal
octane
octave
October
octogenar-
   ian
octopus
ocular
oculist
odd
odd lot
ode**
odious
odometer

odor
odorous
odyssey
OECD
Oedipus
Oedipus
   complex
OEM
oenophile
o'er**
oeuvre
of**
off**
offal**
offbeat
offense
offer
offering
offhand
office**
officer
official
officious
off-line
offload
off-price
off-putting
offset
offshore
offspring
off-the-
   record
off year
often
ogle
ogre
oh**
ohm
oil
ointment
okra**
old
old-boy
   network
older**
old-
   fashioned

old-girl
   network
old-line
old-timer
olé
olfactory
oligarchy
oligopoly
olive
Olympic
om
ombudsman
omelet
ominous
omission
omit
omnibus
omnipotent
omnipresent
omniscient
omnivorous
once**
oncogene
oncologist
oncology
one**
one-liner
one-man
onerous
oneself
one-sided
one-up
ongoing
onion**
on-line
onlooker
only
onoma-
   topoeia
onshore
onslaught
ontogeny**
ontology**
onus
oocyte
ooze
opaque
op. cit.**

OPEC
op-ed
open-ended
opener
opening
open-
   minded
openness
opera**
operant
operate
operative
operator
operetta
ophthal-
   mologist
ophthalmol-
   ogy
opiate
opinion
opium
opponent
opportune
opportunist
opportunity
oppose
opposite**
opposi-
   tion**
oppress
oppressor
opprobrium
opry**
opt**
optic
optical
optician
optimism
optimum
option
optional
optometrist
opulent
opus
or**
oracle**
oral**
orange

orator	ostracize	ovary	**P**
orbit**	ostrich	over	pacemaker
orchard	OTC	overall	Pacific
orchestra	other	overbearing	pacification
orchid	otherwise	overbite	pacifist
ordain	otter**	overboard	pacify
ordeal	ottoman	overcome	package
order	ouch	overcompen-	packed**
orderly	ought**	sate	pact**
ordinance**	ounce**	overdo**	pad**
ordinary	our**	overdue**	paddy**
ordination	ours	overexpo-	padlock
ordnance**	ourselves	sure	padre
ore**	oust	overhead	paean**
organ**	out**	overkill	paella
organic	outage	overlie**	pageant
organism**	outboard	overlook	paginate
organist**	outbreak	overly**	pagoda
organization	outcast	overnight	paid
organize	outclass	overrate	pail**
orgasm**	outcome	overreach	pain**
orgy	outcry	override	painstaking
orient	outdated	overrule	painter
oriental	outdo	overrun	pair**
orientation	outdoor	overseer	paisley
orifice**	outer	overt**	pajama
origin**	outfield	over-the-	Pakistan
original	outfit	counter	palace
ornament	outgoing	overthrow	palatable
ornate	outing	overtime	palate**
ornery	outlaw	overture	palatial
ornithologist	outlay	overview	pale**
orphan	outlet	overwhelm	paleon-
orthodontist	outline	overwrought	tology
orthodox	outlook	overzealous	Palestine
orthopedist	out-of-date	ovoid**	palette**
Oscar	outpatient	ovulate	palindrome
oscillate**	outpouring	ovulation	palisade
oscilloscope	output	ow**	pall**
osculate**	outrageous	owe**	pallbearer
osculatory	outreach	owed**	pallet**
OSHA	outsider	own**	palliative
osmosis	outspoken	oxen	pall-mall**
ossify	outstanding	oxygen	pallor
ostensible	outward	oxymoron	palm
ostentatious	outwit	oyster	palmistry
osteopath	oval	ozone	palomino
osteoporosis			palpable

palpitate
palsy
paltry**
pamphlet
pan**
panacea
panache
panatella
pancake
pancreas
panda**
pandemic
pandemon-
  ium
pander**
pane**
panel
panhandle
panicky
panjandrum
panoply
panorama
pansy
pantheism
pantomime
pap
papacy
paparazzi
papaverine
paperback
papier-
  mâché
papilloma
paprika
parable
parabola
parachute
parade
paradigm
paradise
paradox
paraffin
paragraph
parakeet
paraldehyde
parallel
paralysis
paralyze

paramecium
parameter
paramount
paranoia
parapherna-
  lia
paraphrase
paraplegic
paraprofes-
  sional
parapsy-
  chology
parasite
paratha
parathion
paratrooper
parcel
parcheesi
pardon
pare**
parent
parenthesis
paresis
parfait
parietal
pari-mutuel
pari passu
parish**
parity**
parking
parking
  meter
Parkinson's
parlay**
parley**
parliament
parlor
Parmesan
parochial
parody**
parole**
parquet
parrot
parse
parson
partheno-
  genesis
partial

participate
participle
particle
particular
particulars
parties
partisan
partition**
partner
parturition
party
passable**
passage
passé
passed**
passenger
passible**
passion
passive
Passover
passport
password
past**
pasta
pastel
pasteurize
pastille
pastime
pasting
pastor**
pastoral**
pastorale**
pastrami
pastry
pasture**
patchwork
pâté**
pâté de foie
  gras
patella
patent
paternal
pathetic
pathing
pathology
pathos**
patience**
patient

patients**
patina
patio
patriarch
patrimony
patriot
patriotism
patrol
patron
patronage
patronize
pattern
patty**
paucity
Paul**
pause**
pavement
pavilion
paving
paw**
paws**
payback
paycheck
payee
payload
payment
payoff
payola
payout
payroll**
PC
peace**
peach
peak**
peaked**
peal**
peanut
pear**
pearl**
peasant
pecan
peccadillo
pecks**
pecs**
pectoral
peculiar
pecuniary
pedagogue

pedal** Pennsyl- perjury petite
pedant vania perks petition**
peddle** penny** permanent petit mal
pederast penology permeate petrify
pedestal pension permissible petroleum
pedestrian pent** permit petticoat
pediatrics Pentagon permutation petty
pediculosis pentagram pernicious petulant
pedigree pentameter peroxide pew
pedophilia Pentateuch perp phallocracy
peek** pentathlon perpendicu- phallus
peeked** Pentecostal lar phantasm**
peel** pentobarbi- perpetrate phantom
peephole tal perpetrator phantom
peer** pent-up perpetual limb
peerless penurious perpetuity Pharaoh
peevish peon** perplex pharmaceuti-
pegged people perquisite cal
peignoir pepper persecute** pharmacy
pellagra peptic persevere pharyngitis
pellet** per** persistence pharynx
pell-mell** per annum person phase**
pelvis perceive personal** phenobarbital
pen** percent personality tal
penal** perception persona non phenomenal
penalty perch grata phenome-
penance** percolator personnel** non
penchant percussion perspec- phial**
pencil per diem tive** philanderer
pendant** peremptory perspica- philan-
pendent** perennial cious thropy
pendulum perfect** perspiration philately
penetrate perfecta perspire philhar-
penetration perfidious persuade monic
penguin perforate PERT Philippines
penicillin perform pertain philosophy
penile** perfume pertinent philter**
peninsula perfunctory perturb phlebitis
penis perhaps peruse phlegm
penitent peril pervade phobia
penitentiary perimeter perverse** Phoenix
penknife period perversion phonetic
penmanship periodontal pervert phonics
pennant peripheral peso phonograph
pennants** periphery pessary phony
penne** periscope pessimist phosphate
penned** perish** pesticide phosphores-
penniless peritonitis petal cence

phosphorus
photo
photogenic
photograph
photogra-
  phy
photosynthe-
  sis
phrase**
phreak**
phrenetic**
phrenology
physic**
physical**
physically
physician
physics
physiog-
  nomy
physiology
physiother-
  apy
physique**
pi**
pianist
piano
piazza
pica**
picaresque**
picayune
piccolo
picket
pickle
pickpocket
picks**
pickup
picnic
picture
pictur-
  esque**
pidgin**
pie**
piece**
piecemeal
piecework
pied-à-terre
pier**
pierce

piety
pigeon**
piggin**
piggyback
pigment
piker**
pilfer
pilgrim
piling
pillage
pillar**
pillbox
pillory
pillow**
pilot
pimento
pimple
pin**
pince-nez
pincers
pineapple
pink eye
pinnacle**
pinochle**
pinpoint
pinstripe
pinup
pioneer
pious**
pipeline
piping
piquant
pique**
piqued**
pirouette
pistachio
pistil**
pistol**
piston
pitch
pitcher**
pitfall
pitiful
pittance
pituitary
pity
Pius**
pivot

pixel
pizza
placard
placate
placebo
placement
placenta
placid
plagiarism
plague**
plaid
plain**
plaintiff**
plaintive**
plait**
plane**
planed**
planet**
planetarium
planned**
plant**
plantation
plaque**
plasma
plaster
plastered
plastic
plate**
plateau
platelet
platform
platinum
platitude
Platonic
platoon
platter
plaudit
plausible
playa**
playback
player**
playoff
playwright
plaza
plaza**
plea
plead

pleas**
pleasant
please**
pleasure
pleat
plebe
plebeian
plebiscite
pledge
plenary
plentiful
plenty
plethora
pleurisy
pliable
pliers
plight
plod**
plodding
plop
plot**
plow
ploy
pluck
plug
plum**
plumb**
plumber
plunder
plural
pluralism
plus
plutonium
ply
plywood
PMS
pneumatic
pneumonia
pneu-
  monic**
pocket
pocketbook
podiatry
podium
poem
poet
poetry
pogrom**

poignant
poinsettia
pointless
poise
poison
poison pill
poker**
polar
Polaris
polarize
Polaroid
pole**
polemic
police
policy
polio
poli-sci
polish
polite
politically
   correct
politics
polity
polka**
poll**
pollen
pollute
pollution
Pollyanna
poltergeist
polycentric
polyester
polyethylene
polygamy**
polyglot
polygon
polygraph
polygyny**
polymer
polyp
polyun-
   saturated
pomade
pompadour
pompous
poncho
Pontiff
pontiff

ponytail
pool**
poolside
poop
pooped
poplar**
populace**
popular**
population
populist
populous**
porcelain
pore**
pores**
pornogra-
   phy
porous
porpoise**
porridge
portable**
portal
portend**
porter
portfolio
porthole
portico
portion**
portrait
portray
poseur
position
positive
positron
posse
possess
possession
possible
postage
postal
postcard
posterior
posterity
posthumous
postman
postmaster
postmortem
post office
postpaid

postpone
posture
potable**
potassium
potato
potent
potential
pothole
potion**
potpourri
pottery
pouch
poultice
poultry**
pounce
pound
pour**
pout
poverty
powder
power
practical
practice**
practise**
pragmatic
prairie
praise
pray**
prayer
preach
preacher
preamble
preamplifier
precarious
precaution
precede**
prece-
   dence**
precedent**
precedents**
precept
precinct
precious
precipice
precipitate
précis**
precise**
precisian**

precision**
preclude
precocious
predator
predecessor
predicament
predicate
predict
predictable
prednisone
predominant
preemie
preeminent
preempt
prefabricate
preface
prefect**
prefer**
preference
preferred
pregnant
prejudice
preliminary
prelude
premarital
premature
premen-
   strual
premier**
premiere**
premise
premium
premonition
preoccupa-
   tion
preparation
prepare
preponder-
   ant
preposi-
   tion**
preposterous
prepubes-
   cent
prepuce
prerogative
presage
Presbyterian

prescient
prescribe**
prescription**
presence**
present
presentation
presentiment**
presentment**
presents**
preserve**
preside
president**
presidents**
pressure
prestige
presume
presumption
pretend**
prettify
pretty
pretzel
prevail
prevalent
prevaricate
prevention
preview
previous
prey**
priapism
priceless
prickly
pries**
priest
prima donna
prima facie
primal
  scream
primarily
primary
primate
primative
prime
primer**
primeval
primitive

prince**
princess
principal**
principle**
prints**
priority
prism
prison
privacy
private
privatization
privatize
privilege
privy
prize**
pro
proactive
probable
probate
probation
probe
probity
problem
pro bono
procaine
procedure
proceed**
process
procession
processor
pro-choice
proclaim
procrastinate
procreate
proctologist
proctor
proctoscope
procure
prod**
prodigious
prodigy**
produce
product
production
productivity
profess
profession

professor
proffer**
proficient
profile
profit**
profligate
profound
profuse
progenitor
progeny
progesterone
prognosis
prognosticate
program**
programmer
progress
prohibit
project
projection
prole
pro-life
proliferate
prolific
prologue
prom
promenade
prominent
promiscuous
promise
promissory
prompt
pronounce**
pronouns**
pronto
pronunciation
propaganda
propagate
propel
propensity
proper
property**
prophecy
prophecy**
prophesy**
prophet**

prophylactic**
prophylaxis**
propitious
proponent
proportion
proposal
propose
proposition**
proprietary**
proprietor
propriety**
propulsion
prosaic
proscribe**
proscription**
prosecute**
prospect
prospective**
prospectus
prostate**
prosthesis
prostitute
prostrate**
protagonist
protect
protégé**
protein
protest
Protestant
protocol
proton
protoplasm
prototype
protrude
proud**
prove
proverb
provide
providence
province
provincial
provision

proviso
provoke
provost
proximity
proxy
prude**
prudence
prurient
pruritis
pry
psalm
pseudo
pseudonym
psittacosis
psoriasis
psyche
psychedelic
psychiatrist
psychic
psycho
psychoanaly-
  sis
psychobabble
psychology
psychosis
psychoso-
  matic
psychother-
  apy
psycopath
ptarmigan
pterodactyl
pterosaur
ptomaine
pub
puberty
pubes
pubescent
pubic**
public**
publication
publicity
pudding
pudgy
pueblo
puerile
Puerto Rico

pugnacious
puisne**
pulchritude
pull**
pullet
pulley
pulmonary
pulp
pulpit
pulsar
pulse
pulverize
pummel
pumper-
  nickel
pumpkin
punctilious
punctual
punctuate
puncture
pungent
punish
punitive
punk
punks
punned**
punt**
puny**
pupal**
pupil*
puppet
purchase
pure**
purée
purgatory
purge
Purim
purl**
purloin
purple
purport
purpose**
purr**
purse
purser
pursue
pursuit
purview

pus**
push-up
pusillani-
  mous
puss**
pussyfoot
put**
putative
putrefy
putrid
putsch
putt**
puzzle
pyelitis
pyorrhea
pyramid
pyre
pyromaniac
pyrotechnics
Pyrrhic vic-
  tory

Q

quack**
quad
quadrangle
quadrant
quadratic
quadrille**
quadril-
  lion**
quadripar-
  tite
quadriplegic
quadroon
quadro-
  phonic
quadru-
  ped**
quadruple**
quadrup-
  let**
quaff
quake
Quaker
qualify

quality**
qualm
quantity**
quantum
quarantine
quark**
quarrel
quarreled
quarry**
quarter
quarterback
quarterly
quartet
quarts**
quartz**
quasar
quasi**
quatrain
quaver**
quay**
quean**
queasy**
queen**
queer
queerest**
quench
querist**
QUERTY
query**
question
question-
  naire
queue**
quibble
quiche
quick
quicksand
quid
quid pro
  quo
quiet**
quietude**
quietus**
quill
quince**
quinella
quinine

quinsy** radiologist rapt** real estate
quintet radish rapture realism
quints** radium rarebit** reality
quintuplet radius rarefy realize**
quire** radix rarely really
quirk** radon rarity realm
quit** raffia raspberry Realtor
quite** raffle ratable ream
quiver** raft ratchet reap
quixotic raga** rate reappear
quiz raged rather reason
quizzed ragged ratify reasonable
quizzes raglan rating reassure
quizzical ragout** ratio rebait**
quorum railing ratiocination rebate**
quota** railroad ration rebel
quotation rain** rational** rebellion
quote** rainbow rationale** rebirthing
quotidian raincoat rationalize rebound**
quotient rainmaker rattle rebuff
 rainy rattlesnake rebuke
 raise** rattrap rebuttal
R raisin ratty recalcitrate
rabbi raison d'être raucous recall
rabbis** rakish raunchy recapitulate
rabbit** rally ravage recapture
rabble RAM** ravel recede**
rabid** Ramadan raven receipt
rabies** ramble ravenous receivable
raccoon ramification ravish receive
race rampage ravishing receiver
racetrack rampant raw** recent**
racial rancid rayon reception
racism random rays** receptionist
racist range raze** receptor
racket ranking razor recertify
racketeer rankle reach recess
raconteur ransack react recession
racy ransom reaction recessive
radar rap** reactionary recidivism
radial rapacious reactor recipe
radiant rape read** recipient
radiation rapist reader reciprocal
radiator rapped** readily reciprocity
radical rappel read-only recital
radio rapport ready recitation
radioactivity rapproche- reaffirm reckless
radioisotope ment real** reckon

202

reclamation
recline
recluse**
recognize
recollect
recombinant
  DNA
recommend
recompense
reconcile
reconnais-
  sance
reconnoiter
reconstruct
record
recorder
recoup
recovery
recreation
recrimina-
  tory
recruit
rectal
rectangle
rectify
rectum
recuperate
recurrence
recuse**
recycle
red**
redden
redecorate
redeem
redemption
red-handed
redhead
red herring
redirect
redline
redound**
redress
red tape
reduce
reducible
redundant
reed**

reek**
reel**
reelection
reenact
reenforce
reentry
reestablish
reevaluate
reexamine
refer
referee**
reference
referendum
refined
refinement
reflection
reflex
reform
reformation
refraction
refrain
refresher
refrigerator
refuel
refuge
refugee
refund
refurbish
refusal
refuse
refute
regal**
regale**
regard
regardless
regatta
regency
reggae**
regime
regiment
region
register
registrar
registration
regression
regrettable
regular
regulate

regurgitate
rehabilitate
rehearsal
rehearse
reign**
rein**
reincarna-
  tion
reindeer
reinforce-
  ment
reinvent
reissue
REIT
reiterate
reject
rejoice
rejuvenate
relapse
relater**
relation
relative
relator**
relax
release
relegate
relent
relentless
relevant
reliable
reliant
relic**
relict**
relied
relief
relies**
relieve
religious
relinquish
relish
relocate
reluctance
rely
REM
remain
remark
remarkable
rematch

remedial
remedy
remember
reminisce
remission
remit
remittance
remnant
remonstrate
remorse
remorseful
remote
removable
removal
remunerate
renaissance
renascence
rendezvous
renegade
renege
renew
renounce
renovate
renown
rental
reorder
reorganize
repair
reparable
reparation
repartee
repatriate
repeal
repeat
repel
repellent
repent
repercussion
repertoire
repertory
repetition
repetitive
replacement
replay**
replenish
replete
replica
replicate

reply**   resistance   retro   rhinoceros
report   resistible   retroactive   rhizome
reporter   resolution   retrofit   rhododen-
repose   resolve   retrogres-   dron
repository   resonance   sion   rhubarb
repossess   resort   retrospect   rhumba
reprehensi-   resource   retroussé   rhyme**
  ble   respectable   retrovirus   rhythm**
represent   respect-   return   ribald
repressed   fully**   reunion   ribbon
reprieve   respec-   reunite   rich
reprimand   tively**   reuse   rickety
reprisal   respirator   revaluation   rickshaw
reprise   respite   reveal   ricochet
reproach   response   reveille**   ricotta
reprobate   responsible   revelation   riddance
reproduce   rest**   revelry**   riddle
reproductive   restaurant   revenge   ridge
reprove   restitution   revenue   ridiculous
reptile   restoration   revere   riffle**
republic   restrain   reverend**   rifle**
Republican   restrict   reverent**   rig
repudiate   restriction   reverie**   right**
repugnant   restrictive   reversible   righteous
repulsive   restructure   revert   rightful
reputable   result   review**   right-to-
request   resume   revise   work
requiem   resumption   revision   rigid
require   resurrection   revisionism   rigmarole
requisite   resuscitate   revival   rigor
requittal   retail   revocation   rigorous
resalable   retain   revoke   rime**
rescind**   retaliate   revolt   ring**
research   retard   revolution   ringer
resection   retch**   revolve   ringworm
reseed**   retention   revolver   rinse
resemblance   reticent   revue**   rinsing
resend**   retina   revulsion   riot
resent**   retire   reward   riotous
reservation   retirement   rewind   ripe
reserve   retool   rewrite   ripen
reservoir   retort   rhapsody   rip-off
residence   retouch   rheostat   ripple
residual   retraction   rhetoric   risc chip
residue   retread   rheum**   rise
resign   retreat   rheumatism   rising
resilience   retribution   rhinestone   risqué
resin   retrieve   rhinitis   rite**

ritual
rival
rivet
road**
roadblock
roam**
roar**
roaring
roast
robber**
robbery
robin
robot
roc**
rock**
rock and roll
Rockefeller
rocket
rococo
rode**
rodent
rodeo
roe**
Roentgen
rogue
roguish
roil**
role**
roleplay
roll**
rollout
roll out**
rollover**
roll over**
ROM**
Roman
romance
Rome**
roofs
room**
roomer**
roommate
Roosevelt
root**
Rorschach
rosary
rose**
rosé**

Rosh Ha-
  shanah
rosin
rosy
rotary
rotate
rote**
rotten
roué
rouge
rough**
roughneck
roulette
rouse**
route**
routine
roving
row**
rowdy
rowed**
rows**
royal**
royally
rubber**
rubbish
rubeola
rudder
rude**
rue
rued**
ruff**
ruffian
ruin**
ruler
rumble
rummage
rummy
rumor**
runaway
rundown**
run down**
run-down
rune**
rung**
runner
running
rupture
rural

rushes
russet
Russia
rustbelt
rustic
rustle
rusty
Rwanda
rye**

S
Sabbat**
Sabbath**
sabbatical
sabotage
saboteur
sac**
saccharin
sachet**
sack**
sacrament
sacred
sacrifice
sacrilegious
sadist
safari
safe
safety
saffron
sage
said
sail**
saint
sake**
saki**
salacious
salad
salami
salary**
sale**
salesperson
saliva
salmon
salmonella
salon**
saloon**
salsa

salud**
salutation
salute**
salvage**
salvation
salve
Samaritan
samba
sample
samurai
sanctimoni-
  ous
sanction
sanctity
sandbag
sandlot
sandstone
sandwich
sane**
sanguine
sanitary**
sanitation
sanitory**
sanity
santeria
saphire
sapphire
sarcastic
sarge**
sarsaparilla
sashay**
sassy
Satan**
Satanism
sateen**
satellite
satin**
satire**
satisfaction
satisfactory
saturated
Saturday
satyr**
sauce**
saucy
Saudi Ara-
  bia
sauerkraut

sausage	scissors	sedan	sensor
sauté	sclerosis	sedative	sentence
savage	scofflaw	sedentary	sentiment
saver**	scone	Seder	separate
saving	scope	seduce	Sephardim
savior**	scotch	see**	September
Saviour**	scout	seed**	sequel
savor**	scrabble	seedy	sequence
savvy	scratch	seeing	serendipity
saw**	scream	seem**	serf**
sawed-off	screw	seen**	serge**
saxophone	scrip**	seer**	sergeant
says	script**	sees**	serial**
scab	Scripture	segregate	series
scalable	scroll	segue	serif
scam**	scrub	seine**	serious
scan**	scrupulous	seismic	sermon
scandal	SCSI port	seismograph	service
scanner	scuba	seize**	serviceable
scapegoat	scull**	seizure	sesame
scar	sculptor**	seldom	session**
scarce	sculpture**	select	settee
scarcely	scum	self-	settler**
scarcity	scurrilous	discipline	settlor**
scare	scuttle	self-esteem	seventh
scarf	scythe	self-help	several
scavenger	sea**	selfish	severe
scenario	seal	sell**	sew**
scene**	sealing**	seller**	sex**
scenery	seam**	seltzer	sexcapade
scenic	seamen**	selvage**	sexism
scents**	sear**	selves	sexy
schedule	search	semantics	shack
schematic	seas**	semen**	shake**
scheme	season	semester	shalom
schism	seatbelt	semiauto-	shampoo
schlock	secede	matic	shamus
schmuck	secession	seminar	shanty**
schnaps	second	seminary	shareware
scholar	second-rate	Semitic	sharif**
scholastic	secret	senator	shear**
school	secretary	senior**	sheath
schoolmate	secretive	señor**	shed**
schooner	sects**	sense**	she'd**
sciatica	secular	senseless	sheer**
science	secure	senses**	sheik**
sci-fi	securities	sensitive	shelter
scintillate	security	sensitivity	shelves

shepherd	SIDS	Slav**	solicit
sherbet	siege	slave**	solidarity**
sheriff**	sieve	slavery	solo
shield	sighed**	slay**	solution
shillelagh	sighs**	sleigh**	some**
shining	sight**	sleight**	somebody
shipment	sign**	slight**	someone**
shipped	signature	slim	some one**
shirk**	signet**	slippery	son**
shirt**	significant	sloe**	sonata
shish kebab	silence	slope	soon
shmear	silhouette	slow**	soothe
shock	silicon	slowdown	sophisticate
shoe**	silicone	sluggish	sophomore
shoestring	silver	smother	sore**
shofar**	silverware	smudge	sorrow
shone**	similar	smug	sorry
shoo**	SIMM	snack	sought
shoot**	simulate	snafu	soul**
short	sin	snap	sound
shorthand	since	snapshot	source**
shot	sincere	snarl	southern
should	sincerely	snorkel	souvenir
shoulders	sine**	snort	sovereign
shouldn't	sinecure	snowbird	sovereignty
shove	singeing**	snowmobile	sow**
shown**	singing**	so**	spaghetti
shriek**	single	soaps	Spanish
shrike**	sinus	soar**	sparrow
shrine	sis	social	spasm
shrubbery	sisterhood	socialist	spastic
shtick**	site**	society	spat
shun	situation	sociology	speaker
shutdown	sixth	sociopath	speaker-
shutout	size**	sodality**	phone
shuttle	sizzle	sodium	spear**
si**	skateboard	sofa	special**
sibil	skein	soften	speciality**
sibling	skeleton	software	specialty
sic**	skeptical	solace	specie**
sick**	skew	solar	species**
sickle	skiff	sold**	specify
sickly	skillful	solder**	specimen
side**	skull**	soldier**	specious
sidearm	slack	sole**	spectacle
sidebar	slacks	soled**	spectacular
sideline	slain	solemn	spectator
sidetrack	slaughter	solenoid	spectrum

207

speculate
speech
speed
speller
sperm
sphere**
sphinx
spiffy
spin
spinoff
spiral
spirit
spiritual
splash
sponsor
spoof
spooler
sportscast
sportswear
spotlight
spousal
spouse
spree
spryly
spumoni
spur
spurious
spy
squad
squalid
square
squash
squat
squeeze
Sri Lanka
stab
stability
staff**
staid**
stair**
stake**
stakeout
stale
stalk**
stamp
stampede
standard
standby

stanza
staph**
staphylococ-
cus
starboard
stare**
stark
starship
startup
statement
static
stating
stationary**
stationery**
statistic
stats
statue**
stature**
status
status quo
statute**
stayed**
steak**
steal**
stealth
stealthy
steel**
stein
stench
step**
steppe**
stereo
stereotype
sterilize
stick**
stiff
stigma
stile**
stiletto
stimulus
stipend
stipulate
stock
stockbroker
stocks
stodgy**
stogie**
stomach

stooge**
stopped
storage
stork**
story
straddle
straight**
strait**
strait jacket
strategic
streaker
strength
strenuous
stretch
strictly
stricture**
strife
strike-
breaker
striptease
strobe
stroke
structure**
strudel
struggle
stubble
study
studying
stuff
stupid
stupor
style**
stylus
suave
sublimate
sublime
subliminal
submarine
subordinate
suborn
subpoena
subscription
subsistence
subtile**
subtitle**
subtle**
subtract
suburb**

suburban
subversive
succeed
success
successor
succinct
succor**
succumb
sucker**
sued**
suede**
sufficient
suffix
suffrage
sugar
suggest
suggestion
suit**
suite**
suitor
sulfa**
sulfur**
sulphur**
sum**
summary**
summery**
summit
summons
sumptuous
sun**
sundae**
Sunday**
super
superb**
supercom-
puter
superfluous
superintend-
ent
superior
superman
supernatural
supersede
superstitious
supervise
supplies
supply
support

208

suppose	syndication	tantrum	technical
suppress	synergetics	tape**	technics**
sure	synonym	taper**	technique
surf**	synopsis	tapeworm	techniques**
surface	syntax	tapir**	technology
surfeit	synthetic	tarantella**	tedious
surfing	syringe	tarantula**	tee**
surge**	syrup	tardy	teem**
surgeon	system	tare**	teenager
surgery		target	teeter
surgical		tariff	teeth**
surmise	**T**	tarnish	teethe**
surplice**		taro**	telecast
surplus**	tab	tarot**	telecommun-
surpress	taberbacle	tartar**	ication
surprise	tableau**	tartare**	telecompute
surrogate	tablespoon	Tarter**	telegram
surround	tablet	tasteless	telemarket-
surveillance	tabloid**	tasting	ing
survey	taboo	Tater**	telephone
survival	tabulate	tatter**	telescope
survive	tacit	tattered	telethon
suspect	tacked**	tattle	television
suspend	tackle	tattoo	telex
suspicion	tacks**	taught**	telltale
swayed**	taco	taunt**	temerity
swear	tact**	taupe**	temp**
sweatshirt	tactics	taut**	tempera**
sweatshop	tactile	tavern	tempera-
sweeps	taffeta	tawdry	ment
sweepstakes	tail**	tax**	temperance
sweet**	taillight	taxable	temperature
sweetheart	tailor	tax lien	template
swirl	taint**	taxpayer	temporal
sword	take-out	T-bills	lobe
swordfish	takeover	t-cell	temporarily
sycophant	taking	tea**	temporary
syllable	talc**	teach	tempt**
syllabus	tale**	team**	temptation
sylph	talent	teammate	tempura**
symbol**	talk**	teamster	tenable
symmetrical	Talmud	teamwork	tenacious
symmetry**	tamale	tear**	tenacity
sympathy	tamper	tearful	tenant**
symphony	tampon	teas**	tendency
symptom	tandoori	tease**	tendentious
synagogue	tangent	teaspoon	tenderfoot
syndicate	tangible		
	tantalize		

tender-hearted	tête-à-tête	thong**	tight
tendinitis	tetracycline	thorax	tightfisted
tendon	text	thorough	tightrope
tenement	textbook	thorough-fare	till
tenet**	textile		timber**
tenor**	texture	though	timbre**
tension	thalamus	thought	time**
tentacle	thalidomide	thoughtful	timetable
tentative	than**	thousand	timid
tenuous	Thanksgiving	thrash**	timing
tenure**	theater	thread	timorous
tepee	theft	threat	timpani
tepid	their**	thresh**	tincture
tequila	theirs	threshold	tine**
terabyte	theme	threw**	tingle
teriyaki	themselves	thrifty	tinnitus
terminal	then**	thrilling	tinny**
terminate	thence**	thriving	tinsel
termite	theology	throat**	tint**
terms	theorem	throe**	tiny**
tern**	theoretical	thrombosis	tip-off
terra**	theory	throne**	tirade
terrace	therapeutic	through**	tissue
terra cotta	there**	throw**	titan
terrain	thereafter	thrown**	tithe
terrestrial	thereby	thug	titillate
terrible	therefor**	thumb	title
terribly	therefore**	thumbtack	titular
terrific	thermometer	thunder	to**
territorial	thermonu-clear	thunder-storm	toady
territory	thermostat	Thursday	tobacco
terror**	thesaurus	thwart	toboggan
terrorist	these	thyme**	tocsin**
terse	thesis	thymus	today
tersely	they're**	thyroid	toddler
tertiary	thick-skinned	tiara	toe**
testament	thief	Tibet	toehold
testicle	thieves	tibia	toga
testify	thimble	tic**	together
testimony	thinkpad	tick**	toggle key
testis	thin-skinned	tickle	toil**
testosterone	third person	tide**	toile**
test tube	thirsty	tidings	toiled**
test-tube baby	thirteen	tied**	toilet**
	thirty	tie-in	toilette**
tetanus		tier**	token
		tiff	tokenism
			told**

210

tole**
tolerant
toll**
tolled**
tomato
tomb**
tomboy
tombstone
tome**
tomography
tomorrow
tong**
Tong**
tongue**
tonic
tonight
tonnage
tonsil
tonsillec-
tomy
too**
tooth
toothpaste
toothpick
topee**
topic
topical**
topogra-
phy**
Torah
toreador
torment
tornado
torpedo
torpor
torque
torrent
torrid
torso
tortious**
tortuous**
torture
torturous**
tot**
totaling
totalitarian
tote**
totem

touchdown
touché
tough
toupee**
tour**
tourist
tourniquet
tow**
tower**
toxic
toxin**
tracer
trachea
track**
trackball
tract**
traction
trade-in
trademark
trade name
tradition
traffic
tragedy
trail**
train
traitor
trajectory
tranquilizer
transaction
transcend
transcript
transcription
transfer
transference
transfusion
transient
transistor
transit
transition
translate
translator
transmit
transparent
transplant
transport
transposi-
tion
transsexual

transvestite
trauma
traumatic
travail**
travel**
travesty
tray**
treacherous
treachery
treason
treasure
treasurer
treasury
treaties**
treatise**
treaty
trek
trekkie
tremendous
tremor
trespass
trey**
triad
triage
triangle
tribe
tributary
triceps
tricycle
tried
tries
trigger
trilogy
trim
trimester
trio
triplicate
triumph
trivial
troll
troop**
tropical**
trouble
troupe**
trousers
trousseau
truly

trumpet
trustee**
trusty**
truthfully
tryst
tsetse
tuba**
tubal
tuber**
tuberculosis
Tuesday
tuition
tulip
tumescence
tummler
tummy
tumor
tumult
tunnel
turban**
turbine**
turbojet
turf
turkey
turmoil
turn**
turnaround
turncoat
turndown
turnip
turnover
turnpike
turntable
turpentine
turpitude
turquoise
tush
tutti frutti
tutu
tweak
tweezer
twelfth
twilight
twitch
two**
tycoon
tying
tympani

211

type
typewriter
typhoid
typhus
typical
typist
typogra-
phy**
tyrannical
tyranny
tyrant

U

ubiquitous
udder**
ufology
Ukraine
ukulele
ulcer
ulterior
ultimate**
ultimatum**
ultrasound
ultraviolet
umbilical
umbrage
umbrella
umpire**
unable**
unaccept-
able
unaccus-
tomed
unadul-
terated
un-
American
unanimous
unappealing
unattached
unavoidable
unaware**
unawares**
unbelievable
uncertain
uncle
unclouded

uncomfort-
able
uncommon
uncondi-
tional
unconscious
uncontrolla-
ble
unconven-
tional
uncouth
unctuous
undeniable
underdog
undergo
undergrad
undergradu-
ate
under-
ground
under-
handed
underlay**
underlie**
underline**
under-
privileged
understand
undertaker
underwear
underworld
underwriter
undesirable
undo**
undoubtedly
undress
undue**
unduly
undying
unearned
unearth
uneasy
unemployed
unequal**
unequaled**
unequivocal
unerring

unexception-
able**
unexcep-
tional**
unfair
unfavorable
unfinished
unfit
unfold**
unforgetta-
ble
unfortunate
unfriendly
unfurl
ungainly
ungird**
ungirt**
ungodly
ungrateful
unguarded
unhealthy
unholy
unicorn
uniform
unify
unilateral
unimpeach-
able
uninhibited
unintelli-
gent**
unintelligi-
ble**
union**
unique**
unisex**
unison
unit
Unitarian**
unitary**
United Na-
tions
United
States
unity
universal**
universally
universe**

university
Unix**
unkempt
unknowable
unknown
unlawful
unlicensed
unlike**
unlikely**
unload
unmistak-
able
unnamed
unnatural
unnecessary
unobtrusive
unoccupied
unorganized
unparalleled
unpleasant
unpopular
unprece-
dented
unpreju-
diced
unprincipled
unread**
unready**
unreal**
unreel**
unroll**
unruly
unscrupu-
lous
unsex**
untidy**
untied**
until
untitled**
unveil
unwanted**
unwonted**
unwrap**
upgrade
upped**
uppers
uppity
upright

212

uproar
uproot
upticks
uptight
uranium
urb
urban**
urbane**
urbs
urchin
urea
urge
urgency
urinal
urinalysis
urine
urn**
urologist
usable
usage
used to
useful
Usenet
user-friendly
using
usually
usurious**
usury
uterus
utility
utopia
utter**
u-turn
uxorious**

V

vacancy
vacant
vacation**
vaccination
vacillate
vacuous
vacuum
vagina
vaginitis
vague**
vain**

valance**
vale**
valedictory
valence**
valentine
valet**
valid
validate
Valium
valley**
valor**
valuable**
valve
vampire
van**
vandal
vane**
vanguard
vanilla
vanish
vanity
vanquish
vantage**
vapid
vapor
variable
variance**
variants**
varicose
variety
various
varnish
vary**
vase
vasectomy
vaseline
vassal**
Vatican
vaudeville
VD
veal**
vector**
veer
vegetable
vegetarian
veggie
vegie
vehement

vehicle
veil**
vein**
velcro
vellum
velocity
velour**
velvet
venal**
vendor
veneer
venerable**
veneration
venereal**
Venetian
vengeance
venial**
venom
venomous
venous
ventilate
ventilation
ventricle
ventriloquist
venture
venue
veracious**
veracity**
verb
verbal
verbally
verdict
verifiable
verification
verify**
verité**
verity**
vermin
Vermont
vermouth
vernacular
Versailles
versatile
verse
verses**
versify**
version
versus**

vertebra**
vertebral
vertebrate**
vertical
vertigo
very**
vessel**
vest
vested
vestibule
vestige
veterans
veterinary
veto
vetoes
vex
viable
viaduct
vial**
vibrant**
vibrate**
vibrato**
vibrator**
vicar
vicarious
vice**
vicinity
vicious
victim
victor**
victory
victuals
video
videocas-
sette
vie
Vienna
Viet Nam
view
viewfinder
viewpoint
vigil
vigilance
vigilant**
vigilante**
vignette
vigor
vigorous

vile**
vilify
villa**
village
villain
vindicate**
vindictive**
vinegar
vintage**
vintner
vinyl
viol**
viola**
violate**
violation**
violent**
violet**
violin
violinist
viper
viral**
virgin
virile**
virility
virtual**
virtual real-
  ity
virtue**
virtuoso**
virtuous**
virulence
virulent
virus
visa**
visage
viscera
viscid
viscous
vise**
visible
vision
visionary
visor**
vista
visual
vital
vitally
vitamin

vitiate
viva
vivid
vixen
viz.**
vizier**
vocable**
vocabulary
vocal**
vocation**
vociferous
vodka
vogue**
voice
voice mail
voilà**
volatile
Volga**
volition**
voluble**
volume
voluntary
voluptuous
vomit
voodoo
voracious**
voracity**
voucher
vowel
voyageur
voyeur
vulgar**
vulnerable**
vulture
vulva
vying

W
wade**
wafer
wage
wagon
wail**
waist**
waistline
wait**
waive**

waiver**
waken
wallet
wallop
walnut
waltz
wan**
wander**
wane
wannabee
wanton**
war**
warble
ward**
warden
ware**
warehouse
warm-
  blooded
warm-
  hearted
warning
warp
warrant
warranty
warred**
warrior
wart
wary**
WASP
wassail
wastage
waste**
wasteful
watch
watchdog
watermelon
waterproof
WATS**
watts**
wave**
waver**
wax**
way**
waylaid
waylay
wayside
we**

weak**
weal**
wealth
weapon
wear**
weary**
weather
web
wed**
we'd**
wedding
Wednesday
wee**
weed**
week**
weigh**
weighed**
weight**
weightism
weird
welch**
welcome
welfare
we'll**
well-heeled
well-known
Welsh**
welsh rabbit
welter
wen**
were**
we're**
western
wet**
wetware
whacks**
whale**
whaler
what
whatever
what's**
wheel**
when**
whence**
where**
whereof
whet**
whether**

whey**   wild**   work station

whey**	wild**	work station	**X**
which**	wilderness	workup	Xavier
Whig**	wile**	world	xenophobia
while**	willful	World Wide	xerography
whiled**	wince**	Web	Xmas
whine**	windfall	worm	x-ray
whiplash	windjammer	worry	xylophone
whipper-	windows	worse	
snapper	windshear	worship	
whippoor-	windshield	worst**	**Y**
will	wine**	worsted	
whir**	wintry	worth	yacht
whirl**	wire	would**	yahoo
whisk	wiretap	wound	yak
broom	Wisconsin	wraith	y'all**
whiskey	wisdom	wrangle	yang**
whisper	wisteria	wrangler	yank**
whistle	wistful	wrap**	Yankee**
whistle-	wit**	wrapped**	yanqui**
blower	witch**	wrath	yawl**
whit**	withdraw	wreak**	yaws**
white	wither**	wreath	ye**
white collar	withhold	wreck**	yea**
whitewash	witness	wrest**	yearn
whither**	wives	wrestle	yearned
whittle	wizard	wretch**	yeast
whiz kid	wolves	wriggle	yellow
who	womanizer	wright**	yen**
whole**	womb	wring**	yeoman
whole-	women	wrinkle	yeshiva
hearted	won**	wrist	yesterday
wholesale	wonder**	writ	yew**
wholesome	wondrous	write**	Yiddish
wholly**	wont**	write-in	yield
whoop**	won't**	write-off	yin**
whore**	wonton**	write-protect	yodel
who're**	wood**	writer	yoga**
whores**	woolly	writhe	yogi**
whorey**	word	writing	yogurt
who's**	wore**	written	yoghurt
whose**	workable	wrong	yokel
wicked	workers'	wrote**	yoke**
widget	compensa-	wroth	yolk**
widow	tion	wrought	Yom Kip-
wield**	workfare	wrung**	pur
wiener	workforce	wry**	yonder
wig**	workload	wurst**	yore**
wiggle room	workaholic	WYSIWYG	

you**	yucca	zenith	zing**
you all	Yule**	zenology	Zionist
you'll**	yuppy	zephyr	zip code
young		zero	zither
youngster		zero-coupon	zodiac
your**	**z**	Zeus	zoftig
you're**	zaftig	zilch	zoning
yours**	zany	zillion	zoology
yourself	zapping	zinc**	zoom
youth	zeal	zine	zoster
yowl**	zealous**	'zine	zucchini